The United States and Viet Nam
from War to Peace

The United States and Viet Nam from War to Peace

Papers from an Interdisciplinary Conference on Reconciliation

EDITED BY
ROBERT M. SLABEY

McFarland & Company, Inc., Publishers
Jefferson, North Carolina, and London

British Library Cataloguing-in-Publication data are available

Library of Congress Cataloguing-in-Publication Data

The United States and Viet Nam from war to peace : papers from an
interdisciplinary conference on reconciliation / edited by Robert M.
Slabey.
    p.   cm.
    Includes index.
    ISBN 0-7864-0227-X (library binding : 50# alk. paper) ∞
    1. Vietnamese Conflict, 1961–1975—United States. 2. Vietnamese
Conflict, 1961–1975—Literature and the conflict. 3. American
literature—20th century—History and criticism. 4. Indochina—
History—1945–   I. Slabey, Robert M.
DS558.U55 1996
959.704'3373—dc20   96-28830
                                                   CIP

Manufactured in the United States of America

McFarland & Company, Inc., Publishers
Box 611, Jefferson, North Carolina 28640

For W. D. Ehrhart

TO A FRIEND WHO STILL INSISTS
ON WRITING ABOUT THE WAR

The war poet in you
just will not die—
lines run through your days
like tracers, marking your past,
searching out the targets of your hate:
the hypocrite, the liar, the bullshitter,
death wardens of assorted colors,
all hit with incendiary rounds until
they're just a jellied mass
the size of a scrawny chicken.
You haven't got the decency to stop
though others wish you'd go away
and write of how the light
shines through the trees
and other pretty things the decent
ones can read at tea.

In their niceness let them rot.
Here's some gun oil and a patch:
clean out the barrel of your weapon
and fire line after line
of copper-jacketed truth into every
ignorant bastard who puts his hand
on your shoulder and says, "Now, now,
take it easy, forget about it,
the war is over for us all."

—DALE RITTERBUSCH

Acknowledgments

The participation of the principal speakers, as well as the Notre Dame Conference "The United States and Viet Nam: From War to Peace" December 2–4, 1993, itself, was made possible by major university grants from the Paul M. and Barbara Henkels Endowment, the College of Arts and Letters (Harold W. Attridge, dean), the Kellogg Institute for International Studies, the Kroc Institute for International Peace Studies, the Center for the Study of Contemporary Society, the Notre Dame Student Union Board, and the Indiana Humanities Council.

My work was expedited by a leave sponsored by the L. J. and Mary C. Skaggs Foundation and supported by the Institute for Scholarship in the Liberal Arts. Joseph Buttigieg and Christopher Fox, successive English Department chairmen, were unstinting in their encouragement and assistance. I am grateful to my Notre Dame colleagues Jim Collins, David Cortright, Wilson Miscamble, C.S.C., Martin F. Murphy, and H. Ronald Weber who helped plan the program. External scholars—Jane Hamilton-Merritt, Southern Connecticut State; William H. Kenney, Kent State; Ben Kiernan, Yale; John Root, Illinois Institute of Technology; Larry Rottmann, Southeast-Asia–Ozark Project; Charles Lindquist, Lexington (KY) Veterans Center; and Kali Tal of *Viet Nam Generation*—offered valuable advice and cooperation. The Decio Hall Faculty Services staff provided their usual cheerful and efficient assistance in the preparation of this book.

To W. D. Ehrhart, witness and preeminent figure at the center of writing about the war and its aftermath, whose contributions to our understanding are enormous, this volume (which he engendered) is dedicated.

Merritt's *Tragic Mountains: The Hmong, The Americans, and the Secret Wars for Laos* (Indiana University Press, 1993). "A Farmer from Vinh," from *Voices from the Ho Chi Minh Trail* (Event Horizon Press, 1993), appears courtesy of the author, Larry Rottmann. "Making Friends," by Lynda Van Devanter, is reprinted from *Visions of War, Dreams of Peace*, edited by Lynda Van Devanter and Joan A. Furey (Warner Books, 1991). "How Dare She Have a Baby in the Middle of a War?," part of "The United States, Viet Nam, and the 'Interconnectedness of All Life'" by Kim Worthy, appeared in *Common Sense*, November 1994, a student publication at Notre Dame.

—*RMS*

A Note on Nomenclature

Viet Nam is an independent nation in Southeast Asia with its own people, language, and culture.

Vietnam is an American formulaic identifying a continuing "experience" in Southeast Asia (including Laos and Cambodia), in the United States, and elsewhere.

Vietnamese is the adjectival form of both above terms and is the language of Viet Nam.

Viets are the ethnic majority people of Viet Nam who have called themselves and been called "Viets" for over 2,000 years.

Viet Kieu are "Overseas Viets" including but not limited to those in the United States.

Contents

III. LITERATURE OF RECONCILIATION: POETRY

IV. LITERATURE OF RECONCILIATION: PROSE

V. VIETNAM VETERAN WRITERS SYMPOSIUM

VI. EPILOGUE

VII. POSTCONFERENCE SUPPLEMENTS

Preface

ROBERT M. SLABEY

The Vietnam War, fought in Southeast Asia, in the streets of America, and in the American conscience, dominated life during the sixties and early seventies. Understanding our longest, strangest war is difficult, though it continues both as the subject of profound intellectual and emotional appeal and as a politically divisive issue. As Walter Capps wrote, "The Vietnam War did not mean what wars have meant before. Previous frameworks of interpretation did not count." On the other side of the globe, the war left a land devastated and millions dead, homeless, impoverished or in flight. Viet Nam has not recovered physically, though its people have "put the war behind them"; America has not recovered spiritually or emotionally, and segments of the populace appear fixated on war issues. "Vietnam" has become an American metaphor for a wound that will not heal, a syndrome for which no cure exists, and an event which will not end.

The conference at the University of Notre Dame entitled "The United States and Viet Nam: From War to Peace" brought together representatives of groups for whom the war is of vital concern: American historians, Asia scholars, writers, artists, filmmakers, journalists, psychiatrists, government officials and antiwar leaders, veteran-activists, reconciliation advocates, Viet Kieu, war veterans. The principal speakers and events of December 2–4, 1993, projected an awareness of the present state of Vietnam studies. Attention was given to the ongoing process of understanding the American culture that created the war and the American culture created by the war as part of a true national healing. Urgent needs were to counter stereotypes and misrepresentations (e.g., those of *Rambo* and *Miss Saigon*), to understand both veterans' needs and Viet Nam's culture and people, and to get beyond ethnocentric perspectives and to build cultural bridges.

For three days over 200 persons participated in 46 sessions. Those attending included scholars in various disciplines from American universities and the professions as well as from Canada, China, England and Viet Nam. Speakers discussed reconciliation issues regarding Laos and Cambodia, topics rarely included in such conferences. Generous attention was given to gender issues and to literature and films on reconciliation themes. In addition, films, poetry readings, photography exhibits, and performance pieces were presented.

As an introduction to this selection of conference papers, Larry Heinemann's personal essay describes the war as divisive for American society and senseless for most soldiers in the field. After his return to the United States Heinemann began to write because the war "would not go away" and he needed to validate his experience by writing blunt realism with crude language. Crucial to understanding the war as both an event and an expression of our national character, he suggests that future writers should turn to broader human issues and understand Viet Nam not as an American event but as a place, a people, and a culture.

Southeast Asia scholar Kristin Pelzer has been following this injunction for years; her poem "Song of Land and Water" demonstrates her current commitment. Her title alludes to the most intimate Vietnamese word for "nation" (*Dat Nuoc*, literally "land and water"). Her poem is one of the original creative pieces included. Other poems by participants Gerald McCarthy, Dale Ritterbusch, and Phoebe S. Spinrad are published here for the first time. Thus the scholarly and the creative will be blended as they were at the conference. The last line of John Balaban's poem ("After our war, how will love speak?") forcefully announces a motif in this collection.

In Section I two of the most qualified authorities on Indochina examine reconciliation issues. Craig Etcheson, executive director of the Campaign to Oppose the Return of the Khmer Rouge (formerly the Cambodia Campaign), authoritatively describes Cambodian issues. Three twentieth-century Indochina wars have left Cambodia facing reconciliation issues involving internal political factions, other Southeast Asian nations and world powers. Since September 1993 a popularly elected coalition government has been functioning, but instability continues and reconciliation has not been achieved. And Jane Hamilton-Merritt, from the perspective of a long-term involvement and personal observations and interviews, records American activities during the "secret war" in Laos and the postwar abandonment of our loyal allies, the minority Hmong people of remote mountain regions. Updating her magisterial *Tragic Mountains*, she describes gross violations by the Lao government (with U.S. complicity) of human and civil rights, forced repatriations, executions, atrocities, and genocide.[1]

The final paper in the "Indochina: Reconciliation Issues" section describe American failures to perceive and understand the Viets. David Hunt's examination of a dozen college survey texts on the war published since 1975 reveals unfinished business. In particular, ethnocentric American historians have given only cursory attention to the NLF (National Liberation Front), reducing it to an image of a foreign "other" or eliding it with the other Vietnamese factions. Hunt apprehends the tension between historical agency and narrative structure as textbook authors work to situate the NLF within the war. The section concludes with a poem by W. D. Ehrhart and the speech that Earl Martin, conference participant and Mennonite missionary who worked with the people of Viet Nam during and after the war, delivered to a gathering at My Lai village on March 16, 1993, the twenty-fifth anniversary of the massacre. He reported that the villagers are still sad but not bitter.

The second section deals with reconciliation issues that are primarily domestic ones for Americans and American society. Paul Lyons, in "Clinton, Vietnam, and the Sixties," confronts America's continuing difficulties in "getting past" Vietnam. He identifies the factions in the Sixties generation: those who fought in the war (the New Right), those who protested the war (the New Left) and those who did neither (Baby Boomers). In "M.I.A.: 'The Last Chapter'?" H. Bruce Franklin argues that President Bush tried to win reelection by turning what Bill Clinton did during the war into a campaign issue. Bush also claimed to be writing "the last chapter of the Vietnam War," but Franklin feels that the last chapter can never be written so long as the POW/MIA myth continues to possess millions of Americans. And after more than a decade of government neglect, the Clinton administration has initiated measures to address the condition of the estimated 100,000 Vietnam combat veterans who sleep on the streets of America. Marc Jason Gilbert confronts this long suppressed issue. Using documents and interviews, Gilbert defines the combat-related trauma characteristic of the majority of the homeless veterans. Furthermore, he commends the Veterans Outreach Centers for the holistic approach they take to helping troubled veterans. Until the battles for the sanity and well-being of homeless veterans are won, the process of healing from the war and the process of reconciliation will remain incomplete.

To understand veterans, sometimes elusive and troubling figures, Americans often construct stereotypes, or even social, political, and literary agendas. These responses and their outcomes, as well as the veterans' own ways of coping with their war experiences, are represented, according to Tobey C. Herzog, by three images—the blank page, the tripwire, and the interstate nomad—which are the core of two post–Vietnam novels: Philip Caputo's *Indian Country* and Larry Heinemann's *Paco's Story*. Furthermore, an essential part of the healing process for many who were in Viet Nam is a return to the land that has haunted them since the war. Catherine Calloway's "To Live in the Past Is to Walk in Darkness" examines books by men and women, American and Viet Kieu, who can only come to terms with the war, years later, by making a return trip; she discusses books by Frederick Downs, William Broyles Jr., Lynda Van Devanter, and Le Ly Hayslip. Most of the contentious post-war issues, both international and domestic, have been and will be encountered: diplomatic recognition, cultural and economic possibilities, POW/MIAs, PTSD (Post–Traumatic Stress Disorder), homeless veterans, the plight of the Amerasians, the effects of Agent Orange on people in both countries, and continuing attempts to write "the last chapter" and exorcise "the Vietnam syndrome."

Writing about the war and its aftermath, especially in poetry, constitutes an unprecedented flowering in American letters. The next two sections of the book present seven vigorous appraisals of the literature. Six films, American and Viet, were screened, and three filmmakers participated in the conference. But because much has already been published about film the focus here will be on poetic and prose projections. The first section on the literature of reconciliation includes three perceptive analyses of the poetry, which has become a unique corpus. First, Dale Ritterbusch finds that the aftermath poetry, unlike film and many novels, is an instrument of moral discourse. Vietnam has stayed with the poets longer than previous wars have stayed with their respective generations of writers. Vietnam poets depict a feeling of loss and a concern for lessons learned and unlearned, and they debunk American myths of virtue and manifest destiny and offer cultural and personal values to replace corrupted values.

In his study of women's poetry Vince Gotera finds that Viet and Viet Kieu women poets reach towards reconciliation more often than American women poets. However, Trinh Minh Ha's notion of "conflicting identities" within the writer implies the possibility of rapprochement. Finally, in "What Shall We Give Our Children?," Lorrie Smith analyzes gender and parenthood in poems by John Balaban, W. D. Ehrhart, and Bruce Weigl. The poems reveal how male veterans have overcome masculine codes of behavior and embraced more culturally feminine expressions of tenderness, nurturing, and reciprocity. Writing for and about their children leads these poets towards wholeness and authenticity by opening up connections between their own childhoods, the trauma of Vietnam, and the redemptiveness of loving parenthood. The poetry panel's commentator, Lynda Van Devanter, said that she felt that women exploring traditional male roles and men exploring women's were positive steps towards reconciliation. "For women, it was our masculine side that helped us survive the war, and our feminine side helped us heal."

In a panel on prose, Joseph T. Cox and Thomas G. Bowie concentrated on the intersection of fact and fiction. The two other papers printed here, by James Campbell and Marie S. Bonn, ponder "aftermath" narratives. Cox argues that in our collective Vietnam meta-narrative we have replaced a geographical place with an Americanized zone of consciousness that excludes, among others, the experience of women veterans and Viets. Moreover, in trying to find the truth of their war experiences veterans have had to contend with older national myths: individual heroic idealism and a divinely justified national purpose. Many Vietnam writers record disenchantment and portray the self as anti-hero: Ron Kovic, Philip Caputo, Robert Mason, Frederick Downs, and Tim O'Brien. Cox has not found any narratives of national reconciliation. Thomas G. Bowie Jr. traces Tim O'Brien's narrative journey from factual vignettes (*If I Die in a Combat Zone*) through magical realism (*Going After Cacciato*) to "factual fictions" in *The Things They Carried* and *In the Lake of the Weeds.* O'Brien struggles to narrativize the "Truth" of an experience in memory and in imagination that haunts both an individual and a national journey from war to peace. Through his narratives O'Brien invites us to consider the complex reality exposed by the stories we tell—the reality we must face as individuals and as a nation if we ever hope to understand and reconcile this experience.

James Campbell's "Coming Home" examines the reconciliation between veterans and American civilians in several texts—Bobbie Anne Mason's *In Country*, Larry Heinemann's *Paco's Story* and the film *Coming Home.* He concludes that if civilians are to offer reconciliation, it must be one which respects how different the veteran's experience has been from the civilian's. In the final paper Marie S. Bonn finds the war embedded in a larger context of violence and fragmentation in contemporary American narratives not directly about the war, with PTSD becoming a natural postmodern condition in narratives of trauma. Within these four sections, complementary poems—original and reprinted—by conference participants are placed.

The last section, Marc Leepson's edited transcript of the concluding symposium "The Arts of War and Peace," records the reflections of four veteran writers: John Balaban, Robert Olen Butler, W. D. Ehrhart, and Larry Heinemann. Both Balaban and Butler stressed that their vision of the world was profoundly shaped by having been to Viet Nam. W. D. Ehrhart and Larry Heinemann described their books as a "writing of witness." Heinemann said, "I simply couldn't shut up about what I had seen and what I had become." Ehrhart added, "We should go on talking and writing until people learn something."

The Epilogue presents creative pieces by two veterans read at the conference, Larry Rottmann's poem "A Farmer from Vinh" and Robert Olen Butler's story "Salem." Both writers speak from the minds and sensibilities of Viets in remarkable cross-cultural exchanges emblematic of reconciliation achieved by many veterans and writers on both sides. "A Farmer from Vinh" and "Salem" are by writers whose war and postwar experiences have led to compassion for the other side, now reflected in writings that imagine the consciousness of former enemies. Two decades after the war the speakers in the creative pieces are ordinary men who live in memory and with the residual belief that the souls of the dead need prayers. Rottmann's Buddhist farmer burns incense at the American crash site and Butler's ritually smokes the cigarette the American he killed left half-smoked.

Both of these creative works exemplify Butler's impression that in a "deep place," we "are neither male nor female, Vietnamese nor American.... We are simply human." Both Viets seek healing, peace, and closure, and communion in spirit between former enemies, living and dead. Butler's character, in response to a call for evidence about American MIAs, will turn in the American's photograph but keep the pack of Salems for "someday, when I know it is time."[2] Rottmann's farmer, defying the cadres, will continue his ritual. Appropriately Butler's narrator evokes the Hebrew greeting and farewell "Shalom" ("peace") as a peacemaking gesture.[3]

Two personal accounts of the Notre Dame conference appear as supplements. W. D. Ehrhart and Kim Worthy write subjective essays as Timothy Lomperis did for an Asia Society conference in *"Reading the Wind."* Neither tries to give a comprehensive overview; each highlights individual speakers, panels, and events, along with serendipitous occurrences and personal reflections. Although some past encounters with academic approaches had left W. D. Ehrhart bewildered, he felt exhilarated after the Notre Dame conference and acknowledges that academics must teach the next generations about the war.

Kim Worthy argues that transcendence of race and gender are necessary for reconciliation. She quotes from Lynda Van Devanter's presentation: "Healing from this war will come for America when a spiritual direction returns, not just a physical, mental, or emotional direction." Van Devanter finds that the works of women and Viets provide this transcendence. Another supplement, "Viet Nam and the United States" presents a concise chronology of historical and cultural events relating to the war.

In his conference keynote address, Neil Sheehan said that the lessons of the war are pivotal. He acknowledges that American policy regarding Viet Nam was based on self-confidence, arrogance, illusion and "bright shining lies." Unless we can confront the truth, the lives of 58,000 Americans will have been wasted. To forget Vietnam is to forget the "fallibility" which Americans share with the rest of humanity, the capacity to do evil as well as good. The United States and Viet Nam are, according to Viet Kieu filmmaker Tiana/Thi Thanh Nga, two nations "tied in blood." Her film-journey *From Hollywood to Hanoi* attempts to reconcile her Vietnamese and American identities.

Two 1995 events evoked passionate responses from several segments— veterans, the antiwar left, the revanchist right, and the Viet Kieu. Robert S. McNamara, military promoter of the war, published his *mea culpa, In Retrospect: The Tragedy and Lessons of Vietnam* in which he admitted that "we were wrong, terribly wrong." And President Clinton, who avoided the draft, was both praised and cursed for his decision to establish relations with Viet Nam. A year earlier, W. D. Ehrhart wrote that "the American war ... goes on and on, an open sore on the body politic, a powerful and evocative talisman whose meaning is as multifarious and incomprehensible as the tongues that emerged from the rubble of the Tower of Babel." The struggle to understand the meaning and the "lessons" continues.[4]

The writers in this book make original and substantial contributions towards the goal of closure and reconciliation among divisive elements in both Viet Nam and the United States.

Notes

1. For this book, some of the contributors have revised their essays. The two international essays are essentially new pieces, in which Craig Etcheson and Jane Hamilton-Merritt update their assessments of reconciliation issues to late 1994. And Thomas G. Bowie includes Tim O'Brien's 1994 novel *In the Lake of the Woods* in his analysis.

2. At the Notre Dame conference, James L. Brazee, president of the Vietnam Veterans of America, announced his organization's sponsorship of a parallel initiative calling for the submission of objects removed from dead enemies as well as information about burial sites. In Viet Nam during April 1994, veterans from both sides exchanged artifacts and information. In addition, Americans learned that Viets burned incense at battle sites to honor all the dead. Cf. "Vietnam Journal," *The VVA Veteran*, August 1994: 24–30. See also Kristin Pelzer's conference paper published as "United States and Vietnam: On the Need for Spiritual Reconciliation," *Buddhist-Christian Studies* 13 (1993): 188–195, and the chant of invocation by Viet Nam's national poet Nguyen Du: "Calling the Wandering Souls" (reprinted in Pelzer's article).

3. In a conversation with me on 10 October 1994, Robert Olen Butler said that he was not aware of the Hebrew origins of "Salem." The Hebrew connection, of course, would not be known to Butler's narrator who parses the word into its Vietnamese components (*sa* "to fall" and *lem* "to blur").

4. W. D. Ehrhart, "Old Ghosts and Doubts Linger from the Vietnam War," *The VVA Veteran*, August 1994: 8. Ehrhart concludes that "Americans will put the Vietnam War behind us only when the last surviving member of the Vietnam generation is shoveled into the ground." One of my students, an Amerasian, added that children of the Vietnam generation will continue the heritage.

Prologue:
Vietnam After All These Years

LARRY HEINEMANN

The Vietnam War was a benchmark of American history if there ever was one. It was a cusp, a strangely shaped event through which the Vietnam survivors—the whole country, for that matter—were extruded. We lost our naiveté—had it ripped out of our throats; had it beat out of us most dramatically with the buckle end of the belt—understanding finally and full well that Lyndon Johnson's and Richard Nixon's were governments of selfish, arrogant old men, jolly well ready to eat their own young, both here and overseas, to preserve their own shabby honor and specious dignity. Richard Nixon's "Peace with honor" is as hollow and shallow, and laughable, a phrase as Chamberlain's "Peace in our time."

In its own way the Vietnam War was as extraordinary, divisive, and evocative as our own Civil War—with *its* senseless blood-feud self-destruction, draft riots, bungled military stupidities, and eager but doomed young volunteers. The war was dirty, sloppy, ball-breaking, ugly, grueling, and mean-spirited; not a pleasant business, and we—the soldiers in the field—were not pleasant people. We learned to hate people on sight for the slant of their eyes and the black pants they wore.

Parenthetically, there is nowadays circulating the oddly revised notion that the United States could have won that war. Where did this bizarre notion come from? Lifers and housecats, no doubt. Certainly not from any 11-Bravo grunt *I* know. To say we could have won the war is to say that we didn't fill our hearts with enough hate; didn't napalm or strafe or frag them hard enough; didn't Zippo enough hooches or turn enough of their women into whores; didn't bomb them with B-52 air strikes into small enough pieces far enough back into the Stone Age—the bomb craters as big as house lots.

I was drafted, submitted to conscription with what can only be described as soul-deadening dread, and trained for "Europe" at Fort Knox in the armored cavalry, reconnaissance—recon, we called it. "The eyes and ears of the combat arms," they told us, trying to hide their smirks. A hundred years ago I would have been a scout in the horse cavalry. You know, the guy in the John Wayne movies mounted on the best horse in the troop, some big-ass, steady-

9

as-a-rock eager chestnut plow horse. I'd wear a buckskin fringe jacket, a big brushy mustache, and a rawhide cowboy hat with the brim turned up (decorated with feathers and other Wild West fetishes). I'd ride out into the tall savannah grass of the Dakota plains or some such place to scare up some Indians. Then ride back and come booming up to Mr. Wayne (as we called him on the set; John dressed fit to kill in a bright yellow bandanna, spit-shined riding boots, and non-regulation spurs), my hair-a-flying and eyes wild, whooping and shouting (the horse drooling and snorting lather), "Kunnel! Injins! Lots of 'em. Atta way!"

I did my tour on an armored personnel carrier. We rode roughshod over the countryside around the Michelin Rubber Plantation and Tay Ninh; part of War Zone C—Cochinchina, the French called it. And, to make a long story short, I have no doubt that we radicalized more Vietnamese to Ho Chi Minh's revolution than we "saved." There is an old saying, you know, "Sometimes the best way to disobey an order is to obey it to the letter," and what Michael Herr said in *Dispatches* was true: we wanted to give you a Vietnam you could put in your ashtray. Nevertheless, it seemed especially ominous and foreboding—not to say ironic—when we came upon ruined, long-abandoned French trucks and tanks in the jungle—abundant foliage growing out of the turrets and hatches and horsehair seat cushions. We weren't so bone-numb exhausted and grunt-work stupid that the inference was lost on us: This is what happened to the French, and they hadn't been in Southeast Asia since 1954; what the hell are *we* doing here?

We drove ordinary convoys hell-for-leather, as the saying goes, blowing through roadside hamlets full-bore flat-out. Busting jungle in the Hobo and Bo Loi woods—pushing over trees as big around as you can reach. Search-and-destroy missions—booming into back-country hamlets, *looking* for VC. You could stand buck naked in the middle of a village street and piss in plain sight of 100 people, and as long as you were an American GI with a rifle and a steel pot, no one dared say boo. We tracked the Viet Cong and North Vietnamese soldiers down like dogs and shot them on sight (those we could actually find, though most of the time they found us). We measured our battlefield success by the peculiar institution of the body count, as if the corpses were so many road kills. Standing naked taking a whiz in public was the least of our atrocities; such were the broad and generous permissions in the field. A modern army does not want warriors, you understand, it wants killers, capable of berserk viciousness. And to our shame there was a lot of "looking the other way."

We were sternly warned not to "fraternize" with the Vietnamese; *not* to learn the language; *not* to eat the food; *not* to drink the beer; *not* to listen to their music, or in any way come to appreciate them as people. With the result that "Vietnam" is most often spoken and thought of as an event that *happened* to us, rather than a place or a people or a culture several thousand years old.

The War was unwinnable in any case. Such was the Vietnamese's extraordinary ambition to discover the "Mandate of Heaven" and rid their country of foreigners that we would have had to kill them all and burn their country to the ground. The Vietnamese accomplished their victory with sheer courage and organized patience, common sense and simple tools, and an ideology only too well suited to their culture and their gifts (not unlike ourselves during our own revolution). We have no reason to despise the Vietnamese for their single-minded self-determination.

We prosecuted the war refusing to believe the writing on the wall about our defeat. Our inability, or to be more precise refusal, to understand the movement of Vietnamese history has cost us dearly, and resulted in two simple facts (among many). William Westmoreland has no idea why he lost, while Vo Nguyen Giap understands superbly why he won. And if General Giap has been criticized for needlessly squandering the lives at some of his troops at Dien Bien Phu, the A Shau, the Tet Offensive of 1968, and other campaigns (the droll, old-fashioned phrase being "a waste of good infantry"), it can also be said with a straight face that General Westmoreland squandered *all* of his. Giap is one of the great military minds of the twentieth century; Westmoreland is the ultimate, boorish careerist (a ticket-punching lifer, as we used to say). There were a lot of people like him who went to Viet Nam to cash in on the rank and medals (given out like popcorn, you understand); the war was *good* for their careers.

In the field, if there was an overall spirit of atrocity (and it did take many forms), there was also another, almost opposite, spirit among the troops which became more apparent as the war dragged on. I can only speak of it in this way: When Tolstoy wrote *War and Peace* he put this perception into the mind and martial spirit of General Kutuzov, commander of the Russian armies who fought Napoleon, a fat old guy with one good eye who would fall asleep at meetings, briefings, and the like. It is the *spirit* of the troops, a willingness to surrender your body and your life to an idea larger than yourself (a motherland, say, or a profound and elegant democratic assumption about the equality and justice), which wins a nation's war or loses it. Tolstoy's Kutuzov understood this superbly. During the Vietnam epoch there were no large ideas, aside from the exaggerated and pathetic military propaganda about "saving the world from Communism," and other such lifers' nonsense; I think it's safe to say the only thing fought for in Viet Nam were those things a soldier could actually *see*, the ground around him and his fellows (with whom he shared a gracious intimacy not permitted among men in this culture, and no doubt not possible in any other circumstance). By the way, we never referred to ourselves as "buddies," that irksome journalist's cliché; "buddy-up" was something you did at boy scout camp when it was time to go down to the lake for a swim, and Vietnam was many things, but it certainly wasn't the annual jamboree.

And if it is true that two-thirds of the U.S. troops in Viet Nam were volunteers, it is also true that we learned of our betrayal as soon as we set foot in the field. The war was a shuck, as the saying goes, and ordinary soldiers understood well enough that we had been fucked—to say it clearly and unmistakably.

Our most vulnerable and trusting impulses had been betrayed—squeezed out of us; burned out—by a solid year's tour, by a government that would rather kill us all than admit a mistake. We were worse than so many numbers, worse still than so many bricks in the wall. We were so much meat on the slab to be butchered. The same had happened on a much grander scale in World War I when virtually an entire generation of men was put to death in the trenches of France—English, French, German; a remarkable, unconscionable waste—by leaders whose unimaginative stupidity would, as Mark Twain once said, go around the world four times and tie. (Indeed, the workaday, daily British casualties were tallied under the category "Wastage.")

We can metaphorically speak of the government as a "father," who you assume loves you and wishes you only the best—and being betrayed by your father, not once but 365 times, is a powerful, unforgettable lesson. Vietnam veterans as a rule feel used, wasted, and dumped, even all these years later. We are not victims and we are not heroes; there is nothing ennobling or enriching or manly about the infantry, mind you. We are treated like meat and expected to behave like meat, and returned home reeking with what has been called the "death taint," which seems the perfect word for it.

Taken all around, the survivors can only say we lived. We cannot say that we did our work well. We cannot say that we feel good about the work we did; combat as "work" simply cannot be as satisfying as ordinary-wages work. War produces an astonishing, pervasive ugliness, and that's all.

I left Vietnam with the wistful notion that when I got home I could act as if my war year was as unremarkable and unreal as if it had happened to someone else, and I could pick up my life where I left off. That didn't happen, of course, but that is the impulse which got me aboard my plane at Tan Son Nhut.

It is a roaring ironic understatement to say that the 1960s and early 1970s were a time of great social change, if not downright upheaval. By and large, I think that we veterans scared people—the thousand meter stare is a most uncomfortable gaze. The hard and shrunken, hollowed-out look (carriage, stance, "attitude") of just-returned veterans did not rub off quickly, and genuinely took people aback.

I was not one of those guys who went to "his room," and never said boo about the war. I couldn't shut up about what I'd seen and what I'd done and what I had become. I told anyone who asked, and without the polite dashes, the tasteful euphemisms, or the discreet ellipses. The power to name is extraordinary—that's what racism and sexism are all about—and during and after the war veterans were called many things. I wanted to name myself, thank you, and be precise; not a hero, not a victim, just a man trying to deal with an extraordinary circumstance and come out the other end of it in one piece.

So, I began writing; and it *is* more elegant and articulate than a simple "fuck you." And I think the writers who emerged from the Vietnam War had an advantage over the men who wrote about World War II, those writers most accessible to us. The advantage was their fresh example, of course (these men of my father's generation), as well as the gritty, close-to-the-bone, walk-the-plank Beat writers of the late 1950s and early 1960s. We also had the considerable advantage of the broad permissions of the time for language and subject matter, and the attitude to *take* advantage. To leave nothing out. To take to heart Joseph Conrad's imperative to, above all, make you *see*. In Paul Fussell's seminal work *The Great War and Modern Memory*, he makes clear that the soldier-writers of World War I struggled to find the language and the way to tell the story of their trenches—that hell-bound squalor and madness—but found themselves culture-bound (and self-censored) by propriety and "taste," and a class-bound sentimentality that simply refused to hear. The results were stories that come to us considerably diminished.

Not so Vietnam, and the blunt realism and frank language of ordinary soldiers leaves very little of the realities of the work of the war to the imagination.

I think the writing has come in three distinct movements.

First of all, it deserves to be mentioned that very little imaginative literature, and by that I mean poetry and prose and plays, was published before 1975. To be sure, there was a good deal of writing about the war, but it took the form of political and historical reportage; very little was published by the soldiers themselves. You can count the number of works during that time practically on the fingers of one hand. The war was still pounding and lurching along to its inevitable, pathetic conclusion, and the raw ambivalence of most Americans was at its most touchy extreme. (After 1975, or should I say since, the bibliography has reached well into the hundreds.)

During this time there occurred two concrete events that we can clearly identify as milestones. The first was in 1973 when the Paris Peace Accords were signed, and the American POWs returned—that event dutifully and rightly broadcast live from Guam in the middle of the night. And secondly, the absolutely final, once-and-for-all, distinctly abrupt end to the war in April 1975 when the last Americans scrambled up that paint ladder to the last bit of embassy roof to the last waiting helicopter (galling to watch for the crowds of ordinary Vietnamese in the street), and the North Vietnamese Army drove their tanks into the city and asked for the surrender of the last South Vietnamese government. (I don't know about anyone else, but I felt as if a personal, almost physical agony had ended and a stone had been lifted from my heart, even though I'd been home from the war for seven years.)

To return to my point, the writing immediately before the end and after the war were true "war stories." Most in the form of personal, fictionalized memoirs. Most writers of my acquaintance had simply to take the time to educate themselves to the craft. I myself was among them. It is a topic of no small irony that I, and other veterans, became writers because of the war. And the overarching ambition of the writing during this stage was simply to, above all, validate an experience for ourselves. At least that was my motivation; this *did* happen, *this* is what *that* was; and I am certainly not the first person to write a thing down because I want to discover and understand what it was I thought.

I wrote two novels about the war because the subject simply would not go away. I wanted to make as clear as I was able that *this* is what awaits you, or something similar; that the work of the infantry will transform you into something you don't even recognize; that *this* is what you make when you make war. And perhaps I should add that those first two books were in no way cathartic, as many people would like to suppose (writing as "therapy," God help us). The world doesn't work that way.

I understand that there have been comments made about the absence of the Vietnamese point of view in much of the war literature of this period; all I can say is that the perception and humanity of the enemy is almost never the point of the modern war story form. (Robert Olen Butler's work is a vivid exception to the rule.)

The second movement was an exploration of the inevitable reverberations of the war. Still war stories, perhaps, but of a more reflective and considered kind, and many of these writers waited, as Joseph Heller had to wait. Like Tieg O'Kane of the Irish folktale, they had first to go for one thing, then another, until the impulse finally came together with the opportunity to tell their part of the story.

Now, of course, there is a third milestone to regard, the end of the United States' embargo against Viet Nam, lifted on February 3, 1994. If the first wave of writing was flat-out war stories, and the second wave had to do with the aftermath (still largely concentrating on the American experience), then the third wave calls attention to contemporary Viet Nam, or to put it another way, "Who-are-these-guys?"

Americans, largely veterans, have been returning to Vietnam since the middle 1980s. We began going back for the broadest variety of reasons, but I think it's fair to say that these have not been "guilt" trips. I lately read an article in the *New York Times* about Americans going to Viet Nam, business people, émigré Vietnamese, travelers interested in the exotic, as well as a category labeled "old soldiers" attracted to "battlefields they cannot forget." Are we *old* soldiers simply hankering for the good old days? Are we sentimental, middle-aged jerks who can't get enough of that nostalgia for adolescence, which amounts to regret—regret at aging along with the rest of humanity?

Are we locked up so tightly into a memory that little else has been able to penetrate? Do we long for the days when we were built like brick shithouses, could drink all night, our peckers never went limp, and we were immortal? Is that how we are perceived?

There is something more keenly fundamental to our travels back to Viet Nam, another kind of validation; just as the Vietnamese who travel here seek some deeper connection with us. These have not been journeys of rediscovery, because the Viet Nam we saw during the war turned out, as you might expect, not to be Viet Nam at all. What these trips (and the writing which results) have been is discovery of the Vietnamese as a people in a place, language and song, poetry and story, and a way of life that has persisted for many centuries. And it has already become a considerable cliché among veterans who travel there that we received a warmer welcome and more heartfelt hospitality going back to Viet Nam than we received from the American culture when we returned from the war. To their credit the Vietnamese have always been able to make the important distinction between the American government who tried to bomb them back to the Stone Age and the American people, who wanted no part of the war.

Isn't there something we can learn from them?

But after nearly twenty years, so earnest still is the rancor and resentment and aggressive misunderstanding of the Vietnamese in this country, as well as their embargo-imposed isolation, that any writing on the subject is regarded as exotic.

American war literature has turned from the blunt and frank self-examination (and self-explanation) to the broader human issues; not questions we had to ask ourselves after World War I or World War II. We Americans are famous for not picking on ourselves. But the unfinished business of the war, the social and political and moral reverberations, are still with us *and* the Vietnamese. Not the least of it has to do with our understanding of their extraordinary fortitude and patience for independence, as well as their passion for all things lively, their deep fellow-feeling, and their rich appreciation and affection for Americans—that has nothing to do with the war, mind you.

I don't know that any reasonable, sensible person thinks the Vietnam War was a good and righteous undertaking. It is crucial that we come to understand the war as an event and expression of our national character, and accept the responsibility. And I am not talking about making it right, not at all; such a thing cannot be made "right."

What I am saying is that if we have any claim to morality, as many European countries insist, we have to discover what it was, that epoch of arrogant greed and self-destruction, and be honest with ourselves.

At a time when the Vietnamese seek to move out into the world, and Americans seek to discover, again, who we are, the political and social rewards to be had from this cultural rapprochement cannot be measured.

Song of Land and Water

The earth is moist
With tears

The tears of a wife
Left by her husband

The tears of a child
Teased by her older brother

The tears of foreign soldiers
far from home
Chinese, French, American, Thai, Korean
Soldiers
Stepping, bleeding, killing, weeping, shooting, shouting
on the soil of Vietnam

The turmoil
of ancient battles
and recent conflicts
hum in the land

Defeats unforgiven
Anger unprocessed
Disturb the sleep
of children

Babies
cry out
as they are tossed
by the night-mares
dream she-horses
of the land
on which they sleep

If you lie as quiet
As a child
Sleeping in
Her mother's arms

You may hear
As from a great distance

The sigh of the land
The song of the land

—KRISTIN PELZER

After Our War

After our war, the dismembered bits
—all those pierced eyes, ear slivers, jaw splinters,
gouged lips, odd tibias, skin flaps, and toes—
came squinting, wobbling, jabbering back.
The genitals, of course, were the most bizarre,
inching along roads like glowworms and slugs.
The living wanted them back, but good as new.
The dead, of course, had no use for them.
And the ghosts, the tens of thousands of abandoned
   souls
who had appeared like swamp fog in the city streets,
on the evening altars, and on doorsills of cratered
   homes,
also had no use for the scraps and bits
because, in their opinion, they looked good without
   them.
Since all things naturally return to their source,
these snags and tatters arrived, with immigrant
   uncertainty,
in the United States. It was almost home.
So, now, one can sometimes see a friend or a
   famous man talking
with an extra pair of lips glued and yammering on
   his cheek,
and this is why handshakes are often unpleasant,
why it is better, sometimes, not to look another in
   the eye,
why, at your daughter's breast thickens a hard
   keloidal scar.
After the war, with such Cheshire cats grinning in
   our trees,
will the ancient tales still tell us new truths?
Will the myriad world surrender new metaphor?
After our war, how will love speak?

         —JOHN BALABAN

I.
INDOCHINA:
RECONCILIATION
ISSUES

1. Reconciliation Issues in Cambodia

CRAIG ETCHESON

Twenty years after the United States ended its war in Indochina, "reconciliation" is literally the subject of newspaper headlines in Cambodia on a daily basis: reconciliation with the United States, reconciliation between the Cambodian government and the outlawed Khmer Rouge guerrillas, reconciliation among the factions of the Royal Government of Cambodia, and reconciliation within Cambodia's royalist party. Popular Cambodian citizens' organizations demand reconciliation. Virtually all Cambodian politicians extoll the virtues of national reconciliation. Khmer Rouge guerrilla spokesmen are particularly eloquent on the topic.

Why Cambodia Needs Reconciliation

The history of the twentieth century weighs heavily on Cambodia's leaders. The First, Second and Third Indochinese Wars covered most of this century. The First Indochina War was the war, or rather wars, of French decolonization. This conflict heated up on the heels of World War II, and climaxed with Cambodia and Laos winning full independence in 1954, while Viet Nam was divided between north and south. This division resulted in the Second Indochina War, the war of Vietnamese unification. The violence of this war engulfed not only neighboring Laos and Cambodia but also drew in the United States, China, and the Soviet Union, along with many of their respective allies.

The Third Indochina War also resulted in the rise to power in Cambodia of the genocidal Khmer Rouge regime, and thus planted the seeds of the Third Indochina War.

This third Indochinese conflict was complex, involving both great powers and regional powers. In Cambodia, the Third Indochina War exploded from border clashes with Viet Nam to full-scale combat as the Vietnamese invaded and overthrew the Khmer Rouge regime. It rolled on with a Chinese attack on northern Viet Nam and developed into a 13-year civil war among four Cambodian factions. The conflict was fueled in part by a Vietnamese military occupation of Cambodia, as well as by proxy forces inside and outside of the region supporting the ousted Khmer Rouge and other resistance factions. It ended only after the Soviet Union collapsed, and U.S. and Chinese strategic interests evolved.

These three wars left Cambodia facing a host of reconciliation issues involving various internal political factions and other nations in the region, as well as world powers. Many nations have seen fit to involve themselves in Cambodia's internal and external affairs during the twentieth century. The issue of reconciliation in Cambodia is consequently inextricably bound up in questions reaching far beyond the borders of that benighted land. In part this is so because the convulsions of Cambodia have produced a great diaspora, scattering its people across the planet to regions near and far.[1] In part it is so because of Cambodia's strategic location at the crossroads of Southeast Asia.

Many of Cambodia's reconciliation issues are internal. The last quarter century has witnessed a fracturing of the Cambodian political elite that is unprecedented in modern history. Both the Cambodian diaspora and these internal political fractures reached their climaxes in the Third Indochina War. It is therefore useful in understanding Cambodian reconciliation issues to briefly review the history of this third regional conflict of the century.

The Third Indochina War began before the fall of Saigon to revolutionary forces. Within days of the Khmer Rouge victory over Lon Nol's Khmer Republic on April 17, 1975, Khmer Rouge troops moved to assert revanchist territorial claims in southern Viet Nam. They began by seizing several contested coastal islands in the Gulf of Thailand. During the last weeks of April 1975, the Republic of Viet Nam ("South Vietnam") was in its death throes and unable to resist the predatory actions ordered by the enigmatic Khmer Rouge leader, Pol Pot. Asserting his ambition to recover the lost imperial territories of the Angkor Empire, Pol Pot soon attacked Laos and Thailand as well. The Khmer Rouge state of Democratic Kampuchea was a bad neighbor from the start.[2]

Inside Cambodia, the most radical revolution of the twentieth century unfolded with extreme speed.[3] All cities were emptied. Families were broken up, love was forbidden, and choice of marriage partners became a state function. All personal possessions were outlawed and all activities became communal. The Buddhist religion was utterly obliterated, as were all other religions practiced in Cambodia. Persons associated with the previous regime, most people who had formal education, and anyone who could be linked to Viet Nam were tortured and executed. The unrelenting slaughter gained momentum in 1976.

By 1977, Cambodia's military attacks on Viet Nam resumed and expanded. For several years, the Vietnamese attempted to resolve the "border question" through diplomatic negotiations with Pol Pot's regime. With no resolution in sight, the Vietnamese decided in September 1977 to "teach

Pol Pot a lesson," briefly invading a thin strip along the entire Cambodian-Vietnamese border. The lesson served only to convince Pol Pot that a duel to the death was in progress. Internal purges accelerated and cross-border raids into Viet Nam increased.

By the end of 1978, the Vietnamese had had enough. On Christmas Day, 1978, Viet Nam launched a massive invasion. Pol Pot's eviscerated state, army and society crumbled before the onslaught, and on January 7, 1979, less than two weeks after they attacked, the Vietnamese army entered Phnom Penh. As Pol Pot took to the hills with the rump of his army and administrative apparatus, the Vietnamese installed a new regime made up of refugees and defectors from the Khmer Rouge.[4] The new Cambodian regime established the People's Republic of Kampuchea, and set about attempting to reconstruct a nation shattered by war, revolution and genocide. Their task was made more difficult by a welter of factors, including a continuing Vietnamese military occupation, a tight international economic embargo, and continuing internal military challenges by several rival factions.

In Washington, President Carter's national security adviser, Zbigniew Brzezinski, immediately moved to involve the United States: "I encouraged the Chinese to support Pol Pot. I encouraged the Thai to help" Democratic Kampuchea.[5] By December of 1979, nonetheless, the Khmer Rouge were hard-pressed by the Vietnamese army, and Pol Pot's spokesman Khieu Samphan sent out a diplomatic signal: "All peace-loving, justice-loving countries ought to realize that it is in their interests to stop Vietnamese and Soviet expansionism."[6] This seemingly pitiful plea dovetailed perfectly with what would soon come to be known as the "Reagan Doctrine," the policy of supporting guerrilla wars against the periphery of the Soviet Empire in Afghanistan, Angola, Nicaragua, and Cambodia. Soon the United States was actively aiding Pol Pot's efforts to regain power in Cambodia.[7] Along with China, the ASEAN states and others, the United States arranged a united front between Pol Pot, Prince Norodom Sihanouk, and Cambodian republicans from Lon Nol's regime, creating the exiled Coalition Government of Democratic Kampuchea.

The war lasted 13 long and bitter years.[8] With the collapse of the Eastern Bloc in 1989 and Soviet withdrawal from the Third World in 1990, the Vietnamese army withdrew from Cambodia. The loss of external sponsorship forced the beleaguered Cambodian government to come to terms with the Khmer Rouge–dominated guerrillas. This fact reveals one of the central aspects of reconciliation in Cambodia: when the Russians, Chinese and Americans tired of supporting a proxy war there, they sought to impose a political solution on Cambodia. Yet, the complexities of international intervention in Cambodian affairs over the previous decades combined with the deep bitterness generated within the Cambodian political elite to render an externally imposed reconciliation tenuous at best.

What Kind of Reconciliation for Cambodia?

In the eight months following the September 24, 1993, promulgation of the Royal Government of Cambodia (RGC), the new Royal Army fought and lost ferocious battles against the recalcitrant Khmer Rouge across widespread areas of the country. Finally, on May 27, 1994, top officials of the RGC met to discuss national reconciliation with Khmer Rouge representatives at King Norodom Sihanouk's exile palace in Pyongyang, North Korea.[9] Khmer Rouge spokesman Khieu Samphan told the meeting, "To achieve genuine national reconciliation ... all of us should compromise and make mutual concessions."[10] Such reasonable sentiments could not mask the fact that both the RGC and the Khmer Rouge regarded the other as illegitimate, with each demanding that the other dissolve their political and military organizations. With both sides calling for the preemptive surrender of the other, there was little ground for "mutual concessions." In fact, in a classic Cambodian fashion, in the closing communiqué from the Pyongyang meeting, the only thing the two sides could agree on was something that was not true: they affirmed that Cambodia is undivided and indivisible. Within weeks, the RGC had officially declared the Khmer Rouge to be an "outlaw" organization, and the Khmer Rouge had formally proclaimed a provisional resistance government.[11]

All of this was a far cry from the hopes raised by the United Nations peacekeeping mission in Cambodia. The Paris treaty on Cambodia in October 1991 committed the United Nations to the largest, most expensive and most interventionist peacekeeping operation in history.[12] Idealists argue that the goal of the accords was to bring peace to a land that had known a quarter century of war and genocide. Realists argue the purpose was merely to remove the "Cambodian problem" from the international agenda. In either case, the Agreements on a Comprehensive Political Settlement of the Cambodian Conflict[13] are being seen as a model for collective security in the post–Cold War world order.[14] Consequently, it is essential that we have a clear understanding of exactly what these agreements did—and did not—accomplish. As is clear from the title of the Paris agreements, the central idea of the peace process was to achieve national reconciliation.

The Comprehensive Settlement did achieve numerous significant reconciliation-related objectives. The Cambodian conflict was decoupled from great power geopolitical conflict. Chinese military aid to the Khmer Rouge was terminated, and China has grown closer to the new Royal Government. Cambodia's two decades of international isolation came to an end.[15] Some 362,000 refugees left the camps in Thailand and returned to Cambodia. The three-faction rebel coalition challenging the Cambodian government was reduced to a single faction in opposition, the Khmer Rouge. At the same time, Cambodia's single party state became a multiparty nation, thus marking the fragile beginnings of political pluralism. A free press is flowering in

Cambodia as never before. A dozen or more indigenous human rights groups have been founded and continue to grow rapidly. Ninety percent of eligible Cambodians registered to vote, and 89 percent of those voted during May 1993 in free and fair elections, despite Khmer Rouge threats to kill anyone who participated. A liberal constitution was promulgated in September 1993, and a coalition government has been functioning ever since, more or less. These are huge accomplishments, a tribute to the skill and dedication of the international civil servants who risked and in some cases sacrificed their lives in Cambodia.[16] It is also a tribute to the hopes of the Cambodian people for national reconciliation.

At the same time, one must be clear-headed in assessing the impact of the U.N. peace process in Cambodia. The Comprehensive Settlement laid out numerous central objectives above and beyond the elections. First, the cease-fire must be implemented and maintained. Second, all outside assistance to the warring factions must be terminated. Third, the warring armies must be cantoned, disarmed and demobilized. Fourth, the utterly destroyed Cambodian economy must be rehabilitated. Fifth, the demobilized soldiers, internally displaced persons, and repatriated refugees must be reintegrated into civil society. And sixth, a neutral political environment must be established; which is to say, state institutions must be decoupled from party organs. None of these central objectives of the U.N. peace plan in Cambodia was achieved.[17]

U.S. Secretary of State Warren Christopher called the 1993 elections in Cambodia "the triumph of democracy."[18] But we know that one U.N.-administered election does not make a democracy. In fact, if one examines the transition to stable, liberal democratic systems in western, northern and southern Europe, in central and southern Latin America, and in the emerging democracies of East Asia, it is clear that this process depends on the existence of strong labor movements and a powerful middle class, capable of bargaining with the landed and capital-holding classes.[19] These conditions do not remotely exist in Cambodia, and thus one may confidently conclude that it is quite premature to predict the consolidation of democratic rule in Cambodia. To be completely fair, critics of the U.N. operation in Cambodia should not ascribe such a goal to the operation; likewise, partisans of the U.N. operation should avoid claiming to have achieved that goal.

So, far from the peace and national reconciliation sought through the U.N. peacekeeping mission, Cambodia is wobbling along on the verge of anarchy. Unresolved problems following the November 1993 withdrawal of the United Nations mission to Cambodia are festering and growing unchecked. There is little effective governance in the zones of the country controlled by the Royal Government. At the same time, the zones controlled by the Khmer rouge are again growing through military conquest; 1994 saw the heaviest combat in Cambodia for more than five years, and the Khmer Rouge vowed to escalate the violence in the 1995 dry season. Reconciliation is not among the accomplishments of the U.N. peacekeeping operation in Cambodia.[20]

Great Powers and Cambodian Reconciliation

In the aftermath of the United Nations Transitional Authority in Cambodia, involvement of great powers in Cambodia has indeed undergone a transition. In Moscow, Cambodia has become a non-issue. As previously noted, the dissolution of the Soviet Union was among the principal reasons for the end of the Third Indochina War, leading in turn to the peace process and the beginning of the new war. In one of the few statements on Cambodia to issue from the Russian Federation in the last few years, the Russian Foreign Ministry supported the outlawing of the Khmer Rouge by the Cambodian National Assembly in July 1994, and called for Cambodia's neighbors to "contribute to the cause of protecting peace" by blocking aid to the Khmer Rouge.[21] One measure of the degree to which Cambodia has fallen off the agenda in Moscow is found in comparing pledges for economic aid at the International Conference on the Reconstruction of Cambodia in June 1992. The Russian Federation pledged $1.8 million, or approximately 10 percent of the amount pledged by Canada and less than 1 percent of the amount pledged by Japan.[22]

In Washington, at least according to one Central Intelligence Agency source, "the Cambodian issue is dead." Still, a strong and continuing interest in Cambodia exists among some U.S. agencies. For example, on April 30, 1994, President Clinton signed into law legislation establishing a U.S. State Department Office of Cambodian Genocide Investigations (CGI),[23] which is tasked with putting forward a U.S. proposal for an international genocide tribunal to judge Khmer Rouge crimes against humanity. Some view such a tribunal as an essential prerequisite for national reconciliation in Cambodia; others see it as making reconciliation impossible. Perhaps in response to the CGI project, the Khmer Rouge announced on October 1, 1994, that it was establishing a "Commission to Review the U.S. War of Aggression to Massacre the Cambodian People Between 1970 and 1975."[24] A principal cause of this decision, according to a broadcast over Khmer Rouge clandestine radio, is that the United States has been "conducting all manner of activities to oppose national reconciliation."

The United States has also been active in providing economic, diplomatic and military support to the new Cambodian government. The Clinton administration has threatened a long-standing U.S. ally, Thailand, with military sanctions over the issue of continuing relations between the Thai military and the Khmer Rouge.[25] The Pentagon has recently dispatched several dozen military advisers and trainers to assist the Royal Cambodian Armed Forces. In addition, the United States provided nearly $1 million in non-lethal military assistance in 1994, and has sent military delegations to study lethal aid requirements.[26] The U.S. Agency for International Development is operating rural development and democratization programs in Cambodia on the scale of $25–$30 million per year. Thus, although Cambodia may no longer be a great political issue in the United States, Washington continues to devote much attention to, and exert substantial influence in, that small nation.

Beijing also remains deeply interested in Cambodian affairs. Having recently grown to be the third largest economy in the world, China continues to pursue a massive rearmament program reflecting its economic stature. China's aggressive behavior on such issues as Tibet, the Spratly Islands, Hong Kong and the Missile Technology Control Regime has spurred growing fears among her Southeast Asian neighbors. For thousands of years, China has regarded Southeast Asia as her exclusive sphere of influence, and there are signs China is once again willing to employ force to back up those claims. Even though the Chinese have distanced themselves from the Khmer Rouge, Beijing remains a major factor in the Cambodian crisis. In a significant development, Chinese involvement in Cambodia seems to be transforming itself from military support for the Khmer Rouge (1970–1991) to economic ties with the Royal Government, thus resuming the pre–1970 pattern. In an August 1994 letter to the co–prime ministers of Cambodia, PRC Premier Li Peng affirmed that China continues to deny assistance to the Khmer Rouge, adding that "China will continue to render support and assistance to Cambodia's national reconciliation and reconstruction."[27] The Chinese have backed this assertion by providing a variety of non-lethal assistance to the Cambodian Royal Armed Forces. Chinese state-industrial firms have recently been negotiating to build a large industrial center in Cambodia.[28] China could thus be a major force for reconciliation in Cambodia.

France, Britain and Australia also remain actively engaged in Cambodia. Sadly, however, most of the public notice of this engagement involves their citizens being murdered and kidnapped in attacks attributed to Khmer Rouge guerrillas. Khmer Rouge radio linked the survival of hostage nationals from these countries to political conditions, demanding that the "ambassadors of the three respective countries ... shall publicly and openly declare, on behalf of their countries, that they are halting the provision of military aid" to the RGC.[29] All three of these countries have been providing modest levels of non-lethal aid to the Cambodian government. France has been the most active of the three, attempting to woo her former colony with aid promises linked to Francophone reforms. Australia is planning to rebuild Cambodia's naval forces, and the French have also been active in military and police training. All three have explicitly rejected efforts by the Khmer Rouge to change their Cambodia policies through hostage extortion. Such events would seem to make less likely any possible efforts by these countries to encourage peaceful reconciliation between the Khmer Rouge and the RGC.

The principal combatants in Cambodia—the RGC and the Khmer Rouge—have responded to these various great power initiatives according to their respective situations. The Cambodian government, with its newfound legitimacy and universal diplomatic recognition, has appealed for military assistance from the international community to defend its sovereignty. So far, however, the international community has been unwilling to provide lethal military assistance. For its part, the Khmer Rouge has been displaying its customary creativity and organizational ability. Khmer Rouge intelligence networks in Australia, France, Canada and the United States mounted a strong proactive, preemptive response to the possibility of foreign military aid for the Royal Government of Cambodia early in 1994. This indicated that the Khmer Rouge does not suffer from hubris and over-confidence, and is well aware of its vulnerabilities. It also indicates that it is well-prepared to attempt to neutralize this potential danger to its plans from the international community. For example, as the U.S. Congress began to discuss the possibilities of U.S. military assistance to the RGC, the Khmer Rouge sponsored a May 21, 1994, demonstration in front of the White House in Washington. At the same time, Khmer Rouge–supported publications in the United States launched a propaganda offensive.[30] The bottom line is that based on the interactions among Cambodian forces and the great powers, there is little sign of reconciliation in Cambodia.

Regional Powers and Cambodian Reconciliation

Regional powers also remain very interested in Cambodian affairs. During the Third Indochina War, the Association of Southeast Asia Nations (ASEAN) maintained a united front in the face of what was defined as Vietnamese aggression against Cambodia. Since the withdrawal of Vietnamese armed forces from Cambodia in 1989, however, Thailand's economic and strategic interests in Cambodia have diverged from those of Thailand's ASEAN partners. Countries of the ASEAN are beginning to show strains in their solidarity over the Cambodian issue. Cambodia's prime minister, Norodom Ranariddh, has successfully maneuvered to split Malaysia and Indonesia from Thailand.

Viet Nam, badly burned by its Cambodian invasion, is currently maintaining a hands-off policy in hopes of achieving full normalization of relations with the United States. The Vietnamese, however, cannot indefinitely remain indifferent to events on their western border. Vietnamese intelligence sources have privately indicated they believe the Royal Government is failing to achieve internal consolidation, and they fear the Khmer Rouge military forces may soon menace their border again. This bodes ill for the medium term, especially if the Khmer Rouge should continue to enjoy progress on the battlefield.

Thailand, by contrast, has successfully destabilized the pro–Vietnamese State of Cambodia regime, while largely ignoring U.N. attempts to curb Thai assaults on Cambodia's sovereignty and territorial integrity. Thailand has also engaged in a massive investment program in Cambodia, completely dominating the tourism, banking, transportation, construction, and natural resource extraction sectors of the Cambodian economy. The scale of the Thai program prompted one commentator to remark that Thailand is treating northwestern Cambodia as the seventy-fourth province of Thailand.[31]

The Paris Peace Accords on Cambodia required Thailand and all other signatories to cease any economic or military relations they might have with the Khmer Rouge guerrillas. Everyone did so, except Thailand. After the Cambodian Peace Accords were signed in October 1991, Thai Foreign Minister Squadron-Leader Prasong Soonsiri insisted, "The Thai people have never supported the Khmer Rouge."[32] After the Royal Government of Cambodia was formed in September 1993, Squadron-Leader Prasong asserted, "Thailand no longer supports the Khmer Rouge."[33] When the Cambodian National Assembly formally outlawed the Khmer rouge in July 1994, Prasong promised that Thailand would "cease" its support for the Khmer Rouge.[34] From "never" to "no longer" to "would cease"? It is not difficult to trace the roots of Thailand's tattered credibility on the issue of illegal interference with Cambodia's sovereignty and territorial integrity. Numerous analysts point out that Thailand has always preferred a divided, unstable Cambodia, and has a long history of simultaneously supporting multiple contenders for power there.

Regional reconciliation in Southeast Asia—especially reconciliation between Thailand and Vietnam—is vital to reconciliation in Cambodia. There has recently been an encouraging trend of improved diplomatic and commercial relations between these two states. Thai officials have spoken positively about Vietnam's application for membership in ASEAN, a potentially stabilizing development in the region. Yet, it is important to recall that Vietnam and Thailand have been engaged in a rivalry over Cambodia for nearly 1,000 years. Right now, Thailand enjoys the advantage in this contest after 15 years of Vietnamese advantage. Combined with continuing massacres of Vietnamese civilians by Khmer Rouge forces, the history of the last 1,000 years suggests that it is only a mater of time before there is a response by Viet Nam to Thailand's boldness in Cambodia.

The Khmer Rouge and Reconciliation in Cambodia

Decades of war have riven Cambodia's traditionally small elite class into bitterly opposed factions, and then splintered those factions into subfactions. Thus the most serious challenges to Cambodian reconciliation are political. As King Sihanouk expressed it in May 1994, "There is a civil war between the Khmer Rouge and royal armed forces, civil war within FUNCINPEC, civil war everywhere."[35] If there was any honeymoon for the coalition partners of the Royal Government of Cambodia after the 1993 withdrawal of the United Nations forces, it did not last long. Intra- and inter-party struggles have been proceeding full bore, often in the open. A coup attempt against the RGC in July 1994 was but one indication. Continuing instability with the coalition government has given rise to nearly continuous rumors of major personnel changes among the government's top ministers.

The Royal Government is set up according to a coalition scheme, with ministers and secretaries of state at the national level and governors and vice-governors at the provincial level, one from each of the two major parties. In a sense, this arrangement was a real triumph for national reconciliation in Cambodia. If the objective was to share power, however, it hasn't been working very well. The royalist ministers continue to wield very little power at the national level, and virtually none in the provinces. Most of the royalist ministers have not brought their families to Cambodia from France or the United States or wherever. Some analysts are privately predicting that the coalition arrangement is on the verge of collapse, or at least of open domination by the People's Party.

The political organ of the royalist party, FUNCINPEC, has indeed been in a sort of civil war. The principal princes—Ranariddh, Sirivuth, Sirirath and Chakrapong—have been at each other's throats. Prince Norodom Chakrapong was sent into exile after accusations that he was behind the July 1994 coup attempt. The split among the royals is not merely rivalry for patronage, power, or the question of succession. Their differences are often grounded in serious substantive disputes on policy issues such as corruption, Thailand, the Vietnamese question, how best to handle the Khmer Rouge, land reform, investment regulations, freedom of expression, and even the very nature of market systems. These legitimate differences are magnified by Khmer Rouge agents provocateurs who infiltrated the royalist party during its participation in the exile Coalition Government of Democratic Kampuchea.

Within the "post-communist" People's Party, the political organ of the former ruling regime, there is also much turmoil. The moderate wing of the party under Hun Sen made stunning gains during and after a hardliner-inspired succession attempt in June 1993. Over the balance of 1993, however, the "hardliners" under Chea Sim regained much of their structural advantage. This was not surprising, given Chea Sim's continuing influence over the security forces. The July 1994 coup attempt once again dealt a blow to the Chea Sim faction of the party, removing several of his key allies among the security services. Still, many in the party hold former Prime Minister (now Second Prime Minister) Hun Sen responsible for the party's loss in the U.N.-administered elections, and thus he is vulnerable to other rising stars in the party, such as Co-Minister of Interior and Deputy Prime Minister, Sar Kheng, who also happens to be Chea Sim's son-in-law.

Khmer Rouge battlefield successes in the 1994 dry season exposed the military weakness of the Royal Government of Cambodia. That government is indeed threatened by Khmer Rouge military power, whatever the force level of the Khmer Rouge may be. The Cambodian people are sick of war, and will give almost anything for peace. In the 1993 election, First Prime Minister Prince Norodom Ranariddh campaigned on a peace platform, promising that he would bring peace through negotiation and reconciliation. Instead, he appears to have come to the view that the only solution to the Khmer Rouge problem is war or military containment. Thus, the Khmer Rouge has a political advantage: the government has reneged on its key campaign promise, and many citizens are openly unhappy about it. The RGC may face wrath from voters in the 1996 elections—if, that is, those elections actually take place, and are "free and fair."

Current social and economic conditions in Cambodia are a cause for concern. World Bank and International Monetary Fund (IMF) officials are relatively pleased with the progress of Cambodia's economic stabilization program since the new government took office in 1993.[36] These economists argue that Cambodia's predominantly subsistence-barter economy is being rapidly monetarized, and has achieved a measure of macro-economic stability. Cambodia's own economic officials have also expressed optimism about the progress of the economy.[37]

However, the completely uncontrolled free market economy of the last five years deeply exacerbated the traditionally large disparities between urban and rural income levels, greatly skewing Cambodia's Gini Index. There is a large and growing population of internally displaced persons, un-reintegrated refugee returnees, and underemployed soldiers. Cambodia has a reduced but still significant inflation rate. As a result of these factors, many Cambodians are being driven below the subsistence level. This has contributed to the creation of a large pool of potentially radicalized citizens, more severe than and not structurally dissimilar to the economic conditions in Cambodia during 1970, at the outset of the first Khmer Rouge revolution.

Social indicators of development and well-being in Cambodia are also worrisome, the more so when one compares the situation in 1985—six years before the peace process—to the latest data in 1994, three years after the start of the peace process.[38] In 1985, 24 percent of the rural population (which constitutes some 80 percent of Cambodia's population) had access to safe drinking water; today that figure has fallen by half to 12 percent. The maternal mortality rate per 100,000 live births exploded from 500 in 1985 to 9,000 today; in other words, today nearly 10 percent of Cambodian women die while giving birth. These trends cast a dim light on the rosy scenario offered by Cambodian and international financial institution officials.

Such economic and social trends redound to the benefit of the Khmer Rouge, which has consistently identified the landless, destitute peasantry as its primary constituency. There is no question that Khmer Rouge political behavior over the past few years has shown up a number of tactical errors, such as the fumbled handling of the U.N. elections. Overall, however, its political strategy over the last 15 years has been nothing short of brilliant.[39] In brief, since the early 1980s the Khmer Rouge has adopted the same united front-infiltration-liquidation technique so successful in bringing it to power in 1975.[40] Since the beginning of the endgame of the U.N. peace negotiations, Khmer Rouge strategy has been, "What's mine is mine and what's yours is negotiable." The payoffs are manifest.

During the U.N. protectorate in Cambodia, the Khmer Rouge employed armed force to increase the territory they hold four-fold, from 5 percent to 20 percent of the country. They have also increased the Cambodian population they control four-fold, from about 150,000 to about 600,000. While the size of the Khmer Rouge military forces remains a matter of some dispute, their support by Thailand is clear.[41] The Khmer Rouge continues to enjoy sanctuary, as well as political, economic and military support from Thailand.[42] King Sihanouk lamented in January 1994 that "20 percent of Cambodian territory is today occupied and exploited by an armed and independent, that is, secessionist faction ... the Khmer Rouge."[43] The king should wish the Khmer Rouge goal was secession from Cambodia. Unfortunately, this does not seen to be what Pol Pot has in mind.

Despite its consistent record of extreme violence and its recent declaration that all RGC civil servants should be killed, the Khmer Rouge has proven surprisingly adept at utilizing the popular desire for peace and reconciliation to its own political advantage. Most analysts interpreted the royalist victory in the May 1993 elections as a vote in favor of the royalist platform of peace through reconciliation. This view has been reinforced by multiple voices from within Cambodian society since the elections. In Cambodia's popular media, from indigenous Cambodian human rights organizations, and from coalitions of Cambodian non-governmental organizations, there has been a clear and consistent call for reconciliation among Cambodia's warring political factions. For some reason, popular anger at the fact that this hasn't happened seems to fall more on the government than on the Khmer Rouge.

Perhaps the most dramatic and representative voices for reconciliation in Cambodia have come from the Dhammayietra Center for Peace and Nonviolence, along with its affiliated organization, the Coalition for Peace and Reconciliation. These organizations are coalitions of Buddhists, Muslims, Christians and Jews, inspired by the supreme patriarch of Cambodian Buddhists, the Samdech Preah Maha Ghosananda, who founded the Dhammayietra Center. Ghosananda has organized three large peace marches since the beginning of the U.N. peace process. These marches, called Dhammayietra (or literally, "pilgrimages of truth"), are really demonstrations or prayers in support of peace and reconciliation in Cambodia. Many political analysts discount the practical impact of these events, but the emotion expressed by the huge crowds who have turned out to be blessed by the Dhammayietra marchers belie this cynical view. The Dhammayietra marchers are a physical manifestation of the deep desire for reconciliation in the hearts of the Cambodian people.

On the eve of the third Dhammayietra march, eleven months after the U.N.-supervised election in Cambodia, the Dhammayietra Center issued a poignant plea for peace: "Fighting has only increased and violence remains the only means used to seek national reconciliation."[44] And so it goes in Cambodia.

Conclusions on Reconciliation in Cambodia

In assessing reconciliation issues in Cambodia, one must consider all of the factors, not just whether the U.N. did or did not meet all of the objectives stated in the Comprehensive Agreements. One must examine both long-term factors and short-term factors. Taking into account long-term factors—the continuing ruthless rivalry of Cambodian elites, the continuing Thai-Vietnamese geopolitical competition, and continuing Chinese hegemonic aspirations—it is clear that anarchy in and around Cambodia will persist long after the details of the United Nations mandate in Cambodia have been forgotten.

When one also considers certain short-term factors—such as the predominantly peasant composition of Cambodian society, Cambodia's shattered economic infrastructure, the continued control of most economic activity by a tiny urban elite, the continued control of one-fifth of the country by the Khmer Rouge, and the latter's continued supply by Thailand—it is evident that reconciliation in Cambodia has not yet been achieved. Indeed, reconciliation is a long, long way from realization.

Overall, one must conclude that the U.N. peacekeeping mission has done little to alter the causes underlying conflict in Cambodia. Whether one takes the idealist view that the goal of the peace accords was to bring peace to Cambodia, or the realist view that the goal was to remove the "Cambodia problem" from the international agenda, what is indisputable is that neither goal has been accomplished. Reconciliation remains a goal rather than a reality for the Cambodian people.

Perhaps it is the case in Cambodia that, as Alexander Solzhenitsyn recently commented upon his return to Russia after years in exile, "National reconciliation is a great thing and much needed, but there cannot be national reconciliation without spiritual cleansing."[45] Or, as Rwandan President Pasteur Bizimungu put it, "Reconciliation cannot be built on impunity. Justice must be the pillar of reconciliation."[46]

Notes

1. For an analysis of the Cambodian diaspora, see Judith Banister and Paige Johnson, "After the Nightmare: The Population of Cambodia," pp. 65–139 in Ben Kiernan, ed., *Genocide and Democracy in Cambodia: The Khmer Rouge, the United Nations and the International Community* (New Haven, CT: Yale University Southeast Asian Studies, 1993); see especially Table 4, "Cambodians Outside Cambodia," p. 113, and Table A-1, "Cambodia Assumed International Migration." p. 125.

2. See Chapter 8 in Craig Etcheson, *The Rise and Demise of Democratic Kampuchea* (Boulder, CO, and London: Westview Press and Pinter Publishers, 1984); see also David W. P. Elliot, ed., *The Third Indochina Conflict* (Boulder, CO: Westview Press, 1981); William Turley and Jeffrey Race, "The Third Indochina War," *Foreign Policy* 38 (Spring 1980); and Stephen Heder, "Kampuchea 1980: Anatomy of a Crisis," *Southeast Asia Chronicle* 77 (February 1981).

3. A fascinating look at the thinking upon which this revolution was grounded is David P. Chandler, Ben Kiernan, and Chanthou Boua, eds., *Pol Pot Plans the Future: Confidential Leadership Documents from Democratic Kampuchea, 1976–1977* (New Haven: Yale University Southeast Asia Studies, 1988); a work which does much to place Pol Pot's regime in the context of Cambodian history is Michael Vickery, *Cambodia 1975–1982* (Boston: South End Press, 1984); also of use in this regard is Seanglim Bit, *The Warrior Heritage: A Psychological Perspective of Cambodian Trauma* (El Cerrito, CA: Seanglim Bit, 1991).

4. A useful guide to the regime that replaced Pol Pot's Democratic Kampuchea is Michael Vickery, *Kampuchea: Politics, Economics and Society* (London and Boulder, CO: Frances Pinter and Lynne Rienner Publishers, 1986).

5. Quoted in Elizabeth Becker, *When the War Was Over: The Voices of Cambodia's Revolution and Its People* (New York: Simon and Schuster, 1986): 440.

6. Quoted in Craig Etcheson, "Civil War and the Coalition Government of Democratic Kampuchea," *Third World Quarterly* 9(1) 1987: 196.

7. For a detailed examination of evidence pertaining to U.S. support for the rebel movements during the Third Indochina War, see Craig Etcheson, "The Reagan Doctrine in Cambodia," paper presented to the conference on the United States and Viet Nam: From War to Peace, Notre Dame University, December 2–4, 1993.

8. Useful accounts of this war include Nayan Chanda, *Brother Enemy* (New York: Macmillan, 1986); Michael Haas, *Genocide by Proxy* (Westport, CT: Praeger, 1991) and his *Cambodia, Pol Pot and the United States* (Westport, CT: Praeger, 1991); also see Donald Weatherbee, ed., *Southeast Asia Divided: The ASEAN-Indochina Crisis* (Boulder, CO: Westview Press, 1985); for a pro-Vietnamese view of the crisis, see Wilfred Burchett, *The China-Cambodia-Vietnam Triangle* (Chicago: Vanguard Press, 1981); for a pro-Chinese view of the crisis, see Chang Pao-Min, *Kampuchea Between China and Vietnam* (Singapore: Singapore University Press, 1985).

9. How it came to be that a Cambodian monarch would have palaces not only in communist North Korea but also in the People's Republic of China is told in a fascinating biography of Norodom Sihanouk, by Milton Osborne, *Sihanouk: Prince of Light, Prince of Darkness* (Chiang Mai, Thailand, Silkworm Books, 1994).

10. Quoted in "PDK Team Affirms Desire for Peace," from Khmer Rouge clandestine radio, printed in Foreign Broadcast Information Service (FBIS), EAS-94-120, June 22, 1994: 43.

11. For background on the so-called "Provisional Government for National Solidarity and National Salvation of Kampuchea," see "Khmer Rouge Form Provisional Government," Associated Press, July 11, 1994; and "Khmer Rouge Pick Remote Province as Seat of Provisional Government," Deutsche Presse Agentur, July 13, 1994.

12. For accounts of the Paris Agreements, see Craig Etcheson, "The 'Peace' in Cambodia," *Current History* (December 1992): 413–417; Ben Kiernan, "The Making of the Paris Agreement on Cambodia, 1990–1991," paper presented to the Indochina Project Confer-

ence, Kauai, Hawaii, December 18–20, 1991; and Kiernan's "The Cambodian Crisis, 1991–1992: The U.N. Plan, the Khmer Rouge, and the State of Cambodia," *Bulletin of Concerned Asian Scholars* 24:2 (1992): 3–23.

13. United Nations, Department of Public Information, *Agreements on a Comprehensive Political Settlement of the Cambodian Conflict* (DPI/1180 92077), January 1992, Paris [hereafter, *Comprehensive Settlement*].

14. For example, journalist Elizabeth Becker said during an interview on the National Public Radio program "Talk of the Nation" (May 27, 1993) that the Cambodian U.N. intervention provides a model for collective security in the post–Cold War world order; see also Craig Etcheson, "The 'Peace' in Cambodia," *Current History*, op.cit.: 416, 417.

15. The pernicious effects of the U.S.–led trade and aid embargo against Cambodia are documented in Eva Mysliwiec, *Punishing the Poor: The International Isolation of Kampuchea* (Oxford: Oxfam, 1988).

16. See Craig Etcheson, "Avoiding a New War in Cambodia," testimony before the Sub-committee on Foreign Operations, Export Financing and Related Programs, Committee on Appropriations, U.S. House of Representatives, U.S. Congress, March 1, 1993; see also Frederick Z. Brown, *Cambodia in Crisis: The 1993 Elections and the United Nations* (New York: The Asia Society, May 1993).

17. A more comprehensive account of problems with the implementation of the Comprehensive Settlement can be found in Craig Etcheson, "Anarchy in Cambodia: A Persistent Historical Pattern," a paper presented to the American Bar Association Standing Committee on Law and National Security, Conference on Anarchy in the Third World, Washington, DC, June 3–4, 1993; see also Ben Kiernan, "The Inclusion of the Khmer Rouge in the Cambodian Peace Process: Causes and Consequences," pp. 191–272 in Ben Kiernan, ed., *Genocide and Democracy in Cambodia, op. cit.*; and also Kiernan's "The Failures of the Paris Agreement on Cambodia, 1991–1993," Aspen Institute 8:4, Conference Report on The Challenge of Indochina, April 30–May 2, 1993: 9–21; see also Asia Watch, "Political Control, Human Rights, and the U.N. Mission in Cambodia," September 1992.

18. Interview on "The MacNeil/Lehrer News Hour," Public Broadcasting System, June 1, 1993.

19. See Dan Garst, "Implications for Current Democratic Transitions," in the postscript to an as yet untitled book on comparative democratic development, Ithaca, NY: Cornell University Press, forthcoming.

20. For two recent views on the outcome of the Cambodian peace process, see William Shawcross, *Cambodia's New Deal* (Washington, DC: Carnegie Endowment for International Peace, 1994); and Bertil Lintner, "Cambodia: A Military and Political Overview," *Jane's Intelligence Review*, October 1994: 467–473.

21. Alexander Krylovick and Valdimir Supruns, "Russia Calls to Help Cambodia Solve Domestic Problems," Moscow, ITAR-TASS, July 14, 1994; Russian President Boris Yeltsin offered in August 1994 "his readiness to discuss the cooperation and development of Cambodia in the political and economic spheres," according to Phnom Penh government radio. "Yeltsin Affirms Support for Government Policy," FBIS-EAS-94-162, August 22, 1994: 69.

22. Data from the U.S. Agency for International Development, "USAID Assistance Strategy for Cambodia, FY 1994-95," May 1994. Draft document. See table C.1, page 66.

23. For background on the Cambodian Genocide Justice Act, see Craig Etcheson, "Congress and Administration Negotiate on KR Genocide Investigation," *Indochina Interchange* 4:2 (June 1994): 13.

24. "Commission to Review 'US War of Aggression,'" FBIS-EAS-94-191, October 3, 1994: 69.

25. See, for example, Craig Etcheson, "Sanctions Needed to Curb Thai Military Support of Khmer Rouge," *Indochina Interchange*, September 1994: 8, 9; his "Punish Thai Military Over Khmer Rouge Aid," *The Asian Wall Street Journal Weekly*, June 27, 1994: 16; and his "Dump Pol Pot or You're Grounded," *The Asian Wall Street Journal*, June 23, 1994: 10.

26. See, for example, "U.S. Military Delegation to Visit Phnom Penh," Reuter News Agency, September 16, 1994.

27. "Li Peng Letter Denies PRC Aid to Khmer Rouge," FBIS-EAP-94-157, August 15, 1994: 51.

28. Nate Thayer, "City of Dreams," *Far Eastern Economic Review*, August 11, 1994: 20.

29. "Khmer Rouge Sets Conditions," FBIS-EAS-94-158, August 16, 1994: 66, 67.

30. The author personally attended this Khmer Rouge demonstration at the White House. An example of the propaganda offensive is found in a publication called the *Cambodian Press*, published in Lowell, Massachusetts, a town which is well-known among Cambodian-Americans as a stronghold of Khmer Rouge influence in North America. In its June 1, 1994, edition, the *Cambodian Press* published a front-page story titled, "Stop US Military Aid—Why?" This article recounts the demonstration at the White House, and includes such comments as, "The Khmer Rouge under the leaderships [sic] of Mr. Khieu Samphan is doing right for the country and the people."

31. See, for example, Raoul Jennar, "Before It Becomes Too Late," *Cambodia Chronicles VII*, European Far Eastern Research Center, February 15, 1993: 17–19. Jennar accurately notes that "Thai governments change, but their active sympathy for the Khmer Rouge remains." See also Jennar's "18 Years Later," *Cambodia Chronicles VIII*, European Far Eastern Research Center, April 17, 1993: 12, 13, for additional documentation on Thai disregard for Cambodian sovereignty and violations of the Comprehensive Settlement.

32. Quoted in "Thailand to Abide by U.N. Ban on Cambodia Logs," Reuter News Agency, January 8, 1993; see also *Cambodia Peace Watch*, Folio 2, Volume 1, Number 1, January 1993.

33. See "Prasong Says Thailand No Longer Supports KR," *Bangkok Post*, October 12, 1993.

34. See "Time for Phnom Penh to Prove Its Point or Keep Silent," *The Sunday Post* (Bangkok), July 10, 1994: 22; reprinted in FBIS-EAS-94-134, July 13, 1994: 65.

35. Mark Dodd, "Sihanouk Warns of Khmer Rouge Return to Power," Reuter News Agency, May 12, 1994. Sihanouk went on to say, "The only way to save Cambodia is by helping the royal government and the royal army and by training the soldiers and by giving them lessons in behavior."

36. Michael Ward, Principal Economist, East Asia and the Pacific Country Operations Department, the World Bank, "Recent Developments and Prospects for the Cambodian Economy," paper presented to the Carnegie Endowment for International Peace, Symposium on Cambodia, June 28, 1994; see also Maja Wallengren, "Cambodia Earns High Marks in IMF Study," *Phnom Penh Post*, October 7, 1994: 12.

37. Cham Prasidh, Secretary of State for Economy and Finance, Kingdom of Cambodia, "Macroeconomic Changes in Cambodia: The Positive and Negative Aspects of International Aid Development Strategies," a country case study presented at the U.S. NGO Forum on Vietnam, Cambodia and Laos, Annual Conference, Arlington, VA, June 2–4, 1994.

38. Numerical data taken from The World Bank, *Social Indicators of Development 1994*, Baltimore and London: The Johns Hopkins University Press, 1994.

39. Two excellent studies which amply demonstrate that Pol Pot's goals remain unchanged since the 1970s are Christophe Peschoux, *Enquete Sur Les "Nouveaux" Khmers Rouges (1979–1990), Reconstruction du Mouvement et Reconquete des Villages—Essai de deboussaillage*, unpublished typescript, Paris, March 25, 1991, 173 pp.; and David W. Ashley, *Pol Pot, Peace and the Peasantry: Continuity and Change in Khmer Rouge Political Thinking 1985–1991*, unpublished typescript, London, November 1991, 71 pp.; a revealing look at recent Khmer Rouge methods is Asia Watch, "Violations of the Laws of War by the Khmer Rouge," April 1990.

40. For more detail, see Craig Etcheson, "Pol Pot and the Art of War," *Phnom Penh Post*, August 13, 1993; reprinted in FBIS-EAS, August 19, 1993: 38, 39. According to a Khmer Rouge defector, Pol Pot instructed Khmer Rouge military officers in 1988 that "The fruit

remains the same; only the skin has changed." See David P. Chandler, "The Red Khmer and the U.N. Agreement on Cambodia," Aspen Institute 7:3, Conference Report on the Challenge of Indochina, May 8–10, 1992, p. 14. A captured Khmer Rouge document dated January 10, 1992, emphasizes, "We must concentrate first on accelerating the infiltration of category one forces in order gradually to establish in advance the pre-requisites" for the takeover of his hapless allies. Quoted in Nayan Chanda, "Cambodia: In Search of an Elusive Peace," Aspen Institute 8:2, Conference Report on the American-Vietnamese Dialogue, February 8–11, 1993: 26, 27, note 4; this document has been authenticated by Western Cambodia specialists.

41. U.N. Secretary-General Boutros Boutros-Ghali's Special Representative for Cambodia, Yasushi Akashi, warned on May 19, 1993, that the Khmer Rouge had "increased their military strength by at least 50 percent" and had obtained new weapons. See Reuter News Agency report dated May 19, 1993. Other reports on Thai military and economic support for the Khmer Rouge include "Thai Military Role," *Indochina Digest*, November 6, 1992; "Doing Business with Pol Pot," *The Economist*, November 7, 1992; Ken Stier, "Log Rolling," *Far Eastern Economic Review*, January 21, 1993; "Thai's Supply Khmer Rouge Army," *Cambodia Peace Watch*, Folio 2, Vol. 1, No. 1 (January 1993); and "Thailand Rearms Khmer Rouge Army," *Cambodia Peace Watch*, Folio 2, Vol. 5, No. 1 (May 1993).

42. Author's interviews with confidential U.N. sources in Phnom Penh, Cambodia, March 7, 1993; other sources include a report in the *Bangkok Post* from May 6, reprinted in the Foreign Broadcast Information Service [FBIS], Daily Report—East Asia, May 6, 1993; and a May 7, 1993, report by Raoul Jennar distributed by the International NGO Forum on Cambodia, London. An unnamed diplomat confronted General Charan Kunwalanit, the secretary-general of the Thai National Security Council, with satellite photos of Thai military trucks delivering field artillery and other weapons to the Khmer Rouge in Cambodia in early May, 1993. For Thai rejection of this evidence, see comments by Charan in FBIS, May 13, 1993. Also see Craig Etcheson, "Without any pretensions, dump the KR," *Bangkok Nation*, September 28, 1993; and his "Khmer Rouge Issues Hurt Thai-Cambodian Relations," *Indochina Interchange*, December 1993: 10, 11.

43. Norodom Sihanouk, "Forging Cambodian Nationhood," *Far Eastern Economic Review*, January 13, 1994: 26.

44. "Statement from the Dhammayietra III Walk for Peace and Reconciliation in Cambodia," Dhammayietra Center for Peace and Nonviolence, Wat Bo Viel, Battambang, Kingdom of Cambodia, April 21, 1994.

45. Alexander Solzhenitsyn in May 1994 upon his return to Russian, quoted in Serge Schemann, "Sins of the Father," *The New York Times Book Review*, June 26, 1994: 3.

46. Quoted in Paul Taylor, "Rwanda's New Tutsi Leaders Seek Swift Genocide Trials for Ousted Hutus," *Washington Post*, August 3, 1994: A21; it should be noted that the newly installed President of Rwanda, Pasteur Bizimungu, is himself a Hutu, the ethnic group suspected of perpetrating a genocide in Rwanda.

2. The Abandonment of the Hmong, U.S. Allies in the Lao Secret War

JANE HAMILTON-MERRITT

"To be an enemy of the United States can be unpleasant.
To be a friend of the United States can be fatal."
U.S. Senator Daniel Patrick Moynihan

In the mid–1960s when I arrived in Southeast Asia as a journalist-photographer, the Indochina peninsula was at war. North Vietnam, supported by its Soviet, Chinese, and Eastern Bloc allies, fought against South Vietnam and the United States and its allies from South Korea, Australia, New Zealand, Philippines and Thailand. The two sides raged at each other in the skies, rivers, and rice paddies, on the seas, and in the media.

Critical battlefields of this long and bloody struggle were in the remote northeastern mountainous areas of Laos inhabited by the tribal minorities. Here the war and the U.S. involvement were secret. This secret war pitted Hanoi's General Giap's highly trained and well-equipped North Vietnamese Army and its allies against the mountain men of northern Laos, primarily the Hmong tribe, but also those of the Kmhumu and Mien groups. While some Hmong joined with the communist forces, most Hmong elected to join with the Royal Lao Government and the U.S. to fight to eject North Vietnamese forces from Laos. Hmong forces were led by Vang Pao, a Hmong general in the Royal Lao Army.

In the remote hills where this war was fought, journalists were forbidden. This area included Long Chieng, General Vang Pao's headquarters, the CIA paramilitary base of operations, and the province with the heavy fighting. The war in Laos was embargoed. As a result, few journalists spent meaningful time in Laos. Secrecy and restrictions made significant stories difficult to document. Journalists, accustomed to U.S. military assistance in getting to a story and the freedom allowed the press corps in South Vietnam, found little largesse in Laos. Most journalists concluded that the accolades and prizes would to go those who covered Vietnam. They were right.

Laos and the secret theater of the Vietnam War received little meaningful press. Americans were confused about this faraway place with reported "secret armies" of tribal people and "secret CIA bases" hidden in remote mountains. These "secret" labels stuck, branding the Hmong incorrectly as mercenaries and shielding their true story.

This ignorance, coupled with the barrage of disinformation and propaganda about the virtues of the communist regime that came to power in Laos in 1975 and about the evils of the American imperialists and their "running dog" allies, turned many people away from taking a studied interest in Laos, a little known country halfway around the world.

In 1996, more than twenty years after the communists came to power in Laos, most Americans remain largely oblivious of the details and dimensions of the decade-long secret war in Laos, the contributions and sacrifices of the Hmong in their fight for freedom and of their assistance to the U.S. effort, and of the extraordinary loss of Hmong lives in those endeavors.

At this writing, Laos, along with North Korea, Viet Nam, Cuba, and China, remains one of the last five bastions of dictatorial communism. Laos, known as the Lao People's Democratic Republic (LPDR), remains secretive and repressive with a dismal human rights record over the last 20 years. Laos, a small, land-locked country, played a strategically pivotal, though secret, role for both the North Vietnamese and the Americans during their 15-year-long fight for the control of Indochina. In Laos, the North Vietnamese built and developed their critical supply route complex to South Viet Nam and later to Cambodia, known as the Ho Chi Minh Trail.

During the secret Lao campaigns of the Vietnam War, Thailand counted on the Hmong special forces under the command of Hmong General Vang Pao to keep at bay in northern Laos the North Vietnamese divisions operating there with a strategic eye to Thailand. Thailand did not want to fight any part of the war on its soil. Much better to do battle on Lao soil where Thai and Lao pilots jointly struck enemy targets and Thai and Hmong "irregulars" fought bloody ground battles against communist Vietnamese forces.

In late 1960, unbeknownst to the Americans, Hanoi gave the signal to its people in South Viet Nam to begin the violent stage of the struggle to unite Viet Nam under the North Vietnamese regime. Critical to this goal was the trail complex being constructed by the North Vietnamese inside Laos. This system of supply arteries would provide the means to infiltrate agents, to provide secure communications, and to funnel the weapons, medicines, machines, and troops necessary for a communist victory in South Viet Nam.

The North Vietnamese knew that this operation had to remain secret for two important reasons. If detected, North Viet Nam would be violating the 1954 Geneva Accords that prohibited it from using a second country (Laos) in order to fight in yet another country (South Viet Nam). Secondly—and probably more important—since the strategy was to create the impression of a large indigenous group, known as the Viet Cong, struggling against the government in South Viet Nam independently of North Viet Nam, the detection of massive assistance from the North would destroy this popular and effective underdog, grassroots image.

In July 1962, President Kennedy's efforts to "neutralize" Laos through international guarantees at the Geneva Conference ended with provisions that all foreign military personnel be removed. Between the July 23 signing of the documents and the October 7 deadline for withdrawal of all foreign troops, the United States withdrew 666 military men, accounted for at International Control Commission (ICC) checkpoints. By the deadline, the only American military men remaining in Laos were the military attaché at the embassy and his staff. The Americans had complied with the withdrawal of their military personnel.

Hanoi, while insisting that it had no troops in Laos, publicly withdrew "technicians," "experts," and "advisers." Hanoi had withdrawn a total of 40 men from an estimated force of 7,000 to 9,000. Those remaining were, they claimed, an advisory cadre. It was at this point that the United States decided that the 1962 Geneva Protocol on Laos would not hold. Late in 1962, the CIA paramilitary advisers returned to Laos to advise and equip the counterinsurgency forces. American military men returned to advise and work with the Royal Lao Army.

So the neutralization charade and the "secret war" in Laos had begun. It was not, however, secret to the participants—the Lao, the tribal people (Hmong and Mien particularly), and the communist Pathet Lao and North Vietnamese soldiers.

General Vang Pao, the only Hmong to achieve such rank in the Royal Lao Army, orchestrated front-line defenses for the royal capital at Luang Prabang and the administrative capital at Vientiane. The United States expected him to keep the enemy away from the vulnerable and poorly protected plain that surrounded Vientiane. It was believed that if enemy forces reached this plain, they could roll unimpeded against Vientiane. The Americans reasoned that if this ground fell to the communists, Laos was lost. Thailand would be next. If Thailand were threatened, the United States would lose its rights to use Thai airbases from which to launch airstrikes against North Viet Nam and the Ho Chi Minh Trail. General Van Pao's forces were, then, the front lines and the shield on which the Americans, the Lao, and the Thai depended so heavily.

When President Lyndon Johnson sent ground troops to South Viet Nam, the ante went up. The North Vietnamese expanded their Ho Chi Minh Trail, along which flowed men and materiel to fuel the communist war effort in the South. American aircraft, based in Thailand, flew interdiction strikes against the Trail, trying to stop the traffic.

With the expanded air war over North Viet Nam and Laos, Johnson needed navigational equipment in Laos to direct strikes more precisely in all kinds of weather around the clock against targets both in North Viet Nam and Laos and to avoid Chinese airspace.

Hmong forces guarded the United States' ultra-secret TSQ radar station at Phou Pha Thi—Lima Site 85—that guided U.S. air strikes against targets in North Viet Nam and Laos. They also defended both the staging area at Na Khang for U.S. search and rescue operations and the intelligence gathering base at Bouam Loung that monitored communications in North Viet Nam.

Both President Johnson and President Richard Nixon depended upon the Hmong special forces to rescue downed U.S. aircrews lost over Laos. Hmong soldiers considered it their duty to rescue Americans, and they did so at great sacrifice.

Here is the story of a rescue of two American flyers shot down over Laos who were rescued by a Hmong unit of 100 men. The Hmong lost 60 men to rescue the two Americans.

Vang Kai, who had joined the Hmong "special forces" a year earlier at age 16, was a member of one of these 100 man units. His unit operated near Lhat Sen along the North Vietnamese border. Vang Kai knew it was his duty to rescue American pilots. The order, as he understood it, was to make any sacrifice to get American pilots out. There was never any quibbling about this order.

North Vietnamese forces surrounded Vang Kai's unit. Radios screeched with frightened men calling for "air." American jets responded, swooping in on enemy positions with bombs and strafing runs. During one day of heavy fighting, Vang Kai noticed smoke coming from an American jet.

> Two pilots parachuted. Everyone, including the enemy, could see them. As we watched, an urgent message came over our radio: "Get the American pilots before the Vietnamese!" Quickly coordinates were given to our radio man. It was our turn to rescue Americans.
>
> Since there were so many Vietnamese in this area, we knew we would have to fight to get there. We knew we had to be fast to reach the Americans before the Vietnamese. Our rescue party of 100 started to run. We ran! Fighting! Running! Fighting! More than an hour of running and fighting. We reached the area first, but the Vietnamese were chasing us. One American pilot was hurt from the waist down; the other was also wounded, but could walk. We could not secure the area for the rescue chopper to get in. There were too many Vietnamese—shooting and closing in on us. They would kill us all. We must take the American and run. We took turns carrying the American who could not walk. He was big and heavy. We ran, carrying him, until the two men carrying him couldn't run anymore. Then two other Hmong would pick him up and run. We ran like this carrying one wounded American and helping the other. Still the Vietnamese chased us, firing. For several hours, we ran and fought.
>
> Finally, we outran the Vietnamese and got to the Lhat Sen position. We secured the airstrip long enough to call in a chopper to take out the wounded

American pilots. When we got to Lhat Sen, there were only 40 men left in our rescue party [of 100 men]. The rest were lost.

Years later when I asked Vang Kai, who was living in Montana as a refugee, about the extraordinary loss of Hmong life to save the two Americans, he explained, "When the Americans arrived in Laos, the Hmong respected them and called them 'sir.' We were friends. We had a ba-sii ceremony for every American who came to live and work with us. We did everything we could to help the Americans. When the Americans were in trouble, we Hmong made a path with our blood to save them."

Recently, William E. Colby, former director of the CIA, in congressional testimony recalled Hmong contributions during the Vietnam War: "A measure of the heroism and effectiveness of the Hmong struggle can be seen in the fact that the North Vietnamese forces arrayed against them increased over the years from the original 7,000 to 70,000, including several of North Viet Nam's best divisions." He also noted that Hmong forces "for ten years held the growing North Vietnamese forces to approximately the same battle lines they occupied in 1962. And significantly for Americans, the 70,000 North Vietnamese engaged in Laos were not available to add to the forces fighting Americans and South Vietnamese in South Viet Nam."

The Hmong did this at great loss of life. Not just soldiers, but old people, women, and children also died and suffered in large numbers.

In Laos the Americans, with strong commitments to contain communism at the borders of "Red China" and to keep Laos from falling as the first political domino in Southeast Asia, joined with the Hmong, who disliked the Vietnamese and had a great desire to be free, in a common effort to stop the North Vietnamese in their quest for hegemony throughout Indochina. The long and bloody effort failed. The Americans lost and retreated across the ocean; the Hmong remained behind to be savaged by the conquerors.

When the communists took power in Laos in 1975, they—as in Pol Pot's Cambodia—launched brutal campaigns to eliminate or silence those who had not sided with them, including senior military, police, and civilians of the Royal Lao Government, minorities allied with the United States, and the royal family. The extermination of the beloved royal Lao family is a well-hidden, shameful story.

Laos became a gulag in which opponents were sent to "seminar camps" where they were tortured, starved, denied proper medical treatment and forced to perform slave labor. Intent upon eliminating the old order, communist Vietnamese and Lao soldiers followed the Hmong, hunting them like animals. Tens of thousands were killed in the purges. The LPDR was so ruthless in its "ethnic and political cleansing" that from 1975 to the present over 10 percent of the population fled.

Waves of refugees fled to Thailand in confusion, worry, and fear. Families were separated. Some had fled the country. Others, who feared for their lives, opted to hide in Laos rather than to try to escape. Hmong, trapped inside Laos, ran to their mountains to hide, but the communist soldiers followed them, launching attacks against them with both conventional and chemical-biological toxin weapons.

Tens of thousands of Hmong escaped across the Mekong River where they sought sanctuary in refugee camps in northern Thailand. Hmong refugees continued to flow to Thailand for the next 20 years as the Hmong and other ethnic groups resisted the repressive Lao regime. From Thailand Hmong were resettled in France, Australia, Canada and the United States. Some 150,000 Hmong now live in the United States. Many, however, remain in Thailand.

From 1975 into the early 1980s, most Hmong political refugees and asylum seekers were welcomed by Thailand, but that policy changed soon after the fall of the Soviet Union. With the demise of the Soviet Union, the Lao government lost its major benefactor and turned to the West and other Asian nations for replacement funds. Neighboring Thailand, taking advantage of the weakened position of both Viet Nam and Laos after Soviet support vanished, initiated efforts to better relations with the Lao and perhaps to lure Laos away from Viet Nam and back to Thailand—a relationship with considerable history. Unlike the Vietnamese, ethnic Lao and ethnic Thai share a common culture based on Theravada Buddhism. For centuries the Lao and Thai have traded and fought over land and over Buddhist relics.

So in this Thai quest to better the economic and diplomatic relationships with Laos, the Hmong in refugee camps in Thailand who had fled the communist Lao authorities who had vowed to "wipe them out" when they came to power became an impediment. These Hmong did not want to be resettled in third countries. They wanted to return to their homeland in Laos, but not until they were certain that they would be safe. Many of these refugees and political asylum seekers were former soldiers who during the Vietnam War had fought against the communist forces in Laos. Many had worked with or alongside the Americans. Some had continued fighting the communists after they came to power in Laos. Many of these Hmong believed that they could not return to Laos until there was a multiparty system of government and the basic rights and freedoms—freedom to criticize the government, to assemble, and to travel; academic freedom; and other basic liberties—were reliably established.

In the mid–1990s, U.S. rapprochement and reconciliation with Viet Nam and Laos forced the United States to deal with some 40,000 to 50,000 Hmong political refugees and asylum seekers in Thailand who refused to return to communist Laos. In addition, the United States must also address the troublesome issues of drug trafficking by the LPDR and of accounting for the POWs and MIAs lost in the secret Lao theater of the war.

Over the years, the U.S. Department of State's annual report on human rights in Laos has been damning. The "Country Report for Human Rights Practices for 1994" concluded that the ruling Lao communist party restricts freedom of speech, press, and assembly, and denies the rights of privacy and of citizens to change their government. The LPDR reacts harshly to expressions of political dissent. The Ministry of Interior (MOI) remains the main instrument of state control with the MOI police monitoring international mail and phone calls, Lao society, and foreigners, including foreign officials and diplomats. In recent years, the MOI has made late-night inspections of households to insure that all those in the house were registered with the police.

Arrests are made on unsupported charges: accusers' identities are withheld. Trials are not public. Prisoners, many of whom are held for political reasons, labor on both state and private enterprises. Human rights groups are not allowed. There is no freedom to travel without government permission. Suggesting a multiparty political system brings long imprisonment. Importantly for the Hmong, minority tribes have virtually no voice in decisions affecting their lands. Since human rights groups are not allowed, any organization wishing to investigate and criticize the government's human rights policies or its treatment of refugee returnees would face serious obstacles.

The penal code bars disseminating books and other materials that are deemed indecent or would infringe on the national culture. In December 1992, an American citizen received a three-year prison sentence for having brought politically sensitive and allegedly pornographic material into the country.

Newspapers and the state radio and television are instruments of the government, reflecting its views. Academic freedom remains tightly controlled. Lao academicians are often denied permission to travel abroad for conferences or for training. The government also severely restricts Western scholars trying to conduct research in Laos.[1]

With a 20-year record of gross violations of human and civil rights, documented executions and atrocities by Lao authorities against Hmong forcibly returned in the 1980s by the Thais, and the residual animosity toward the Hmong based on the Viet Nam War, it would seem inconceivable for the State Department to ignore the loud warnings that Hmong feared persecution at the hands of the LPDR and to sponsor and fund a plan to repatriate Hmong political refugees—former staunch U.S. allies, and an ethnic minority—to their sworn enemies who vowed publicly to "wipe them out."[2] But so it has done.

It is disturbing to learn that while one bureau of the State Department can evaluate a particular country—in this case Laos—as a repressive one-party communist state, another bureau—the Bureau of Refugee Programs—can make policies that apparently do not consider the department's own human rights report.

In 1991, the United Nations High Commissioner for Refugees (UNHCR) and the governments of Thailand and Laos, with U.S. Department of State political and financial support, initiated a repatriation program called the Luang Prabang Tripartite Agreement, funded in part by millions of U.S. tax dollars. This politicized and controversial plan has been plagued with problems. Hmong who fled the terror of the LPDR want to return to their mountain homelands in Laos. Most, however, insist that they cannot do so until democracy returns there.

Since 1989, the U.S.–based Lao Human Rights Council has assembled a compendium of information documenting involuntary repatriation of Hmong to Laos, abuses against returnees by the Lao authorities, and an atmosphere of desperate fear in refugee camps in Thailand. The Lawyers Committee for Human Rights in 1989 reported, "Screening [to determine refugee status] is conducted in a haphazard manner with little concern for legal norms. Extortion and bribery are widespread. And despite an observatory role, the office of the UNHCR in Thailand has proven incapable of ensuring a reliable and fair procedure."[3]

The original tripartite plan called for Hmong returnees to be resettled in large groups—5,000 per site—with promises of schools, hospitals, and land. This was not to be. The LPDR took control of the repatriation of its former enemies. The Hmong were not allowed to return to their mountain homelands, and instead of large resettlement sites where returnees might have some protection in numbers, they are resettled in smaller groups on marginal land in unfamiliar and often hostile environments on LPDR–approved sites. Returnees report basic necessities are lacking and many are hungry. Fear continues.

Hmong returnees report that LPDR authorities are suspicious of those who fled the communist regime and accord them a status below that of those who did not flee. Objective, effective, frequent and unannounced monitoring by non–LPDR officials of repatriated Hmong refugees to Laos is impossible. Hostilities between the communist government and the minorities continued in 1994. Some Hmong who have been returned to Laos have re-escaped to describe the brutalities, sometimes fatal, that have been inflicted upon returnees by Lao authorities. Other Hmong have disappeared.

There is the disappearance of Vue Mai, a former Hmong soldier during the time of the Americans. In 1991, he was recruited from a refugee camp in Thailand by U.S. Embassy staff in Bangkok and brought to the United States to promote repatriation to refugees, to the press, to human rights groups, and to U.S. policymakers. With the State Department's blessing, he urged Hmong to return and sought to quell obvious fears and concerns. In 1992, under the auspices of the Lao government, he returned to Laos to lead Hmong repatriation. Vue Mai disappeared in Vientiane in September 1993 and has not been seen since.

Hundreds of forced repatriations of Hmong political refugees have been recorded. One Hmong, a former soldier twice gravely wounded in the fighting in Laos, whose parents, two brothers, and two sisters were killed by communist soldiers, wrote to his congressman about the forced repatriation of his sister on Thanksgiving Day 1993:

> I have just received a telephone call from my sister and brother-in-law [a former soldier]. They said that the U.N. used Thai soldiers to point guns at every family and told them to sign a volunteer repatriation. While I was speaking to my sister on the phone, a [Thai] soldier took the phone and spoke to me. He said that they only do what the U.N. wanted them to do and that my sister will have to be repatriated with force. During the conversation, my sister and brother were crying and yelling for help.

The U.S. embassy in Bangkok responded to a congressional query, admitting that the family was part of a group of 382 to be repatriated but insisting it was voluntary. The embassy claimed, "We have confirmed that the allegation made of Thai soldiers coercing the Hmong to repatriate at gunpoint is simply untrue." There are hundreds—maybe thousands—of similar cases of Hmong coerced into returning to Laos through a repatriation program in which a corrupt and flawed "screening" process selects many who are, in fact, political refugees and asylum seekers.

Philip Smith, a member of former congressman Don Ritter's staff, headed a fact-finding mission to Thailand in 1992. He reported,

> Because of the failure to fully cover-up this scandal, the forced return to Hmong has been accelerated and ... insidious character attacks are made against those who step forward with evidence of human rights abuses. Despite their best efforts to keep this quiet, to suppress the facts, and conduct white-washing investigations, the State Department, Thais, UNHCR, and Lao have not kept the stench of this scandal from causing a stir in Congress.

A few in the media also began to pay some attention. In February 1994, Marc Kaufman, after extensive field research in an investigative article for the *Philadelphia Inquirer Magazine*, documented ongoing involuntary repatriation of Hmong to Laos and described an entrenched and deceitful campaign by State Department and UNHCR personnel to discredit Hmong American leaders and Hmong refugees—and to manipulate congressional investigations.[4]

After April 1994 hearings on Hmong refugee repatriation before the House Subcommittee on Asia and Pacific Affairs, a high-level staff delegation was dispatched to Thailand to investigate reports of reduction of food and charcoal, jailings, and beatings to induce refugees to "volunteer" to return to Laos. In September 1994, this three-member staff delegation sent by congressman Lee Hamilton and Ben Gilman, chair and vice chair of the House Foreign Affairs Committee, were denied access to Na Pho refugee camp by

Thai authorities with acquiescence of the local UNHCR representative and U.S. embassy personnel in Bangkok.

As a result, refugees in Na Pho were forbidden to give to the fact-finding staff their 5,000-signature petition intended for the U.S. Congress begging it to stop their forced repatriation to the LPDR. Later, after their petition did reach Capitol Hill and the State Department, Thai Ministry of Interior police with the assistance of UNHCR personnel arrested six Na Pho camp refugee leaders—five Hmong and one Lao. They were taken to Suan Plu Immigration Jail in Bangkok where they will be kept until they sign up "voluntarily" to return to Laos.

Also in 1994, a growing number of members of Congress in bipartisan efforts have repeatedly voiced grave concerns to Secretary of State Warren Christopher about the efficacy of the Tripartite Agreement in view of the continued fighting in Laos, the evidence of human rights violations against the Hmong, and their forced repatriation to Laos financed with U.S. tax dollars.

In February 1994, Rep. Patricia Schroeder wrote to King Bhumipol Adulyadej of Thailand, asking him to intercede on behalf of these Hmong and to stop repatriation. She pointed out that the 1991 Tripartite Agreement under which the Hmong are being repatriated has been invalidated because of "the ongoing bloody civil war in Laos..., well documented cases of mandatory (forced) repatriations of Hmong to Laos ... [and] gross violations of human rights by the Lao government which has closed Laos to all monitoring by independent human rights organizations." Other U.S. lawmakers also called for an end to involuntary Hmong repatriation to Laos.

On September 22, 1994, U.S. senators Ted Kennedy, Alan Simpson, Paul Simon and Daniel Patrick Moynihan and congressmen Ben Gilman, Howard Berman, Bill McCollum and Charles Schumer wrote to Warren Christopher expressing concern about the disturbing arrest of the six refugee leaders in Na Pho and asked that they be allowed to come to the United States. To date, there has been no response from Christopher.

Then during the final days of December 1994, Wisconsin Congressman Steve Gunderson with the support of Ben Gilman, soon to become chair of the House Committee on International Relations, launched another five-man fact-finding mission to Thailand. Their report seriously criticized the State Department, UNHCR and non-governmental organizations, including the U.S.–based Hmong National Development, Inc., charging them with deception and specifically accusing the Clinton State Department of a whitewash to "cover up misdeeds of officials involved in helping pressure and force Hmong/Lao refugees from Thailand to Laos and also cover up their persecution and murders in the LPDR."[5]

Gunderson's group found " a disturbing pattern of inaccurate and misleading information being provided to Members of Congress through official and NGO channels."[6] It also accused the UNHCR of giving false and misleading information to Congress. In a fall 1994 letter to congressmen Jim Leach, Gunderson, and Gilman about the six Suan Plu prisoners, the UNHCR makes light of their condition: "[they] are in good health and are receiving preferential treatment, including English classes. They are only complaining of boredom."[7]

Gunderston's team visited the six prisoners and found that the UNHCR had misled Congress: "They said they often become sick and suffer from fevers and other symptoms for which they receive no medical care," and they denied receiving English language instruction and special treatment. In fact, the team found the six ill and languishing in prison.[8] Repeated calls for their release go unheeded.

The Gunderson trip report also notes that the State Department, the NGOs it funds and the signers of the Tripartite Agreement (Thailand, Laos, and the UNHCR) pursue a hardline policy on this issue that is "flagrant historical revisionism and is aimed at covering up evidence and proof of forced repatriation and human rights violations against Hmong/Lao refugees so that signers of the Tripartite Agreement and the U.S. Department of State can further their policy objectives."[9]

In an accompanying press release Congressman Gunderson added: "Even more disturbing are apparent attempts by officials in the State Department to discredit credible evidence of persecution of Hmong/Lao returnees to Laos."

In the summer of 1994, *St. Paul Pioneer Press* journalist Brian Bonner documented chilling LPDR abuses against the Hmong; LPDR camps where Hmong prisoners, as in Nazi Germany, were tattooed with numbers; forced repatriation of Hmong to Laos; and obfuscation of evidence by NGOs and the State Department.[10]

In November and December of 1994, Bonner traveled to Laos, describing it as a "totalitarian state where bloodletting never ends" and where Hmong are targets of random executions, village raids and land grabs by the LPDR. He also documented Hmong in Thailand being forced to Laos at gunpoint and under threat of death or starvation; incompetent or absent monitoring of returnees; embezzlement of U.N. money by LPDR officials; and returnees' survival being dependent upon money sent by relatives in the United States.

At this writing in early 1995, Hmong in Thailand continue to fear that they will be forced back to Laos under the Tripartite Agreement. Some 7,000 are held in Thailand at Na Pho, called a "concentration camp" by the Hmong. Another 16,000 to 20,000 have temporary sanctuary at Wat Thamkrobok, a Buddhist temple north of Bangkok. An unknown number—certainly in the hundreds—are held in Si Khiew Detention Center near Korat, jailed because fearing persecution they refused to be repatriated to Laos. Others hide in the hills of northern Thailand to escape being sent back to Laos.

"This is a moral and ethical issue," maintains Eugene Douglas, President Reagan's ambassador-at-large for refugees. "We need to acknowledge that we enlisted the Hmong into the service of the U.S. in an effort to contain communism in Southeast Asia. We promised them protection in exchange for their assistance. They kept their bargain; we broke ours. We owe them a loyalty that has nothing to do with funding pressures, or the convenience of a rapprochement, or the coming together with Hanoi. ... While all refugees merit compassion," he says, "the fighters and employees of the armed forces and the CIA among the Hmong people, their wives, their children, and their immediate families deserve our special support."

On Capitol Hill, some believe the solution must include rescreening and resettlement for genuine refugees inappropriately screened out by the current process. Hmong agree. But the resolve by senators and representatives to help these former loyal and effective allies is unimpressive. Since Hmong Americans have no significant political base and only a few Americans really know the sacrifices of the Hmong during the war and the realities of life for this ethnic minority in Laos under the current dictatorial communist regime, their cries to call a moratorium on the forcible repatriation of their relatives from Thailand to Laos is largely ignored.

On May 20, 1991, Moua Cher Xiong, who had fought communist forces in Laos, recorded this message on a cassette tape for his relatives in the United States. He and other refugees were given no advance warning that they would be forced back from Chiang Kham camp in Thailand to Laos. There was no time to alert relatives, no time or procedure available to petition their fate. This story is similar to the fate of many Hmong repatriated from 1991 through 1994 under the U.S.–sponsored and -financed Tripartite Agreement. Moua's cassette was received by the U.S.–based Lao Human Rights Council on June 2, 1991. Though Moua's plea came in 1991, it is, tragically, still apt in 1996.

> We are on the death road now ... the authorities shall force us to go to Laos tomorrow. We lost all of the addresses of our relatives in America because the authorities did not allow us to take our property and belongings with us when they arrested us.... Our last words to you and people in America are that the authorities used guns and strings [ropes] and wood [sticks] to force us to sign the papers stating we are willing to go to Laos. Please tell the world that there are corruptions and refugees traded in the camp. We will die soon. So you must remember us. We were born in the wrong world and at the wrong time.... Our lives are over. We shall die when we arrive in Laos. We shall not meet and see you and our good friends again. We are sorry. We cry now. Goodbye and good luck to all of you in America.

Unfortunately for the Hmong, Senator Moynihan is correct: "To be an enemy of the United States can be unpleasant. To be a friend of the United States can be fatal."

Sources

1. See "Country Reports on Human Rights Practices," reports submitted to the Committee on Foreign Relations, U.S. Senate and the Committee on Foreign Affairs, U.S. House of Representatives, by the Department of State, Washington, D.C.: Government Printing Office. Released annually, usually in February for the previous year.
2. Radio Pathet Lao, May 6, 1975, in FBIS-APA, May 9, 1975.
3. "Forced Back and Forgotten: The Human Rights of Laotian Asylum Seekers in Thailand." New York: Lawyers Committee for Human Rights, 1989, p. 3.
4. Marc Kaufman. "Allies Abandoned," *Philadelphia Inquirer Magazine*, February 27, 1994.
5. "Report to the Congress of the United States: Fact-Finding Mission to Thailand Regarding the Status of Hmong/Lao Refugee and Asylum Seekers." Tim Bartl, legislative assistant to U.S. Congressman Steve Gunderson; Lao Veterans of America; and Philip Smith Center for Public Policy Analysis, December 28, 1994–January 2, 1995, p. 6. From now on referred to as the Gunderson Report.
6. Gunderson Report, p. 9.
7. Gunderson Report, Exhibit PP.
8. Gunderson Report, pp. 31–32.
9. Gunderson Report, p. 18.
10. Brian Bonner. "Hmong Fight Bitter Return," *St. Paul Pioneer Press*, October 2, 1994.

Additional Source

Jane Hamilton-Merritt's *Tragic Mountains: The Hmong, The Americans, and The Secret Wars for Laos* (Indiana University Press, 1993) details the relationship of Hmong and the Americans during the Vietnam War era, the communist takeover of Laos in 1975, the communist rule from then to 1993, the fate of the Hmong who fought against the LPDR, and the plight of the remaining Hmong political refugees and asylum seekers in Thailand.

moment when southerners made history, but most of the books see the issue otherwise. Lewy recognizes that in the late 1950s militants in South Viet Nam increasingly "demanded a change in policy," but passes quickly to a more schematic formulation, stressing NLF "impotence" on one side, "control by Hanoi" on the other. His conclusion differs only in degree from the view expressed in several texts that "the insurgency was a genuine revolt based in the South, but it was organized and directed from the North." Here as elsewhere, the insurgents appear most frequently in passages where others are the subjects, where they serve as foils for illuminating policy dilemmas in Washington or Saigon or Hanoi.[6]

In any text, some passages carry more weight than others; some only illustrate a point spelled out elsewhere or provide a chronological bridge to get the reader from one crisis to the next. More weighty are sections that frame the presentation, that announce what is coming or sum up what has just been learned. Historical subjects brought forward to participate in these assessments, often situated at the beginning or end of chapters, are promoted above others in the narrative, as their point of view is associated with the truth claim that the author is presenting. In sizing up the Tet Offensive, Lewy turns to Henry Kissinger, whereas Turley quotes NLF General Tran Van Tra, just as he did Do Van Buu when the time came to make sense of the Geneva Accords. Outside of the works by Turley and Young, southern revolutionaries are never included in these framing passages.[7]

In short, fragmented and marginalized references to the NLF do not add up to a coherent narrative. But the images of the enemy that are embedded in such passages cannot be said to lack power. The first such depiction might be termed the "Foreign Other." The story begins with the Saigon government ruling a peaceful Viet Nam, its officials and sympathizers established as the natural leaders of their communities. With no program, nothing to contribute to a better life for the Vietnamese, guerrillas intrude, threatening and murdering those who stand up to them. Whether their origins are traced to the USSR or to China or to Hanoi or to the swamps or mountains or jungles of the South does not matter. They are the Foreign Other.[8]

"People's War" reverses these terms. Here the guerrillas, benefiting from Viet Minh accomplishments of the previous generation, are the natural leaders when the fighting starts, while Saigon officials, primarily absentee landlords and northern Catholics, are aliens, using force to gain control. For the People's War as for the Foreign Other paradigm, the village provides a starting point, a natural order, a vision of peace, one that is threatened by enemies with nothing positive to offer, sowing destruction all around. But People's War reverses Foreign Other, with outsiders recast as authentic Vietnamese and insiders as morally bankrupt invaders.

In between is what might be called a "Crossfire" image of the situation. According to this view, both the GVN and the NLF are outside the villages, and the peasants are caught in the middle as the two factions contend. Cross-fire eschews the utopianism of Foreign Other, which hopes for a world free of subversion, and of People's War, which imagines liberation as the outcome of the struggle. As a battle between right and wrong gives way to mere pathos, solidarity with one of the two camps is set aside in favor of pity for the hapless Vietnamese.

The Foreign Other has a complicated history, predating the Cold War and sure to survive the collapse of the Soviet Bloc. Foreign Others do not belong, they are from somewhere else, but their "foreignness" is more a moral than a spatial construct. The "others" are "foreign" mainly because they are beyond the pale, as when Joes refers to "utterly revolting" atrocities against women and children, demonstrating "to what satanic depths of cruelty human beings could sink in the name of a Communist Viet Nam." Writing in 1978, Lewy argued that Communism was a threat to U.S. interests. His is the only text to begin in 1950 rather than in 1945, a device meant to emphasize simultaneous enemy aggression in China, Korea, and Viet Nam. Taking up the baton for a conservative view of the war, Joes shows less interest in global issues. For him, Communism remains abhorrent, but it poses a moral rather than a strategic challenge to the United States. Hanoi leaders are even more "foreign" in his book than in earlier texts, as they are excoriated with a venom that used to be aimed across the whole front of international communist totalitarianism.[9]

At first glance, the other surveys break with the Foreign Other, especially in their treatment of Ho Chi Minh, whose patriotism is taken at face value and whose potential as a Vietnamese Tito the Americans are castigated for overlooking. A "Great Man" emphasis on Ho provides a solution for both narrative and interpretive dilemmas. Focus on the individual simplifies the expository task (Ho's thoughts and actions are made to stand for a national movement) and blurs the political stakes as well (the man identified by the State Department as a "Commie" and a "Stalinist" was "an awfully sweet old guy," as one OSS agent put it[10]).

But Great Man history does not fully break from Cold War views. Ho Chi Minh carries the argument only so far, and the legitimacy derived from his person evaporates as the action moves from the 1940s to the 1960s, from North to South, from patriotism to the dynamics of a revolutionary movement. When Ho is no longer there, sympathy runs out, and the Foreign Other resumes its ascendancy.

"The Hue Massacre" demonstrate this shift from one paradigm to another. Hue '68 was the bloodiest battle of the war. House-to-house fighting and U.S. bombing and shelling destroyed much of the city and caused civilian casualties. Political murders were also committed, with NLF victims including police and other Saigon officials, while the GVN aimed at Front cadres and sympathizers whose affiliations had surfaced during the occupation of the city.

Going beyond the fact of NLF assassinations, which no scholarly study denies, the "Hue Massacre" is a Cold War narrative construction purporting to demonstrate that enemy terrorism was qualitatively different from GVN and U.S. attacks on civilians and that it resulted in the most heinous atrocity of the war. Bombs and bullets were flying on all sides and killers under every flag roamed the streets, but the "Hue Massacre" signifies that the guerrillas killed more than the Americans and the GVN and that they killed with a uniquely blameworthy premeditation and relish. Their violence was "systematic," meaning that it was constitutive, inevitable, and limitless in scale, in contrast to reactive violence on the other side, intended to halt the depredations of the Foreign Other.[11]

Body counting by Douglas Pike played a central role in formulating the "Hue Massacre." Pike declares that there were 7,600 civilian casualties in Hue, that 1,900 of these were hospitalized or outpatients with "injuries attributable to warfare," and that 944 died "due to accident of battle." He states that 2,810 victims of VC terrorism were found in mass graves after the offensive, leaving 1,946 victims unaccounted for but probably also dead at the hands of the Communists. In the debates that followed, 2,810 was often rounded off to 2,800 or 3,000 and 1,946 to 2,000. Assuming that no amount of evidence will sway critics who believe that the guerrillas were "friendly agrarian reformers," Pike promises not to waste time on word pictures "of Vietnamese communists as fiendish fanatics with blood dripping from their hands." But only "fiends" could have committed the acts that he describes, pinpointing thousands of victims in advance, torturing and executing them, and dumping their corpses into mass graves.[12]

Turley is noncommittal, referring the matter to a footnote, and Young takes her distance from the Pike view, but all the others opt for the "Hue Massacre." Lewy declares that 5,800 perished, in "the most extensive and systematic political slaughter of the war." Hess says as many as 5,000 were "summarily executed," in "perhaps the worst atrocity of the war." Lomperis puts the number at 3,000–5,000 "systematically executed." Olson and Roberts go with 2,800 "systematically slaughtered" and 2,000 presumed killed, and Herring employs the same figures. Karnow speaks of "unprecedented brutality," "ghastly atrocities," "Communist butchery," "the worst bloodbath of the conflict," claiming the lives of at least 3,000 victims. Perhaps the impression is only the result of clumsy phrasing, but he also makes it seem as if the NLF killed "minor government functionaries and other innocuous figures as well as harmless foreign doctors, schoolteachers, and missionaries" in cities other than Hue. Moss and Joes are content with 2,800, the victims executed "often in brutal fashion" or "buried alive," according to Moss, or "shot, bludgeoned to death, or buried alive," according to Joes. Maclear cites a U.S. veteran's comment about enemy "goon squads" and a captured document from the other side taking credit for close to 2,800 executions. Since most of the books say little or nothing about the NLF in the years leading up to the Tet Offensive, these passages have an even greater impact. It is as if, once launched, the Viet Cong stayed in hiding until 1968, then leapt into the open to murder thousands.[13]

Olson and Roberts assert that more than 10,000 civilians died during the battle of Hue and blame "random American bombardment" for those not killed by the NLF, while Karnow and Moss call attention to U.S. firepower, with Karnow noting its "uncommon fury" and Moss indicating that the city "had been blasted into corpse-strewn rubble." Neither supplies a body count for bombing and shelling. Maclear affirms that 5,800 Hue residents died and adds that the U.S. military was later prepared to assign only half of these deaths to "Communist executions." Hess and Herring quote Dave Richard Palmer (Hue was left "a shattered, stinking hulk, its streets choked with rubble and rotting bodies"), in a way that suggests, but does not explicitly affirm, American responsibility. Lewy writes, "there is no doubt that many civilians were killed during the expulsion of the VC/NVA from Hue," but hurries on to rebuke "Hanoi sympathizers" who minimize the "magnitude and ruthlessness of the VC terror." Among the authors, only Karnow and Young mention GVN hit teams.[14]

The picture gets murky when attention turns to causes of the "Hue Massacre." Olson and Roberts remark that "Instead of leaving the bodies on public display, as they had always done in the past with political assassinations," the Communists "buried the victims in shallow graves", and that "There was an ideological dimension to the killings—liquidations of entire groups of people—which had not been seen before." But they do not ask why the NLF might have departed on this occasion from its usual mode of operation. Moss thinks the "Massacre" was intended to send "a stark message" that "no one associated with the GVN was safe from insurgent reprisals anywhere in South Vietnam." This hypothesis—that the killings were intended to intimidate, to terrorize—might be squared with Communist "bragging about the large number of class enemies eliminated in Hue," as Lewy puts it. But it collides with Lewy's adjoining speculation that "the largest number of people were probably eliminated during the cover-the-traces period when the retreating communist troops seized witnesses of the earlier killings and marched them away to be shot and buried in well-concealed places outside the city." Ill at ease in the Foreign Other paradigm and perhaps sensing the futility of the task, the other authors say nothing about possible motives for such an atrocity.[15]

Near unanimity among survey authors on the "Hue Massacre" cannot be explained on the basis of scholarship. Only Lewy footnotes Pike's treatment, which is contained in a pamphlet commissioned and published in 1970 by the U.S. Mission in Saigon and which is, by any definition, a work of propaganda. The mass graves on which Pike lays so much stress were evacuated by the GVN under tight security that ruled out independent oversight and were presented to the public to illustrate communist perfidy. "Captured documents" employed to prove that NLF assassinations were calculated in advance and intrinsic to the guerrilla endeavor have a similar provenance. Bodies recovered long after the Tet Offensive, some in inaccessible mountainous terrain ("the 101st Airborne Brigade burial detail" had to be airlifted to one site), especially ought to arouse skepticism.[16]

Keeping their distance from Pike, the other surveys prefer to cite Don Oberdorfer's book on the Tet Offensive, a device that evades rather than resolves the problem of documentation. Oberdorfer's case studies of NLF terrorism, based on interviews he conducted with survivors and witnesses, are credible, but his treatment of the "Hue Massacre" is just warmed over Pike. Pike recognizes that "We do not know who the dead are, nor even how many," an acknowledgment that Oberdorfer repeats, without seeming to notice that these comments cast doubt on the "Hue Massacre." If we cannot identify all of the victims, how can we be sure that the enemy had named them in advance? If we cannot count the dead, how can we conclude that the Communists killed 2,800?[17]

The occasion when our survey authors are closest to agreement does not show them at their best. Some readers will deplore the "Hue Massacre" as a lapse into anti-communist demonization. Others, more loyal to the Cold War paradigm, will want to know how so many survey authors reconcile their image of a benevolent "Uncle Ho" with their depiction of his terrorist nephews and nieces in 1968. But such critics can at least draw satisfaction from this belated acknowledgment of the Foreign Other.

Often criticized for romanticizing the other side or for repeating communist propaganda, People's War does not exercise the same leverage as does Foreign Other, but its explanatory power is acknowledged, one way or the other, in all the texts. Turley and Young describe political and organizational ties between the guerrilla forces and their rural constituency, enabling the NLF to train and promote recruits, assess and collect taxes, run schools and health clinics, and keep a multilevel armed force in the field. The other surveys lack this detail, but even the most cursory takes note of connections between the Front and the population, as when Olson and Roberts affirm that the guerrillas lived "off the land and the peasants."[18]

Lewy and Joes show a particular interest in People's War. Believing that trouble in South Viet Nam derived from external sources, they are also critical of U.S. preoccupation with infiltration and persuaded that the key battles should have been fought in the villages by police and counterinsurgency specialists, with the aim of rooting out the "Viet Cong infrastructure." Especially insistent on this point, Lewy draws attention to the redistributive, revolutionary character of the NLF and in the process repeatedly strays into the People's War paradigm. Viet Cong assassins targeted "the natural leaders of the community," he argues, borrowing again from Pike. But then, a few pages later, it is noted that, because of landlord control of the GVN, "natural leaders were ignored, good men were not promoted, and cowards and buffoons with connections rose to positions of power." As a result, "frustrated in their ambitions," peasants who might have become natural leaders of the Saigon regime joined the other side, which "promised advancement and rewarded outstanding performance." The Front constitutes a tenacious, haunting presence in Lewy's survey even after the Tet Offensive, when the countryside remained "a society basically in enemy hands."[19]

The authors' uneasiness with People's War is signaled by frequent narrative displacements. Viet Minh land reform is taken out of its proper chronological place and revealed in flashback, during discussion of Diem's failed reform, thereby losing some of its polemical impact. Lewy employs a similar device, acknowledging NLF land policies in a passage on Thieu's Land-to-the-Tiller program of 1970, so that the reader learns about an earlier appeal to peasants at a moment when, in the author's words, "a class conflict which the VC had exploited for years, had been largely neutralized."[20]

Some of the strongest affirmations of NLF legitimacy are situated in comments on their adversaries. Diem "could not comprehend the dimensions of the political, social, and economic revolution being promoted by his Communist foes," Karnow declares. General Westmoreland "refused to recognize that the Communists might represent a tempting alternative to a rural population eager for political, economic, and social change." These affirmations are far more ringing than anything the author says directly about the NLF. The result is that the reader is more focused on what was wrong with Diem's understanding or Westmoreland's understanding than on what the other side was doing right. These passages suggest that the U.S. endeavor was in the nature of things and that the communist triumph was an aberration. As Joes puts it, "stupid errors" by our side constitute the first reason for the success of the enemy.[21]

"Last words" also override People's War. Herring's treatment of the NLF is generally respectful, but the tone shifts in the epilogue, which notes, "Vietnam's indifference to the fate of some 2,500 U.S. servicemen still listed as missing in action"; portrays Viet Nam as an aggressor in the wars with China and Cambodia; and makes no mention of the U.S. embargo. Karnow and Olson and Roberts also leave out the embargo, and the latter text concludes that the communist regime is responsible for transforming Viet Nam "into one of the poorest countries in the world." To sum up, People's War gets a hearing, but also stirs a palpable ambivalence.[22]

With an air of sociological shrewdness and even wisdom about the human condition, the Crossfire metaphor appears to stake out a middle ground. Here the peasants appear as simple folk, caring only about food on the table and a roof over their heads.

In Karnow's words,

The lives of peasants are dictated by the arduous and endless cycle of their crops. They plow, sow, and harvest, resigned to the droughts, floods, pests, and diseases that blight their rice, corn, sugar, peanuts, and potatoes. Their daily tasks bend their backs and age their wives far beyond their years, and the hunger of each day stunts their children. Their every waking hour is concerned with survival. ... I found them muddled, frightened, weary. Again and again as they spoke, one thread seemed to run through their conversation. They were not participants in the conflict, but its victims.

Olson and Roberts make a similar point by citing the *Quiet American* vision of peasant society as static and outside of history. "In five hundred years there may be no New York or London, but they'll be growing paddy in these fields," the novel's protagonist predicts. "Thought's a luxury. Do you think the peasant sits and thinks of God and Democracy when he gets inside his mud hut at night?"[23]

Empty-minded peasants crouching in their huts just want to be left alone, these scholars insist, in a way that suggests their own desire to get away from quarrels between Foreign Other and People's War. Such an approach has an appearance of neutrality, of estrangement from all the parties, allowing an observer of Karnow's inclination to back away from "a war that nobody won—a struggle between victims." But the deeper logic of Crossfire is pro-intervention. Tacitly shifting blame for the carnage to Vietnamese peasants who did not have the strength or the wit to be anything but victims, it shares with Foreign Other a belief in the nullity of the rural population and distances itself from the People's War notion of peasants as patriots and revolutionaries. It implies that country people, who were unable to understand or to resist the Communist threat, needed an outside force to act on their behalf.[24]

I conclude by affirming that our three images of the NLF are implanted in the literature and that none are likely to be dislodged anytime soon. This staying power has emotional and cultural roots, but also mirrors reality. Crossfire does not do justice, but has some relationship, to an *attentisme* that waxed and waned throughout the war among the Vietnamese people. The debate between People's War and Foreign Other views parallels the collision between revolution and counter-revolution, between Communism and its enemies, in Viet Nam.

Most texts move with a seeming lack of self-consciousness from one paradigm to another, as metaphors are shuffled to compensate for a lack of narrative coherence. A more fruitful approach would be to recognize that in every phase some villagers saw the guerrillas as intruders, others joined the NLF, while still others sat on the fence; and that peasants often reassessed their options, moving from support for the Front to neutrality to the government side and back again. The paradigms should be seen not as fixed constructs, but as choices that people made and remade during the war. The literary impulse can work against scholarship, substituting metaphor for analysis, but if not turned into essentialist constructs, our images help build a narrative of agency in the countryside.[25]

Notes

1. See Patrick Hagopian, "Report on the 1990-1991 Survey of Courses on the Vietnam War" (Fairfax, Va: Indochina Institute/George Mason University, 1993). "Vietnam Institutes" organized by the William Joiner Center at the University of Massachusetts at Boston in 1993, 1994, and 1995 attracted high school teachers from all over Massachusetts. Their reports second with respect to the high school scene what Hagopian affirms about colleges: that courses on the war are popular with students and are still being added to the curriculum. The surveys discussed in this essay include George Herring, *America's Longest War: The United States and Vietnam, 1950–1975* (New York: Knopf, 1986; first edition 1979); Gary Hess, *Vietnam and the United States: Origins and Legacy of War* (Boston: Twayne, 1990); Anthony James Joes, *The War for South Viet Nam, 1954–1975* (New York: Praeger, 1990; first edition 1989); Stanley Karnow, *Vietnam, a History: The First Complete Account of Vietnam at War* (New York: Penguin, 1984; first edition 1983); Guenter Lewy, *America in Vietnam* (New York: Oxford, 1978); Timothy Lomperis, *The War Everyone Lost—and Won: America's Intervention in Viet Nam's Twin Struggles* (Washington: Congressional Quarterly Press, 1993; first edition 1984); Michael Maclear, *The Ten Thousand Day War, Vietnam: 1945–1975* (New York: Avon, 1981); George Moss, *Vietnam: An American Ordeal* (Englewood Cliffs: Prentice Hall, 1993; first edition 1990); James Olson and Randy Roberts, *Where the Domino Fell: American and Vietnam, 1945–1990* (New York: St. Martin's, 1991); William Turley, *The Second Indochina War: A Short Political and Military History, 1954–1975* (New York: Mentor, 1986); and Marilyn Young, *The Vietnam Wars, 1945–1990* (New York: HarperCollins, 1991). Of the 83 instructors who responded to a questionnaire Hagopian distributed in 1990-91, before several of the above works had appeared, 58 recommended Herring's book, followed by Karnow (46), Turley (11), Moss (7), and Olson and Roberts (7).

2. This essay on the NLF is part of a larger project. Later installments will deal with survey treatments of the GVN, the DRV, and the American side.

3. The NLF was finished after 1968 according to Hess, *Vietnam and the United States*, p. 108; Joes, *War for South Vietnam*, pp. 96-97; Lomperis, *War Everyone Lost*, pp. 80 and 169; and Moss, *American Ordeal*, p. 252. Less categorical on the point, but also inattentive to the NLF after the Tet Offensive, are Herring, *America's Longest War*; Karnow, *Vietnam*; and Olson and Roberts, *Where the Domino Fell*. According to Turley, the Front "had been weakened" after 1968, but in 1971, "down in the villages and hamlets," it was still "exacting a fearful toll" (*Second Indochina War*, pp. 132). Southerners are portrayed as active in 1975 in *ibid.*, pp. 175-177; and Young, *Vietnam Wars*, pp. 292-295.

4. Young, *Vietnam Wars*, pp. 38, 39, and 54-56. Turley (*Second Indochina War*, p. 21) and Lomperis (*War Everyone Lost*, p. 32) note a communist party presence in the south, with Lomperis arguing that the southern branch was stronger than its counterparts elsewhere in Viet Nam.

5. Turley, *Second Indochina War*, pp. 11-12; Lewy, *America in Vietnam*, p. 10; and Karnow, *Vietnam*, pp. 227-230.

6. Lewy, *America in Vietnam*, pp. 16, 18. The citation on revolt being "organized and directed" from Hanoi comes from William Duiker, *The Communist Road to Power in Vietnam* (Boulder: Westview Press, 1981), p. 198. It is cited by Herring, *America's Longest War*, p. 66; Moss, *American Ordeal*, p. 96; and Olson and Roberts, *Where the Domino Fell*, p. 71. Duiker's treatment is more complex than the summary sentence he provides (*Communist Road*, pp. 183-199). For more on the issue, see David Hunt, "U.S. Scholarship and the National Liberation Front," in Jayne Werner and David Hunt, eds., *The American War in Vietnam* (Ithaca: Southeast Asia Publications/Cornell University, 1993), p. 94.

7. Lewy, *America in Vietnam*, p. 76 (end of Chapter 2); and Turley, *Second Indochina War*, pp. 116–117 (end of Chapter 6). Turley's book is the only one of the 11 to draw heavily on Vietnamese language sources and is also the most balanced in considering the various Vietnamese parties in the war, with 32 percent of the text on the United States, 7 percent on the Viet Minh, 21 percent on the DRV, and 20 percent each on the NLF and the GVN.

8. The scholarly basis for competing images of the NLF is discussed in Hunt, "U.S. Scholarship."

9. Joes, *War for South Vietnam*, p. 47. Joes's views are anticipated in Norman Podhoretz, *Why We Were in Viet Nam* (New York: Touchstone, 1982). The first survey of the Viet Nam War to appear, Lewy's formidable work still commands our attention. I am not sure Joes's volume will wear as well. For a critique, see Edwin Moise's review in *Journal of Asian Studies* 49 (1990), pp. 209–210.

10. Quoted in Olson and Roberts, *When the Domino Fell*, pp. 29 and 18.

11. The key text is Douglas Pike, *The Viet-Cong Strategy of Terror* (Saigon: U.S. Mission, 1970). See also Stephen Hosmer, *Viet Cong Repression and Its Implications for the Future* (Lexington, MA: Heath, 1970); and Robert Turner, *Vietnamese Communism: Its Origins and Development* (Stanford: Hoover Institute, 1975).

12. Pike, *Viet-Cong Strategy*, pp. 3, 30–31. Without elaboration, Pike attributes these statistics to the GVN. "Injuries attributable to warfare" and "accident of battle" might refer to the results of U.S. bombing and shelling, but this hint is not pursued in the text.

13. Turley, *Second Indochina War*, p. 109; Young, *Vietnam Wars*, pp. 217–219; Lewy, *America in Vietnam*, p. 274; Hess, *Vietnam and the United States*, p. 108; Lomperis, *War Everybody Lost*, p. 78; Olson and Roberts, *Where the Domino Fell*, p. 184; Herring, *America's Longest War*, p. 190; Karnow, *Vietnam*, pp. 525 and 530; Moss, *American Ordeal*, p. 249; Joes, *War for South Vietnam*, p. 92; and Maclear, *Ten Thousand Day War*, p. 211. Turley's lack of attention to the "Hue Massacre" (and also to the My Lai massacre, which he does not mention) is in the logic of his rigorously argued survey. It is criticized (and misrepresented) in a review by Timothy Lomperis, in *Conflict Quarterly* 7 (1987), pp. 95–97. Marilyn Young has been assailed from several quarters for her less provocative treatment of events in Hue; see references in footnote 18.

14. On U.S. bombardment, see Olson and Roberts, *Where the Domino Fell*, p. 185; Karnow, *Vietnam*, p. 525; Moss, *American Ordeal*, p. 249; Maclear, *Ten Thousand Day War*, p. 211; Hess, *Vietnam and the United States*, p. 108; Herring, *America's Longest War*, p. 190; and Lewy, *America in Vietnam*, p. 275. On GVN hit teams, see Karnow, *Vietnam*, p. 531; and Young, *Vietnam Wars*, p. 219.

15. Olson and Roberts, *Where the Domino Fell*, pp. 184–185; Moss, *American Ordeal*, p. 249; and Lewy, *America in Vietnam*, pp. 274–275. Both Pike (*Viet Cong Strategy*, p. 31) and Hosmer (*Viet Cong Repression*, p. 50) recognize that the "Hue Massacre" does not fit with normal NLF practice. Pike provides various "hypotheses" to account for this anomaly. My favorite is the notion that

> Since the communist, especially the communist from Hue, takes his dogma seriously, he can become demoniac when dismissed by a Confucian as a philosophic ignoramus, or by a Buddhist as a trivial materialist. Or, worse than being dismissed, ignored through the years. So, with the righteousness of a true believer, he sought to strike back and eliminate this challenge of indifference [pp. 36–37].

Hosmer speculates that maybe the North Vietnamese and not the NLF were responsible for the atrocity, or that soldiers on the run may have assassinated prisoners of war (p. 50). The latter scenario, with killings not planned in advance and not numbering in the thousands, draws readers out of the "Hue Massacre." Pike declares that "the communists made a major effort to hide their deeds" (p. 32), but Hosmer argues for "open communist endorsement of what occurred in Hue" and makes it seem as if the perpetrators were anxious to take credit for what they had accomplished. Body counts from mass graves, he argues, "would seem to lend credibility to communist claims that about 3,000 persons were eliminated during the occupation of Hue" (pp. 50, 146).

16. The title page of *Viet Cong Strategy* notes, "This monograph was prepared by Douglas Pike for the United States Mission, Viet Nam." Gareth Porter, "The 1968 'Hue Massacre,'" *Indochina Chronicle* 33 (1974), pp. 1–14, argues that the mass grave body count was inflated and that it is impossible to establish the circumstances in which many of the victims had been killed. His surmise that others beyond the NLF share responsibility for the deaths of people whose remains were found seems reasonable and even unavoidable. Along these lines, Karnow asserts that Saigon assassins threw the bodies of "many" of the people they had killed "into common graves with the Vietcong's victims" (*Vietnam*, p. 531). See also Porter's discussion of "captured documents." Porter's critique is cited by Turley and Young and ignored by the other survey authors. On the 101st Airborne, see Pike, *Viet Cong Strategy*, p. 29.

17. On the limits of evidence from mass graves, see Pike, *Viet Cong Strategy*, p. 40; and Dan Oberdorfer, *Tet!* (New York: Avon, 1971), p. 249.

18. Turley, *Second Indochina War*, pp. 42–44; Young, *Vietnam Wars*, pp. 66–69, 72–73, and 84–86; and Olson and Roberts, *When the Domino Fell*, p. 149. More than the other paradigms, People's War sends tempers rising, as is evidenced by the reception of Marilyn Young's scholarly, low-key survey. Jonathan Mirsky assails what he takes to be Young's moral obtuseness in excusing crimes committed by Vietnamese Communists, then concludes with the unexpected and—within the context of the review—inexplicable judgment that it is "a useful and interesting book" in "Reconsidering Vietnam," *New York Review of Books*, October 10, 1991, pp. 47–49. David Marr is also scornful, affirming that Young "romanticizes" the other side and parrots "war stories emanating from Hanoi," in *Pacific Historical Review* 62 (1993), pp. 394–395. Andrew Rotter, who liked the book, criticizes Young's failure to condemn "Communist cruelty," in *Diplomatic History* 17 (1993), p. 497.

19. Lewy, *America in Vietnam*, pp. 88, 95, and 194–195; on "natural leaders," see Douglas Pike, *Viet Cong* (Cambridge, MA: MIT Press, 1966), p 248. Jumps from one paradigm to another are especially marked in Lewy's discussion of the war crimes debate. In attempting to exculpate U.S. policymakers, he affirms that civilian victims of American war making were persons the GIs "often had good reason to consider unfriendly," so that there was military justification for the violence the Americans aimed against them (p. 237). In close proximity are passages describing U.S. efforts to provide the villagers with "greater security" from the Viet Cong. I disagree with Lewy's argument about war crimes, but respect his decision to devote 150 pages to the controversy. Most of the surveys do not even take notice of the issue.

20. Flashback constructions are found in Joes, *War for South Vietnam*, p. 68; Karnow, *Vietnam*, p. 231; and Lewy, *America in Vietnam*, p. 189. See also Moss's assertion that "the southern delta region had been a communist stronghold since the days of the Vietminh," in a passage on events in 1962 (*American Ordeal*, p. 115). Going in the opposite direction, Karnow and Lewy flash forward when discussing Hanoi's role in forming the NLF, suggesting that northern suppression of southern activists after 1975 proves they had been in control all along. Karnow's inter-cultural references to the Northerners as "carpetbaggers" underscores the point (*Vietnam*, p. 239), while Lewy has NLF fellow traveler Jean Lacouture speak against himself to express a postwar disillusionment with Hanoi (*America in Vietnam*, p. 18).

21. Karnow, *Vietnam*, pp. 213 and 464; and Joes, *War for South Vietnam*, p. 49.

22. Herring, *America's Longest War*, p. 272; and Olson and Roberts, *Where the Domino Fell*, p. 275.

23. Karnow, *Vietnam*, p. 232; and Olson and Roberts, *Where the Domino Fell*, p. 59. Karnow echoes a similar portrait of Vietnamese peasants, for whom "contentment is a full belly and untroubled rest," in John Mecklin, *Mission in Torment: An Intimate Account of the U.S. Role in Vietnam* (New York: Doubleday, 1965), pp. 78.

24. Karnow, *Vietnam*, p. 11. The authoritarian logic of Crossfire is overt in the testimony of a Saigon official: "It was too early for elections.... The peasants only know about

making a living, they didn't know anything about politics" (quoted in Jeffrey Race, *War Comes to Long An: Revolutionary Conflict in a Vietnamese Province* [Berkeley: University of California Press, 1972], p. 14). But the image crops up everywhere, even in the antiwar movement. See, for example, Loren Baritz, *Backfire: A History of How American Culture Led Us into Vietnam and Made Us Fight the Way We Did* (New York: William Morrow, 1985), underscoring the incomprehension of policymakers when confronted by peasants who cared more about their "water buffaloes" than about war and revolution (p. 91).

25. For example, James Trullinger argues that 80–85 percent of the villagers in one locale supported the NLF in the mid–1960s, while 5 percent lined up with the GVN and 10–15 percent hedged their bets. After Tet, the NLF audience dwindled to 50 percent, the Saigon side advanced to 10–15 percent, and attentisme grew to 35–40 percent. By 1974, the Front partially recovered, to 70 percent, the government fell to 10 percent, and the number of fence sitters shrank to 20 percent. One could quarrel about the numbers. The point is that villagers changed their minds and allegiances, sometimes more than once. See *Village at War: An Account of Revolution in Vietnam* (New York: Longman, 1980), pp. 129, 143, and 193.

Letter

to a North Vietnamese soldier whose life crossed paths with mine
in Hue City, February 5th, 1968

Thought you killed me
with that rocket? Well, you nearly did:
splattered walls and splintered air,
knocked me cold and full of holes,
and brought the roof down on my head.

But I lived,
long enough to wonder often
how you missed; long enough
to wish too many times
you hadn't.

What's it like back there?
It's all behind us here;
and after all those years of possibility,
things are back to normal.
We just had a special birthday,
and we've found again our inspiration
by recalling where we came from
and forgetting where we've been.

Oh, we're still haggling over pieces
of the lives sticking out
beyond the margins of our latest
history books—but no one haggles
with the authors.

Do better than that
you cockeyed gunner with the brass
to send me back alive among a people
I can never feel
at ease with anymore:

remember where you've been, and why.
And then build houses; build villages,
dikes and schools, songs
and children in that green land

I blackened with my shadow
and the shadow of my flag.

Remember Ho Chi Minh
was a poet: please,
do not let it all come down
to nothing.

—W. D. EHRHART

To the People of My Lai,
March 16, 1993

Warm greetings to the people of My Lai, to the people of this district and this province. I come to you this morning with a deep sadness for the tragedy of your village. I sense also that this morning the people of My Lai are sad. The people of this district and province, indeed the people of Vietnam are sad. And peace-loving people around the world, including the United States, are also sad at the memory of what happened in this village. As there has been a gentle rain here this morning, I believe we can say that even the heavens are very sad.

A few days ago my wife and son came here to My Lai. As I sat over here by the irrigation ditch where 170 people, mostly old people, women and children, were killed, the wind in the surrounding pine trees seemed to weep in sorrow for these lost sons and daughters of My Lai.

I come to you this morning as a person who was born in a land far away, the land of America. But I am sad because we can say that each one of those 504 men, women and children who were killed on that fateful day was my brother and sister. For in an ultimate sense, we all have the same father and mother. We are all brothers and sisters in the same family: the family of mankind.

The tragedy of My Lai is the tragedy of war. Each time a person is killed, we can say that person is our sister or brother.

It is my hope and prayer that we all will remember the tragedy of the morning in March 25 years ago, not that we will hold hatred for each other, but that we will thoughtfully learn the lessons of history. And it is my hope and prayer that a tragedy like My Lai will never, never, never happen again.

It is my hope also, that from this day forward, the relationship and friendship between our peoples will grow stronger and deeper. As I see the irrigation ditch here in My Lai, it is my hope that our peoples will not be separated by the ditch of war and misunderstanding, but that we will find ways to build a bridge of friendship and mutual respect over this ditch, and that we shall live together in peace.

Finally, I want to say personally that I am deeply sorry for what happened here in your village 25 years ago. As people who long for peace, we ask your forgiveness for that tragedy.

We honor the people of My Lai, of this district and of this province. We honor the people of Vietnam. We wish for you a future of happiness, of peace and fullness of life.

—EARL MARTIN

Speech to an assembled group of about 1000 farmers, children and officials in My Lai village.

II.
THE UNITED STATES:
RECONCILIATION
ISSUES

4. Clinton, Vietnam, and the Sixties

PAUL LYONS

In this essay, I want to focus attention on the ways in which responses to Bill Clinton's antiwar youth force us to come to grips with the legacy of our Indochina War and with the Sixties generation with which it remains associated. To do so, I would like to begin with two stories, the first of which you already know:

On Memorial Day of 1993, President Clinton spoke at the Wall before an audience which included a vocal minority of hecklers. To such critics, Clinton was insulting the memory of all who served; he was not only a draft-dodger, but a liar and a coward. Some turned their backs to him. Most of the crowd was more respectful, hearing the president reiterating Colin Powell's quoting of Lincoln—"With malice toward none and charity toward all," calling for a binding up of the nation's wounds.

My second story occurred later that same day in a small South Jersey town following its Memorial Day parade. The ceremonies included a color guard of veterans and several patriotic speeches, featuring local dignitaries. What was striking about the service was the invisibility of Vietnam. None of the color guard unit were Vietnam Era veterans; most were Korean or World War II vets. During perhaps 45 minutes of speechifying, all of which was conventionally patriotic, there was only a single mention of the Vietnam War, and that was as a part of a series of the wars we had fought. The keynote speaker, a local Republican politician, spoke about the ways in which the battle of Iwo Jima still speaks to us; it was an eloquent, impressive historical lesson. And yet—the speaker is a baby boomer. He did not serve in the military, he did not get sent to Vietnam. And yet he is a right-of-center conservative, characteristically hawkish, anticommunist—at least until the Berlin Wall came down.

I find the two stories paradigmatic of our continuing difficulties in, as Gerald Ford implored us to do almost twenty years ago, putting Vietnam behind us. We are stuck in the Sixties and a considerable part of that remaining presentness rests on the war; the other aspects I will also address below.

First, the efforts by Ford and others to get beyond Vietnam, the char-

69

acteristic American tendency to view history, à la Henry Ford and Jay Gatsby, as irrelevant, has not worked. Second, the effort by others to transcend Vietnam, to depoliticize it, to establish one big tent within which antiwar activists, war vets, and mainstream patriots could heal the wounds, has had only partial success. The Vietnam Memorial, the Wall, is an extraordinary place; it comes the closest to transcending ideology by focusing on both the particularity of those who died and those who see their own faces reflecting off the black granite. But Clinton's rough experience on Memorial Day suggests that there is only so far that such transcendence can take us.

Just consider another story, that of Katherine Ann Power's attorney, Steven Black, a Vietnam pilot who staged a mock war crimes trial for himself, in which Power served as *his* attorney. He sentenced himself to community service at the same time as he negotiated the terms of Power's surrender.

I believe that to begin to understand, not to speak of resolving, the pain and anger, the wounds still festering, we must reconfigure the involved parties. For much of the past decade, we have been stuck with an unfortunate dualism: those who served, increasingly admired as proles, blue-collar heroes versus those who protested, increasingly criticized as self-serving, hypocritical elitists. From Jim Webb's novels to Jim Fallows' influential article on social class and the draft, from *Platoon* to *China Beach*, the dualism has often *been* the politics of the war in recent years. It has a conservative and a liberal tint; the former tends to believe that we could and should have defeated Communist tyranny; the latter argues that it was, simply, a waste of American lives. The only opponents of the war granted respect in both scenarios are GIs, like John Kerry, and those protesters willing to go to jail for their beliefs (recall Myra MacPherson's important study, *Long Time Passing*).

As discussed elsewhere in this volume, we need, however, to begin with not two but at least three groups—those who fought, those who protested, and those who did neither. My *Class of '66* provides a case study of such people, at least the males, mainstream baby boomers, most of whom supported the war, voted for Richard Nixon, but who found respectable, middle-class ways, i.e., the National Guard and reserves, to avoid possible combat. It is this group who make my second story relevant; they are people who still tend to avoid the issue or, if more hawkish in their adulthood, be more defensive about their own behaviors. Are they Dan Quayles? Not quite, that wouldn't be fair. Few are as flat-out rich, few have been as baldly hypocritical. The flak that Clinton receives is in part a diversion of resentment away from those "silent majority" baby boomers who are uncomfortable with the legacy and, especially, the survivors of the war.

In a similar sense, the mythos of the airport spitting at returning vets allows us to avoid the ways in which mainstream people, and not only baby boomers, made Vietnam vets uncomfortable with their awkward silences.

Instead of fixating on the noisemakers, hissing the president, we need to pay attention to the silences of those who remain haunted by their passivity and insensitivity.

In making sense of the responses to Clinton, we need to emphasize that there is a right-wing agenda, a Sixties-bashing strategy, spearheaded by Newt Gingrich, the Quayles and folks like Bill Bennett. Marilyn Quayle excoriated Sixties activists at the GOP Convention in Houston. She worked to reinforce another myth, that of the irresponsible, hedonistic Sixties radicals whose permissive behaviors ravage our culture. First of all, we need to make certain distinctions. Those who opposed the war fall into two camps: radicals who saw the war as a symptom of American imperialism and liberals who viewed it as a tragic error. Among those radicals, there are splits over approach, levels of militancy. It is important to admit that many of the radicals romanticized the Vietnamese Communists, as they tended to romanticize all Third World liberation movements. This led them to some serious moral failings, some callousness toward human suffering and injustice committed by the Third World "Davids" against the American "Goliath." It's important for these self-criticisms to be part of the story; Susan Sontag was, indeed, right to suggest that the radical press ignored or downplayed or rationalized communist violations of human rights. Those of us who opposed the war, particularly from a radical, anti-imperialist stance, need to face our own blindnesses.

What's most interesting about Clinton is that he was not part of that most radical, militant wing of the movement. He was a dove, an intern in Bill Fulbright's office, a "Clean for Gene," Simon and Garfunkel kind of guy; he probably never did inhale and certainly was aligned with those like Allard Lowenstein who sought to save the system by reforming it.

Those like Clinton who sought to make the system consistent with its own ideals in matters of opportunity, democratization, and human rights, who stood with Gene McCarthy and Bobby Kennedy and Martin Luther King, Jr., need to directly challenge the Sixties-bashing from the Right. They not only have nothing to be embarrassed about, they have much to defend with pride.

The Quayles focus on partial truths. Yes, there was indulgence and permissiveness; yes, there was a mindless rebellion against authority; yes, there was some moral laziness. But examine our world, how far we've come—an end to American apartheid, an enlargement of rights to African Americans, Hispanics, Native Americans, the disabled, women, gays. OK, I know—we've got a long way to go. But those of us who remember Jim Crow, the problem that has no name, the time before anyone would even consider the possibility of the rights of gays in the military, must recognize the achievements generated by the Sixties. Almost every advance came out of the troublemakers, the agitators, the radicals of that era, as their ideas were absorbed by the

Middle, diluted, softened, but integrated. Every survey of opinion sustains this achievement. To counter the real Vietnam Syndrome, to effectively address Sixties-bashing, we must cherish our victories. My goodness, they're rare enough!

The New Right provides another segment of baby boomers, characteristically ignored by most observers. Indeed they came out of the Sixties stronger, for more of the long haul, than did the New Left. As E.J. Dionne and others note, there are some striking similarities between New Left and New Right—a critique of the welfare state as bureaucratic and deadening, a call for liberty and community, a focus on the individual. We must credit the New Right with raising important questions about the dangers of the state and with persisting in a valuing of the role of markets in sustaining both human choice and economic efficiencies.

On the other hand, the New Right has consistently been resistant to the transformations which have moved the USA toward diversity, toward tolerance. Their criticisms of affirmative action, of political correctness, while often astute, are undermined by their suspect track record. Of course, it is a mark against the heirs of the New Left that they have allowed First Amendment rights to be so hypocritically coopted by conservatives.

Regarding Vietnam, the New Right conservative movement also has much to confess. They ideologized a struggle with a particular history, insisting that Vietnam was merely an extension of Soviet or Chinese aggression. They played with martial rhetoric, at the expense of untold lives. And, when it was crunch time, they did not stand up and be counted. No senior level officers—no insiders who believed in invading the North, declaring war, calling up the reserves, nuking Hanoi—came forward and resigned their commissions. And many who played hawk in later events, like Dick Cheney and Bill Bennett and Newt Gingrich and Phil Gramm, somehow managed, like the South Jersey politician in my second story, to avoid service.

And yet there is a compelling conservative issue, one that makes those on the Left uncomfortable, and one that helps to shape the response to Bill Clinton. It's made most eloquently by Jim Webb, John Wheeler and William Broyles: What is worth dying for? What does it say about a nation if it is uncomfortable with sacrifice, whether one is discussing national service or tax increases? One can interpret this challenge as particularly masculine. And in some ways I believe the ultimate gift of modern feminism is precisely a centering on what's worth living for. But the issue remains troubling, and its very nature seems to me to be part of what haunts Bill Clinton, who neither served nor took many risks as an activist, always, as his now famous letter states, maintaining his options. Clinton's difficulties over Bosnia rest to a considerable degree in the ways in which his waffling highlights unresolved questions raised in the Vietnam era.

In all of the above, we are considering elite opinion and behavior. In many ways, the legacy of the Sixties and of the Vietnam War rest on the rivalry between New Left and New Right elites, each seeking to persuade the mainstream of its case. The New Left antiwar side has been charged with elite privileges, most sharply by Fallows' piece on Harvards and proles at the Cambridge draft board. Unfortunately this truth about Vietnam, which Christian Appy appropriately calls a working-class war, seems to be walled off from its broader implications. It's as if Fallows and others discovered that this is a society with social class and racial privileges and then only applied this knowledge to the war. What is unusual, unique about the Sixties and Vietnam is that elite youth, in part, broke with their well-paved paths to success. Most elite youth did not become antiwar activists or even antiwar sideliners; they may have done some dope and grown longer hair, but they remained career oriented, often oblivious to the changes and challenges surrounding them, and used their social class advantages to either get deferments or to get into guard or reserve units.

At the heart of this dispute is the legacy of Tom Wolfe's notion of radical chic, the notion that affluent people who have a social conscience are morally suspect. Wolfe's cutting prose has been a significant factor in the virtual disappearance of political liberalism. One must agree with Wolfe that a politics of guilt generates wonderful material for a social satirist, from Leonard Bernstein parties for Black Panthers to the political correctness of Antioch's dating rules. But such an essentially conservative and cynical posture, what one might also call the P.J. O'Rourke School of Cultural Criticism, lets the country clubs and corporate boardrooms off the hook. Most affluent people don't have bleeding hearts or generous wallets; they live in suburban cocoons, insulated from the squalor of American life. And most powerful people are merely economically correct. The Wolfean metaphor, which stretches to a fixation on yuppies and Big Chilled boomers, shifts the political and ideological ground from a focus on economic to cultural privilege, from power to status, from lives to lifestyles. Recall the assumption by voters, before the Convention, that Clinton was part of the elite, based on his Rhodes Scholarship, his Yale law degree. He still suffers from this conservative framing which, at bottom, suggests that a new class of intelligentsia, yackers, are our cultural elite, remote from mainstream values and behaviors, including patriotism and a commitment to service. Under this cultural framing, the billionaire Ross Perot becomes a populist.

It remains essential to note the racial and gendered distortions of most considerations of Vietnam and the Sixties. Those who served, those who protested and those who did neither is a gendered way of conceptualizing a generation. Hillary Clinton now enters the foreground. She personifies the transformation which the Quayles and such have condemned; of course, Marilyn Tucker Quayle, finally, shares a Sixties story more with Mrs. Clinton than she does with her husband. And the Supreme Court decision on sexual harassment in the workplace, driven by two female justices and supported by the most conservative—Scalia and Thomas—suggests that the center has shifted to the left in terms of women's rights. We owe such shifts to those like Hillary Clinton, who have been in the forefront since the 1960s. What was once radical becomes mainstream.

Clinton's detractors juxtapose Colin Powell, Vietnam vet, with the commander-in-chief, reinforcing the conventional view that the working class and minorities fought while the privileged protested and avoided service. Such an obvious truth should not be allowed to stigmatize those who sought to "bring our boys home," at least without attention being paid to those who simply took a hike, cultivating their private gardens. A strong case can be made that those who protested saved lives, both American and Indo-Chinese. That should be a source of pride to Bill Clinton.

The issue of the Indo-Chinese must be addressed; finally, the least satisfactory aspect of the ways in which we attempt to integrate the war and the decade with which it is associated, is the invisibility of "the other," those at some distance from our attention, those whose over 300,000 missing in action generate no protest, those whose post–traumatic stress disorder veterans pay the heaviest of prices, those who have had to struggle to build a nation following 35 years of warfare, those denied their claim to visibility—and honor—at the Wall.

It must be said plainly and forcefully—it is obscene for Americans to smugly criticize the Vietnamese for their economic screw-ups without at the same time paying attention to the ways in which the war brutalized their society and ravaged their landscape. This is not to return to a romanticization of the heroic Vietnamese; we surely know enough about the evils of communist dictatorship to resist that illusion. They, like all peoples, must be held accountable for their behavior. But so must we. Our obsession with the MIA/POW issue, our vengeful economic warfare upon the Vietnamese, our resistance to the restoration of relations until 1995—we are like Tom and Daisy Buchanan going on with our lives oblivious to the destruction our thoughtlessness has wrought.

Perhaps Clinton's move toward diplomatic recognition, a courageous act, will help us integrate the Indochina war into our historical record. Certainly he has been assisted in this regard by the support of Vietnam veterans like John Kerry, Bob Kerrey, and, especially, conservative Republican John McCain. But the responses to Clinton's move suggest that we haven't been able to get on with our lives, to get past Vietnam, to heal all of the wounds. There's still too much hurt out there. This is what Bill Clinton needs to find a way to address.

At his best, as a new kind of Democrat, he is able to understand the need to get past some of the worn-out rhetoric of both right and left, willing to see that we are in a new ballgame with new challenges. I admired him, standing there at the Vietnam Memorial that Memorial Day, but I was uncomfortable with him almost physically hiding behind generals Powell and Jesse Brown, with his defensive if empathetic words. Why not stand proudly as an heir of the best of the Sixties, its refusal to reduce love of country to knee-jerk allegiance, its expansion of rights to all previously excluded groups? He can be proud of what his segment of a generation has wrought and, at the same time, be generous and ecumenical, with those whose values have led them to other choices. He needs, as well, to continue to criticize the worst legacies of the Sixties, the righteousness and snobbery of the well-educated.

For Bill Clinton to have any chance to win over many, never all, of his critics and to regain the respect of many of his former supporters, he needs to recognize that it's not enough to think about tomorrow; one must speak out on those traditions of the past which can help us get there. Sadly, he may be characterologically incapable of such consistency, as David Maraniss suggests in his biography; but, at the same time, we must be careful about too quickly assuming his demise. He can no longer play "the comeback kid"; that's become tiresome. Most of all, he needs to no longer communicate being merely a "kid," someone without the gravitas, the maturity to lead this nation.

Selected Bibliography

Appy, Christian. *Working-Class War: American Combat Soldiers and Vietnam.* Chapel Hill: University of North Carolina Press, 1993.

Broyles, William. *Brothers in Arms.* New York: Alfred A. Knopf, 1986.

Chafe, William H. *Never Stop Running : Allard Lowenstein and the Struggle to Save American Liberalism.* New York: Basic Books, 1993.

Friedman, Thomas. "Clinton, Saluting Vietnam War Dead, Finds Old Wound Is Slow to Heal," *New York Times,* June 1, 1993.

Horne, A.D. ed. *The Wounded Generation: After Vietnam.* Englewood Cliffs, NJ: Prentice-Hall, 1981.

Maraniss, David. *First in His Class : A Biography of Bill Clinton.* New York: Simon & Schuster, 1995.

Webb, James. *A Country Such as This.* New York: Bantam Books, 1985.

Wheeler, John. *Touched with Fire.* New York: Avon Books, 1984.

Wolfe, Tom. *Radical Chic and Mau-mauing the Flak Catchers.* New York: Bantam Books, 1971.

Zaroulis, Nancy, and Gerald Sullivan. *Who Spoke Up?* Garden City, NY: Doubleday, 1984.

5. M.I.A.:
"The Last Chapter"?

H. BRUCE FRANKLIN

Flush with what seemed America's glorious victory in the Gulf War, President George Bush on March 1, 1991, bragged to a nation festooned in jingoist yellow ribbons, "By God, we've kicked the Viet Nam syndrome once and for all!"[1] Kicked? Syndrome? Had Viet Nam become America's addiction? Its pathology?

The president's diagnosis proved more accurate than his prognosis. Sixteen months after claiming to have cured us of our Viet Nam disease, George Bush was on national TV shouting "Shut up and sit down!" at MIA family members heckling him at the July 1992 annual convention of the National League of Families.

Between these two exclamations by the president, the POW/MIA issue had metamorphosed into outlandish new forms contorting American politics and psychology. One victim was a new Viet Nam policy adopted by the White House; another may have been the president himself, defeated in an election skewed by Ross Perot, the original POW/MIA huckster.

On April 9, 1991, a month after declaring that the "Viet Nam syndrome" had been "kicked," President Bush, perhaps emboldened by his popularity as leader of "Operation Desert Storm," handed Viet Nam a "Road Map" toward normalizing relations within two years. This timetable outlined four phases, each contingent upon Viet Nam making what Washington considered satisfactory progress in resolving "all remaining POW/MIA cases." As part of the process, an office for ongoing joint investigation of American MIAs was opened in Hanoi. The administration hinted that the normalization process might even include limited trade before the end of 1991.[2]

Instantly the smoldering POW/MIA issue was fanned into a firestorm. In Congress the incendiary crew was led by Republican senators Jesse Helms, Charles Grassley, Hank Brown, and Bob Smith. In May, Helms released, in the name of all Republicans on the Senate Foreign Relations Committee, *An Examination of U.S. Policy Toward POW/MIAs*, a hundred-page pseudohistory alleging that *thousands* of U.S. POWs were abandoned in Indochina, and that some are still alive, betrayed by a vast Washington conspiracy.

Helms's treatise claimed that the American POWs "repatriated by the North Vietnamese during Operation Homecoming" were merely "12 percent of the figure of 5,000 held by the North Vietnamese reported by *The New York Times*."[3] Where did Helms and cohort get the figure 5,000? From a March 1973 *New York Times* story as cited in an AP dispatch: "While the North Vietnamese did not list a number of prisoners they wanted freed, *The New York Times* reported from Saigon today that American sources set the demand at 5,000." After it was pointed out that the figure 5,000 in the news story referred not to American POWs but to the number of prisoners North Viet Nam was demanding from Saigon, Helms's staff removed the quotation from later printings but kept the 5,000 count, now documented by unnamed "sources interviewed by the Committee staff."[4] As Deputy Assistant Secretary of Defense Carl Ford was later to testify, the report is so permeated by falsehoods that "to catalogue the inaccuracies would require a document of equal length."[5]

The report's principal author, Helms staffer Tracy Usry, was later exposed as having falsified much of its evidence about abandoned POWs.[6] Finally in January 1992 several embarrassed Republican members of the Senate Foreign Relations Committee, who had not been consulted before the report was issued in their name, forced Helms to fire most of his top staff, including Usry.[7]

Nevertheless, the Helms volume continued to be mailed out daily by the Senate Foreign Relations Committee. By mid–1992, well over a hundred thousand copies were in circulation, all printed and distributed at taxpayer expense and bearing the seal of the U.S. Senate.[8] Referring to it as "The Senate Report on POW/MIAs," POW/MIA activists cite it by chapter and verse.

The report helped the men behind it—including Helms, Grassley, Brown, and Smith—create the Senate Select Committee on POW/MIA Affairs and then shape the committee's assumptions and agenda. Senator Smith's staff had helped engineer the Helms document, and he now tried to set up a Senate committee designed to give this thesis respectability and ongoing media exposure. But he was making little progress and the Senate was due to recess on August 2, 1991.

Suddenly on July 17 began one of the most spectacular media coups in U.S. history, orchestrated largely by Smith and associates. A photograph allegedly showing U.S. POWs from the Viet Nam War still held captive in Indochina exploded as the lead story on national TV and radio networks. Newspapers across the country front-paged the picture under banner headlines. The three men were identified as John Robertson, Albro Lundy Jr., and Larry Stevens, three pilots shot down over Viet Nam and Laos between 1966 and 1970. Within a week photographs ostensibly showing two more POWs in Indochina—identified as Daniel Borah Jr. and Donald Carr—hit the media. According to a *Wall Street Journal*/NBC News poll, 69 percent of the American people now believed that U.S. POWs were being held in Indochina and 52 percent were convinced that the government was derelict in not getting them back.[9] A headline in the August 2 *Wall Street Journal* read, "Bring on Rambo."

The same day a stampeded Senate unanimously passed Bob Smith's resolution to create a Senate Select Committee on POW/MIA Affairs—along with a resolution to fly the POW/MIA flag over federal buildings. The Republicans got as many seats on the committee as Democrats, who included Harry Reid, sponsor of the POW/MIA flag-flying resolution, and John Kerry, named chairman. The six Republicans included Helms, Grassley (who had helped craft the Helms document), former POW John McCain, Hank Brown, who had authored resolutions reiterating President Reagan's 1983 pledge that the POW/MIA issue must be "the highest national priority," and Smith, named vice chairman. Brown and Smith had been working together with shady POW/MIA fundraisers Captain Eugene "Red" McDaniel and Billy Hendon since at least 1987, when they and 19 other Republican members of Congress had each pledged $100,000 toward McDaniel and Hendon's $2.4 million reward for the return of a live POW, an offer that produced a tidal wave of phony live sightings and photographs.[10]

The photos that launched the Senate Select Committee later proved as bogus as all the other "evidence" of live POWs in the last two decades. "Daniel Borah" turned out to be a Lao highlander who had happily posed because he had never had his photograph taken before.[11] "Donald Carr" was a German bird smuggler photographed in a Bangkok rare bird sanctuary.[12] The picture of "Robertson, Lundy, and Stevens" was a doctored version of a 1923 photograph reproduced in a 1989 Soviet magazine discovered in the Phnom Penh national library; the three men were actually holding a poster proclaiming the glories of collective farming (mustaches had been added and a picture of Stalin subtracted).[13]

All of the photographs were the handiwork of notorious scam artists. Each was used by POW/MIA crusaders to blitz the media and the public—and thus help create the Senate Select Committee. Senator Smith provided the "Daniel Borah" pictures to the Pentagon and then went on the *Today* show to display them to a national television audience.[14] The "Robertson, Lundy, Stevens" picture had been released by Red McDaniel, who has been promising the faithful since 1986 that as soon as they contribute enough money he will produce live POWs. McDaniel got it from Jack Bailey, head of a POW/MIA fundraising operation known as Operation Rescue. Bailey, who had conspired to fake the "Donald Carr" photos, assaulted two ABC reporters on camera when they confronted him in the rare bird sanctuary where the pictures had actually been taken.[15]

As vice chairman of the select committee, Smith was able to place fanatical POW/MIA crusaders from his staff in key posts on the committee's staff. Smith staffer Dino Carluccio, a designer of the Helms report, was given the powerful office of deputy staff director. Carluccio worked closely with another

Smith staffer, Billy Hendon, whose shady solicitations of hundreds of thousands of dollars for McDaniel's right-wing American Defense Institute had prompted numerous calls for investigating and possibly prosecuting him. *Time* reported that Hendon's presence was one reason the select committee "made little progress in its inquiry into those who prey on families of missing service personnel." As one insider said, "How can we investigate Hendon when Hendon's on the staff?"[16] Eventually the behavior of Carluccio and Hendon, which included physically strong-arming witnesses, became so outrageous that Chairman Kerry in July 1992 fired both from the committee's staff.[17] Co-Chairman Smith immediately put the duo back in his own office.

John Kerry's own staff unanimously argued against his trying to steer a committee with the Helms-Grassley-Brown-Smith crew on board through the treacherous POW/MIA swamp, but he overruled them.[18] Kerry himself may have been unaware of how the POW/MIA issue had been used back in April 1971, when he joined hundreds of other antiwar Viet Nam veterans to throw their medals at the Capitol. Panic-stricken by these actions and the growing antiwar movement among the POW/MIA wives, top Nixon aide H. R. Haldeman had dashed off a memo to fellow White House staffer General James Hughes, arguing that "after the Veterans' effort last week, we've got to be doubly sure we are keeping the POW wives in line." General Hughes responded: "According to Al Haig, the next eight weeks are critical and the efforts of the Ad Hoc Coordinating Group on POW/MIA matters will be devoted to keeping the families on the reservation in order to buy this time."[19]

Ironically, Kerry now accepted the spurious history of the POW/MIA issue promulgated by those bent on continuing the conflict, including the ludicrous notion that the government during the war and ever since had been minimizing and perhaps concealing the possibility of prisoners being kept after the United States withdrew. Thus POW/MIA crusaders were allowed to define the committee's assumptions, goals, and procedures.

The committee refused to allow testimony about how and why the POW/MIA issue was concocted and used by the government to legitimize hostilities against Viet Nam from 1969 on. The only witnesses allowed to testify were, in fact, either defenders of the government or its attackers from the POW/MIA movement.[20]

The select committee's parade of Pentagon and State Department witnesses put on a strange performance. Former Nixon officials Roger Shields, Frank Sieverts, and Henry Kissinger, who had helped concoct the belief in live postwar POWs, solemnly testified that now they believe there might have been live postwar POWs. In fact, all three men had been key players in the Nixon administration's fabrication of the postwar POW/MIA issue as a pretext for the United States to break its pledge of reconstruction aid to Hanoi, made in Article 21 of the Paris Peace Agreement and spelled out in the president's February 1, 1973, secret letter to Hanoi Prime Minister Pham Van Dong.

When Henry Kissinger went to North Viet Nam in early February, before the completion of Operation Homecoming, he confronted the Hanoi government with "some 80 files of individuals who we had reason to believe had been captured." Because "we are extremely dissatisfied" with Hanoi's accounting for these MIAs, Kissinger had concluded, "we cannot proceed in certain other areas such as economic aid negotiations."[21] In other words, Kissinger and Nixon used the MIA issue to renege on Nixon's secret pledge, whose very existence was denied by the White House until 1976.

Why did Kissinger's list contain 80 names when the highest number of such cases then claimed or secretly listed by the U.S. government was 56? The truth came almost two decades later from Roger Shields, the Pentagon's main POW/MIA man in 1973, who finally admitted in late 1992 that Washington had deliberately included on Kissinger's list a number of cases the Vietnamese could not possibly account for, supposedly as a "control group."[22] Thus the Nixon administration created an issue that could never be resolved.

The select committee acted as though Nixon's boasts that he had liberated all the POWs had been official U.S. policy in early 1973. But Nixon spelled out his actual policy in his 1973 report to Congress, which bragged about pressuring "the Communist side" to adhere to the "unprecedentedly specific" commitment "to secure the fullest possible accounting for each of our men."[23] Indeed the demand for such an accounting of the missing was unprecedented. It is also a demand that can never be satisfied.

Having no intention of honoring their pledge of aid, Nixon and Kissinger therefore made accounting for the MIAs the issue. But accounting is a meaningless issue unless there is some belief in the possibility of live POWs. Hence the Nixon, Ford, Carter, Reagan, Bush, and Clinton administrations each tried to exaggerate—not minimize—this possibility of live POWs. But there is a contradiction between the government's efforts to keep belief in the existence of POWs alive and to keep it comatose, ready to be either disconnected from its life support machine or resuscitated as the circumstances of *Realpolitik* dictate. Seeking to maintain this ambiguous status, the government has fed the paranoia of true believers, thus helping turn a sleeping giant into the Frankenstein's monster of the POW/MIA myth. Hence such grotesque spectacles as the 1992 Senate hearings where POW/MIA fanatics wrestled with Pentagon apologists for the mind of the nation.

The POW/MIA crusaders who created and dominated the select committee were unable to produce a shred of credible evidence of postwar POWs. So it's no surprise that the committee's 1,285-page final report merely restated the ambiguity created by the senators' own Republican and Democratic administrations, while also asserting that the POW/MIA issue should continue to be made the "'highest national priority' by our diplomats ... and by the nation."[24]

Though unearthing no evidence of postwar U.S. POWs, the committee did stumble upon potentially explosive evidence of how the Reagan administration and its right-wing allies had connived to inflate and exploit the POW myth. But "due to time constraints, the Committee was unable to pursue these reports" of how the government used the POW issue and private POW organizations "as a cover for providing ... non-appropriated funds" to anti-government mercenaries in Indochina.[25] Before being halted by the pretext of "time constraints," the investigation produced something the media failed even to notice, much less recognize as the committee's only major discovery: a byzantine, illegal government scheme for Indochina strikingly similar to the Iran-Contra scandal.

To help transform the POW/MIA issue into what he designated "the highest national priority," Ronald Reagan had placed Carol Bates, original coordinator of VIVA's bracelet campaign and later head of the National League of Families, into his expanded POW/MIA section of the Defense Intelligence Agency, and positioned right-wing activist Ann Mills Griffiths as the central figure in the IAG (POW/MIA Interagency Group). Meanwhile, as the committee confirmed, "the Government sanctioned, encouraged, funded, approved, and provided logistical support" to Bo Gritz, for "some of his overseas reconnaissance and rescue operations."[26] In early 1981, while Gritz was beginning to organize for raids into Laos, the administration sent congressmen Billy Hendon and John LeBoutillier to Laos, ostensibly to "establish a dialogue on POW/MIA issues."[27] LeBoutillier's conception of "dialogue" was revealed when he was caught purchasing weapons for Laotian mercenaries. The Bureau of Alcohol, Tobacco, and Firearms' recommendation that he be prosecuted for firearms violations was overruled by a Justice Department official who affirmed that "LeBoutillier's activities had been sanctioned by the U.S. Government."[28]

LeBoutillier, working closely with Ann Mills Griffiths and Colonel Richard Childress, NSC Director of Asian Affairs and Political Military Affairs from 1981 to 1989, set up "Skyhook II," an organization that raised large sums of money, ostensibly to free POWs. Griffiths got Betty Bartels, an official of Support Our POW/MIAs, Inc., a moribund California organization with tax-exempt status, to set up bank accounts in Bangkok and elsewhere to receive the funds. According to Bartels's sworn deposition, Carol Bates and Griffiths insisted that the "entire matter be kept in strictest confidence.... Only a U.S. Senator, to remain unnamed, and the White House, Ann, Carol and myself were aware." The funds were moved through a Bangkok bank account to mercenary forces in Laos known as the "Lao resistance."[29]

This unauthorized roundabout funding of covert operations outdid Iran-Contra in ingenuity, for it included a self-sustaining mechanism. The "Lao resistance" produced a stream of phony evidence of live POWs for LeBoutillier to use in his Skyhook II propaganda to raise more funds for the "Lao resistance," which was then able to supply still more phony evidence of live POWs to raise still more funds and so on.[30]

The media circus invoked by the select committee and other assorted POW/MIA crusaders in 1992 soon featured two spectacular novel acts—one by a newcomer to the big top, Russian President Boris Yeltsin, the other by its original ringmaster, now would-be U.S. president Ross Perot.

On Monday, June 15, Yeltsin told NBC-TV that "our archives" show that some U.S. POWs from Viet Nam "were transferred to the territory of the former USSR and were kept in labor camps. We don't have complete data and can only surmise that some of them may still be alive." He must have forgotten that on Friday, June 12, he personally reported to the committee that Soviet archives had disclosed absolutely "no data" about any "U.S. citizens listed as missing in action in Viet Nam and other countries of South-East Asia."[31] Or maybe the Russian president thus showed how much he had learned from U.S. presidents about how to manipulate the POW/MIA issue to implement his own political agenda.

Yeltsin had three goals. First, he wanted to turn the issue into a weapon to use against those forces in Russia hostile to his rule, particularly the remnants of the Communist Party. Second, by presenting himself as the champion of the American people seeking to liberate their POWs from the clutches of these evil communists, he hoped to gain billions of U.S. dollars to support his rule. And third, recognizing that normal political and economic relations between the United States and Viet Nam would wipe out what remained of Russian economic interests in Viet Nam, he was firing a well-aimed salvo at the process of normalization.

While President Yeltsin was fighting for his political life, so was President Bush. And so now the very man who boasted about healing America's Viet Nam wounds tried to win reelection by reopening them, eventually turning what Bill Clinton had or hadn't done during the Vietnam War into the Republicans' main campaign issue. Meanwhile Ross Perot launched his own campaign as the wartime champion of the POWs and a Rambo-like hero who would rescue not only the dozens allegedly still alive in Indochina but also the nation itself. John LeBoutillier called the POW issue "the metaphor for Perot's campaign."[32] As one astute commentator put it, "The country is the prisoner, held hostage by lobbyists and professional politicians, and he and the American people together will create a commando team to rescue it."[33]

Unlike the Republican and Democratic candidates, Perot had no national party apparatus. What he used as a remarkably effective substitute was a ready-made national infrastructure, a network of activists motivated by near religious fervor and coordinated by grassroots organizations: the POW/MIA movement. A master of symbolism, Perot chose ex–POW James Stockdale as his running mate and ex–POW Orson Swindle as his campaign manager. Homecoming II, an organization leading the Rambo faction of the POW/MIA movement, illegally turned the Viet Nam Veterans Memorial into a perpetual campaign prop for Perot.[34] At his typical rally, Perot sat with former POWs and family members on a stage bedecked with POW flags, and POW activists and their organizations were central to the petition campaigns that got Perot on the ballot in every state.[35]

Without the Perot candidacy, Bush would probably have beaten Bill Clinton in a one-on-one race. Certainly in the televised debates, Perot's ferocious attacks on the administration—ranging from his remorseless exposure of the national debt to his shrewd debunking of the glorious Gulf War—inflicted major damage while allowing Clinton to keep the blood off both his hands and his face. The demographics of the Perot vote also suggest that he drew disproportionately from Republican voters. If indeed Perot was responsible for Bush's defeat, then certainly the POW/MIA issue was central to the election's outcome, for without it Perot would surely not have been a national political figure, much less a presidential candidate. In fact he would not have even made his first billion dollars, which largely came from favors accorded to him by the Nixon administration for selling the POW/MIA issue to the American people in the first place.

During the war, Perot claimed that his POW campaign was entirely his own idea and had no connection with the Nixon White House.[36] Later he claimed that he was merely recruited into the campaign by Nixon and Kissinger.[37] The historical record in the Nixon Archives proves that both claims are false.

Ross Perot began telephoning Richard Nixon daily two weeks before the presidential inauguration.[38] By April 1969, the Nixon staff was pressuring government agencies to award contracts to Perot's EDS corporation because "H. R. Perot of Dallas, Texas, was a most substantial Nixon backer in 1968."[39] When the president in May 1969 created the Richard M. Nixon Foundation, Perot was named as one of its trustees along with John Ehrlichman, H. R. Haldeman, Nixon's brothers, Herbert Kalmbach, and John Mitchell.[40] The main item on the agenda for the president's meeting with Perot a few days later was "the best use" of Perot's offer of "$50 million in the purchase of television time."[41] Ehrlichman pressured the IRS to overrule the tax examiner who disallowed Perot's deduction for the services of EDS employees to the 1968 Nixon campaign.[42] Thanks to the intervention of the White House with government agencies and sweetheart contracts that allowed EDS to get 90 percent of the computer work on Medicare claims, by 1971 Perot had become what one writer accurately dubbed "the first welfare billionaire."[43]

In June 1969, Perot was proposed to head the pro-war committee that would coordinate Nixon's newly announced POW campaign.[44] Henry Kissinger advised the president that while "the State and Defense Departments" are doing everything possible "to keep the heat on" in "the propaganda offensive in the POW issue with North Vietnam," they needed what seemed an independent citizens' movement, and he stressed the need to make it appear that "there is no U.S. Government involvement with the ladies," i.e., the organization of

POW/MIA wives being set up with help from the Pentagon.[45] Perot then presented his plan to create a public uproar demanding that Hanoi immediately release the POWs. This would include "full-page ads in the nation's 100 largest newspapers" and all major national magazines, "credit card billing enclosures," and "service station handouts (with the cooperation of oil companies)."[46]

A November national advertisement demanding that Hanoi immediately release all the POWs, run in the name of Perot's United We Stand, was planned jointly by Perot and the White House. A week later, television stations in 59 cities broadcast "United We Stand," a heartwrenching program about POWs and MIAs. It ended with narrator Frank Borman calling upon every American to send a check pledging "100% support" for the president's Viet Nam policies to United We Stand, Box 100,000, Dallas, Texas. Perot had submitted Borman's entire script for approval by the White House, where Alexander Butterfield forwarded it to his boss Bob Haldeman with the hope that it would help sustain "at least a moderate level of flag waving and other visible rallying of the masses to the support of the President."[47] The president followed up by having Perot and Borman meet with him in the Oval Office on December 4 to plan more of what Charles Colson referred to, without a trace of irony, as "the outside efforts we are trying to organize."[48]

The meeting focused on "Perot's ideas for various outside activities in support of the Administration," including tax-exempt status for various pro-war organizations, as well as "continuation of United We Stand and other Perot efforts to mobilize massive popular support." According to Haldeman's notes, "It was agreed that Borman should stay in the general television area under Perot's sponsorship."[49] Butterfield submitted to Nixon a report on the POW campaign, including Perot's "plan of action for future months." The plan laid out in detail actions that Perot would indeed perform right on schedule, including "Christmas Plane to Hanoi ... or Vientiane" to generate "worldwide publicity"; "charter plane to transport to Paris approx. 100 wives and children of American POWs"; a Christmas vigil by the wives in Paris "with heavy press and television coverage" to embarrass Hanoi's delegation; appearances by Perot on *Meet the Press*, the *Today* show, *Here's Barbara*, *Mike Douglas*, et al.; and a national conference to launch the National League of Families.[50] Perot soon was off to Vientiane with two chartered jets filled with Christmas presents for the POWs and, according to Butterfield's report to the president, "reporters from *Time, Life, Newsweek*, AP, UPI, *Los Angeles Times, Reader's Digest, Look, New York Times, Washington Post, Dallas Morning News*, and some five–six other publications." Butterfield explained how "we were able to give Ross a good bit of behind-the-scenes assistance."[51]

Perot's use of the POW/MIA issue in 1992 was even more wily. Despite making the POW/MIA issue his crucial symbol and subtext, Perot kept it out of the debates and his own television commercials. In fact, he chose to make his national presentation on the POW/MIA issue as a witness before the select committee during the summer interlude when he was supposedly not a candidate. Why? Perot associate Jeffrey Donahue was sure that Perot would later produce major evidence of live POWs while fellow POW/MIA crusader John LeBoutillier, who referred to Perot as "a clever snake" and "a pathological liar," thought he was accepting Billy Hendon's advice not to "be typed as a one-issue candidate."[52] But the real reason came out during that select committee appearance when Perot, masterfully playing the role of the lone outsider from Texas ready to ride into Washington to save us from its sleazy bureaucrats and politicians who had betrayed the POWs and the American people, failed to produce a shred of evidence. Perot, who had taught some of these bureaucrats and politicians how to create and manipulate the POW/MIA issue, showed his awareness that its profound power comes not from Vietnamese reality but from American culture.

The most revealing symptom of the Viet Nam syndrome in election year 1992 was that no national candidate ever made an issue of America's ongoing economic and political warfare against Viet Nam. Yet in the closing days of the campaign, the Pentagon and White House claimed that they were on the verge of ending hostilities by forcing Viet Nam into resolving the POW/MIA issue. So George Bush now presented himself as the man who was about to lead the nation to "begin writing the last chapter of the Vietnam War."[53]

The president was responding to two events. One was Viet Nam's all-out efforts to resolve the POW/MIA issue, including actions utterly unprecedented between belligerent states, such as opening their military archives and museums to U.S. inspection, conducting joint searches and interviews of witnesses throughout their country, and allowing short-notice U.S. inspection of suspected or former prison sites. The other was pressure from some U.S. corporations anxious not to lose lucrative business opportunities to foreign competitors already swarming into Viet Nam.[54]

But neither corporate anxiety nor Vietnamese cooperation could overcome the potent forces wielding the POW/MIA issue, forces still including its original engineer, Richard Nixon. On December 30, 1992, Nixon sent a judiciously leaked memo to the select committee, insisting that "it would be a diplomatic travesty and human tragedy to go forward with normalization" until Hanoi "fully accounts for the MIAs." As the *Los Angeles Times* observed, "Nixon's written statement provides the strongest evidence so far that he and officials of his former Administration constitute a powerful and determined, though largely hidden, lobby against normalization."[55]

So instead of following his own "Road Map," Bush merely allowed U.S. enterprises to begin negotiating for future business, which "only made matters worse," according to the *Wall Street Journal*, for "Mr. Bush's action sent a wake-up call to the Asian and European businesses," causing them to "accelerate their efforts before the Americans come in full force."[56] This left a curious situation in the early months of the Clinton administration: U.S. corporate interests, which had supported and profited from the Viet Nam War, furtively leaning on the former antiwar demonstrator to end the war. Even the *Wall Street Journal*, for decades one of the master builders of the POW/MIA myth, ran a major story headlined "President Clinton, Normalize Ties with Vietnam" and arguing that "by any account, the Vietnamese have more than met" all the conditions of the Road Map, including the requested "help in resolving the fate of American MIAs."[57]

Ending the embargo and eventual normalization now seemed inevitable. Why, then, such a slow and secretive process? A few corporations frankly acknowledged one roadblock: their own fear of the POW/MIA movement. Some companies scheduled for a trade mission to Viet Nam dropped out after receiving a faxed message from the National P.O.W. Strike Force summed up by its leader: "We will go out of our way to destroy your company because you want to do business with filthy Communists who are holding American prisoners."[58] The government also seemed frightened. When French President Mitterrand condemned the U.S. embargo, Clinton White House spokesman Stephanopoulos replied, "We want to make sure that we have a full accounting of all MIAs, and that's the policy we'll continue."[59] All this suggests the profound effects of the POW/MIA myth on American society.

Just as it once covertly slid into the Viet Nam War, the government was now covertly sliding out of it. The secrecy came from the same motive: fear of the American people. But in the 1960s, the government feared popular opposition to *war* with Viet Nam. Now, with the history of the war thoroughly rewritten by the POW/MIA myth, which has thus helped radically militarize American culture, the government feared popular opposition to *peace* with Viet Nam.

In early April 1993, the Clinton administration was exploring some quiet, timid steps toward normalization, such as allowing the IMF meeting scheduled later that month to release funds to Viet Nam. "Bill Clinton may be on the verge of finally ending the Vietnam War," declared the April 12 *Wall Street Journal*, which went on to warn, however, of "an orchestrated campaign" to stop him.[60]

Right on cue, in the same day's *New York Times*, came a sensational front-page story: "Files Said to Show Hanoi Lied in '72 on Prisoner Totals": a "top secret" document "discovered" in Moscow by "Harvard researcher" Stephen J. Morris "has been authenticated by leading experts" (all unnamed) as a Russian translation of a September 15, 1972, report to Hanoi's Politburo. This so-called "smoking gun" supposedly proved Viet Nam withheld "hundreds" of American POWs. For an "expert" opinion, the *Times* turned to Zbigniew Brzezinski, the main man responsible for persuading Jimmy Carter not to normalize relations with Viet Nam in 1978. Since, as Brzezinski well knew, there has never been any credible evidence of postwar U.S. POWs in Viet Nam, he offered an explanation which was sooner or later destined to become part of the POW/MIA mythology: "the great likelihood is that the Vietnamese took hundreds of American officers out and shot them in cold blood."[61]

In a replay of the phony photos of 1991, the "smoking gun" now exploded as the lead story on every television network, including PBS, whose balanced coverage showcased a MacNeil/Lehrer panel consisting of three disinterested "experts"—Brzezinski, Kissinger, and Morris himself.[62] Brzezinski's massacre scenario was repeated in newspaper editorials across the country. Headlines blared "North Vietnam Kept 700 POWs After War: 'Smoking Gun' File Exposes '20 Years of Duplicity'"; "Viets May Have Lied About POWs in 1972"; "POWs: The Awful Truth?"; "We Can't Set Up Ties with Killers of Our POWs."[63]

Not a single one of the "facts" about POWs in this spurious document conforms to the historical record.[64] Yet this clumsy hoax helped maintain the trade embargo for almost a year. And when President Clinton finally did call off the embargo on February 3, 1994, he claimed that he was doing so to get more "answers" about the fate of the MIAs, because "any decisions about our relationships with Vietnam should be guided by one factor and one factor only—gaining the fullest possible accounting for our prisoners of war and our missing in action."[65]

A 1993 *Wall Street Journal*/NBC News poll indicated that two-thirds of Americans believed that American POWs "are still being held in Southeast Asia."[66] The poll did not measure how many of the other third believe in Brzezinski's fable of hundreds of American officers being massacred in "cold blood." Though conveniently disposing of the chimera of live POWs—which eventually would be biologically impossible anyhow—this scenario may become the primary fantasy preventing true closure of the Vietnam War.

Some day—for the first time ever—there will be normal diplomatic relations between the United States and Viet Nam. But the last chapter of the Viet Nam War cannot be written so long as millions of Americans remain possessed by the POW/MIA myth.

Notes

1. "Kicking the 'Vietnam Syndrome,'" *Washington Post*, March 4, 1991.

2. "'Road Map' to Renew Ties with Hanoi Could Lead to Some Trade by Year End," *Wall Street Journal*, April 15, 1991; "Concerned Citizen Newsletter," *National League of Families of American Prisoners and Missing in Southeast Asia*, May 31, 1991.

3. U.S. Senate Committee on Foreign Relations Republican Staff, *An Examination of U.S. Policy Toward POW/MIAs*, May 23, 1991, pp. 5–8.

4. *Ibid*, November 1991 edition, pp. 5–8.

5. Testimony of Carl Ford, November 15, 1991, *Hearings Before the Senate Select Committee on POW/MIA Affairs*, Part I of II (Washington, U.S. Government Printing Office, 1992), p. 641.

6. *Hearings Before the Select Committee on POW/MIA Affairs*, Part I of II, November 5, 6, 7, and 15, 1991, pp. 443–447.

7. "Panel's Top G.O.P. Staff Is Dismissed by Helms," *The New York Times*, January 8, 1992.

8. Telephone conversation on July 21, 1992, with Senate Foreign Relations Committee staff member who declined to give her name.

9. Poll reported in "Minor Memos," *Wall Street Journal*, August 2, 1991.

10. "Lawmakers Pledge Cash to POW Reward," *Los Angeles Times*, July 16, 1987; *Report of the Select Committee on POW/MIA Affairs, United States Senate* (Washington: U.S. Government Printing Office, 1993), p. 319. McDaniel acknowledged raising "several million dollars ... in addition to the $2.4 million" thanks to his appearances on the "Morton Downey, Jr., Show" ("POW/MIA Debate," *Vietnam*, February 1992, p. 56).

11. Telephone interview with Commander Gregg Hartung, Public Affairs Office, Department of Defense, September 23, 1991. Since then, the Lao highlander has been extensively interviewed and photographed.

12. Interview with James Bamford, the investigative reporter who led the ABC team that exposed the fraud, February 28, 1992. Bamford played for me the extensive videos showing the bird sanctuary, the bird smuggler, and the unmasking of the scam.

13. Defense Department press conference, July 2, 1992; "U.S. Is Sure Photo of Missing Is Fake," *The New York Times*, July 19, 1992.

14. "Baker Presses Vietnam on MIAs, Cambodia," *St. Louis Post Dispatch*, July 25, 1991; UPI story datelined Olney, IL, story tag "mia-borah," July 22, 1991; *Report of the Select Committee on POW/MIA Affairs*, p. 319.

15. ABC World News with Peter Jennings, February 11 and February 12, 1992.

16. "Trouble on the MIA Committee," *Time*, May 4, 1992, p. 13. Even fellow POW/MIA crusader John LeBoutillier had presented evidence of Hendon's possibly illegal activities to the National League of Families (Monika Jensen-Stevenson and William Stevenson, *Kiss the Boys Goodbye*, New York: Dutton, 1990, pp. 139–140).

17. "Bui Tin: My 'Detention' at Dulles," *Washington Post*, October 20, 1991.

18. "The Avenger. Love Him or Hate Him, Senator John Kerry Has Always Been a Man on a Mission," *Boston Globe Sunday Magazine*, February 9, 1992.

19. Memorandum from H. R. Haldeman to General Hughes, April 26, 1971, and "POW/MIA Wives," memorandum from General James D. Hughes to Haldeman, April 29, 1971, Nixon Presidential Materials Project, White House Special Files, Haldeman, Box 77, General Hughes folder.

20. My own efforts to testify, which persisted from February to December 1992, were officially rebuffed not only by the staff and in letters from Senator Kerry but also by Senators Kerry and Grassley when I appeared with each of them on national television.

21. Confirmation Hearings of Dr. Henry Kissinger as Secretary of State, September 7, 10, 11, and 14, 1973, as reprinted in "Americans Missing in Southeast Asia," hearings before the House Select Committee on Missing Persons in Southeast Asia, Part 5, June 17, 25, July 21, and September 21, 1975, p. 175.

22. "Long Shadow of the M.I.A.'s Still Stalks a Pentagon Official," *The New York Times*, September 20, 1992.

23. Richard Nixon, "Fourth Annual Report to the Congress on United States Foreign Policy. May 3, 1973." *Public Papers of the Presidents*, 1973, Document 141.

24. *Report of the Select Committee on POW/MIA Affairs*, p. 164.

25. Ibid., p. 221.

26. Ibid., p. 302.

27. Ibid., p. 155.

28. Ibid., p. 310.

29. Ibid., pp. 305–310, 334–335.

30. Ibid., pp. 221, 276–280.

31. Letter from Boris Yeltsin to Senate Select Committee, June 12, 1992.

32. Telephone interview with John LeBoutillier, June 25, 1992.

33. John Taylor, "Commando-In-Chief," *New York*, June 15, 1992, pp. 27–29.

34. "Veterans Raise Perot Banner," *New York Daily News*, June 11, 1992.
35. David Jackson, "MIAs' Kin Want Perot as President," *Dallas Morning News*, May 19, 1992; interview with David Jackson, May 18, 1992; interview with LeBoutillier, June 12, 1992; "It's Businessman Perot and Not War Hero Bush Who Attracts a Following Among U.S. Veterans," *Wall Street Journal*, July 2, 1992.
36. "Money Talks," *Newsweek*, December 8, 1969, 57; Fred Powledge, "H. Ross Perot Pays His Dues," *New York Times Magazine*, February 28, 1971, pp. 22, 24.
37. Lawrence Wright, "The Man from Texarkana," *New York Times Magazine*, June 28, 1992, pp. 40, 43; "Road to the White House" (transcript of interview with Perot on C-Span), May 17, 1992, p. 14.
38. Richard Nixon telephone log, Nixon Presidential Materials Project, White House Special Files, Peter Flanigan Box 9.
39. Memorandum from Office of Arthur Burns, April 9, 1969, White House Special Files, Haldeman File Box 133, Ross Perot Folder.
40. "Richard Nixon Foundation," White House Special Files, Haldeman Box 133, Perot Folder; *The New York Times*, "Nixon Worth Put at $596,900," May 13, 1969.
41. "Agenda for Ross Perot Meeting with the President, May 16," White House Special Files, Haldeman Box 133, Perot Folder.
42. "H. Ross Perot," memorandum from Gordon Strachan to H. R. Haldeman, January 12, 1971, White House Special Files, Haldeman Box 133, Perot Folder.
43. Robert Fitch, "H. Ross Perot: America's First Welfare Billionaire," *Ramparts*, November 1971, pp. 42–51.
44. Memorandum from Peter Flanigan, June 30, 1969, White House Special Files, Haldeman Box 133, Perot Folder.
45. "POW Policy in Vietnam," memorandum for the president from Henry A. Kissinger, October 2, 1969, White House Special Files, President's Office Files, Series A: Documents Annotated by the President, Box 3. In response to the first edition of my book, Sybil Stockdale and Richard Capen alleged that the government was not involved in their activities in creating the National League of Families. The Nixon Archives prove the opposite. The first major media event using the wives was a methodically planned meeting to be held on December 12 between the president and a carefully selected delegation led by Sybil Stockdale. "Dick Capen and his people have worked hard to put together the package," Alexander Butterfield wrote to fellow White House staffer Colonel Hughes on December 4, but "a final decision has been made that there will be no fathers among those invited so wives and mothers must be substituted for the 2 sets of parents," the "demographic spread" must be widened, and "there must be at least 1 and preferably 2 more enlisted men represented, without exceeding a total of 23 ladies" (memorandum from Butterfield to Colonel Hughes, December 4, 1969, White House Select Files, Haldeman Box 55, Hughes folder). Lyn Nofziger asked Butterfield for "a brief bit on each POW wife we might be able to make use of ... on the Hill." (Nofziger to Butterfield, December 4, 1969, White House Special Files, Butterfield Box 8.) Butterfield asked Hughes to forward the president's preplanned answers to possible questions from the press "so that I can complete the required scenario" (Butterfield to Hughes, December 8, 1969, Haldeman Box 55, Hughes Folder).
46. "Projects Proposed by Ross Perot," memorandum from Butterfield to Haldeman, Ehrlichman, Kissinger, and Harlow, October 24, 1969, White House Special Files, Haldeman Box 133, Perot Folder.
47. Script for "United We Stand," list of TV stations, and "Perot's Project" (November 14 memorandum from Butterfield to Haldeman), White House Special Files, Haldeman Box 133, Perot Folder.
48. Memorandum from Colson to Butterfield, December 3, 1969, Butterfield Box 8.
49. White House Special Files, Presidential Office Files, Memoranda Box 79.
50. Haldeman Box 55, John Brown folder.
51. "Message from Perot," Memorandum for the president from Alexander Butter-

field, President's Handwriting Files Box 4. Nixon has written a big double-underlined "Good!" on this.

52. Interview with Jeffrey Donahue, June 23, 1992; interview with LeBoutillier, June 25, 1992.

53. "Bush Sees Gain in Vietnam Ties," *Los Angeles Times*, October 24, 1992.

54. "Corporations Ask Bush to Lift Vietnam Ban," *The New York Times*, May 9, 1992; "Vietnam: The Big Buildup Begins," *Washington Post*, December 9, 1992.

55. "Nixon Opposing U.S.–Vietnam Normalization Policy: He Could Influence Any Move by Bush Administration to End Trade Embargo," *Los Angeles Times*, January 9, 1993.

56. "U.S. Firms Gear Up for Vietnam Business Once Trade Ban Ends," *Wall Street Journal*, February 9, 1993.

57. "President Clinton, Normalize Ties with Vietnam," *Wall Street Journal*, March 8, 1993.

58. "U.S. Businesses Turning to Vietnam," *The New York Times*, February 8, 1993; "Heading for Hanoi: U.S. Firms Gear Up for Vietnam Business Once Trade Ban Ends," *Wall Street Journal*, February 9, 1993; "U.S. Firms Losing Out in Emerging Vietnam," *Chicago Tribune*, March 7, 1993.

59. "U.S. Won't Heed Mitterrand Plea to Rush Vietnam Trade," Reuters News Agency, February 10, 1993.

60. "Clinton Prepares to Relax Policy on Vietnam as U.S. Business Urges Access to New Market," *Wall Street Journal*, April 12, 1993.

61. "U.S. to Press Hanoi to Explain '72 P.O.W. Report," *The New York Times*, April 13, 1993.

62. *MacNeil/Lehrer News Hour*, April 13, 1993.

63. *Washington Times*, April 12; *USA Today*, April 12; *Washington Post*, April 15; *Jersey Journal*, April 18 (respectively).

64. References are to a photocopy of the English-language text sent by fax from the Moscow Bureau of *The New York Times* to the *Times* Foreign Desk with a cover letter referring to it as a "Sept. 15, 1972 Vietnamese Top Secret report, recently discovered in Soviet Communist Party archives—confirming that Vietnam was holding on to far more U.S. POWs than it had pubicly [*sic*] admitted." I am grateful to *Times* reporter Steven A. Holmes for this copy. For detailed exposés of the document, see Nayan Chanda, "Research and Destroy," *Far Eastern Economic Review*, 6 May 1993, p. 20, and H. Bruce Franklin, "M.I.A.sma," *The Nation*, May 10, 1993, p. 616.

65. "In Clinton's Words: 'Fullest Possible Accounting' of M.I.A.'s," *The New York Times*, February 4, 1994.

66. *Wall Street Journal*, April 23, 1993.

6. Lost Warriors: Viet Nam Veterans Among the Homeless

MARC JASON GILBERT

In August 1988, Ken Rose a Marine veteran, barricaded himself in historic Fort Vancouver, Washington, in an effort to draw attention to America's neglect of its growing population of homeless Viet Nam veterans. He surrendered to police in return for the opportunity to make a statement to reporters. The message Rose risked his freedom to convey was that these veterans had "paid their dues," and that it "was a disgrace to see them sleeping on the sidewalk." He wanted America to understand that these lost warriors faced "a lot of emotional, psychological and physical problems that are unlike any other segment of the population in America."[1]

Rose was not the first to make such an appeal. In 1969, a disabled veteran, Max Clelland, had warned Congress that Viet Nam veterans would require special assistance in making the adjustment to civilian life.[2] Yet the federal government joined most Americans in riding the economic and political winds of the 1970s and 1980s that swept much-needed health care, public services and economic opportunity beyond the reach of many of those who saw military service in Southeast Asia. By the early 1980s homelessness among these veterans had become chronic. Each passing winter brought more stories of veterans perishing from the cold in vacant lots, doorways or cardboard boxes.[3] Nonetheless, as late as 1987, the federal government had no programs directly addressing this problem. Only in 1994, six years after Rose's sacrificial gesture and more than twenty-five years after the majority of Americans who served in Viet Nam had returned from that theater of war, did an American president commit the country to address the suffering of these men and women. By then, it was acknowledged that any effort to ameliorate their condition would be through support groups and caregivers drawn from those Americans who had fought this last battle of the Viet Nam War for so long and so often alone, the veterans themselves.

Approximately 3 million Americans served in Southeast Asia. Many of them, particularly the 750,000 who survived continuous combat operations, saw a face of battle that was particularly harsh. It mated close-quarter guerrilla warfare with unprecedented conventional firepower capable of butchering combatants and noncombatants, friends and foes alike. On the other hand, it witnessed advances in medical services that ensured that all but the most seriously wounded could be quickly returned to the killing ground. It was fought by Americans whose average age was 19, compared with 26 in the Second World War. These young soldiers often initially engaged their opponents as part of small units operating at enormous numerical disadvantage, where survival depended upon a high degree of mutual trust and reliance between individuals. Yet these crucial intimate relationships were undermined by the one-year rotation system and high casualty rates.

Further, American policy in Viet Nam pursued a war of attrition that lacked meaningful tactical objectives and whose overall strategy was so poorly articulated in the field and at home that it deprived those Americans engaged in combat of a moral compass with which to view their own suffering, the suffering of Vietnamese friends, or the suffering they inflicted on foes often as young and brave as themselves.[4] This loss of moral compass deepened upon their return to the United States, where the value of their war was open to debate and where they "encountered a social taboo that in effect decreed that the most searing experience of their lives was not to be discussed."[5]

The impact of such a war on its American combatants became apparent after the veterans returned home. While the vast majority who served experienced little difficulty in readjusting to civilian life, a disproportionate number of those veterans who served in combat units or were otherwise exposed to combat stress[6] suffered high rates of alcoholism, psychological illness, divorce, suicide, lower incomes, higher unemployment, and, as time progressed, homelessness.[7] Statistical analyses of the problems of veterans have rarely included the homeless in their survey samples, leading to profound and politically volatile under-reporting of veterans' employment rates and health conditions. However, a carefully and conservatively drawn Columbia University research project commissioned by the American Legion in 1986 concluded that the average annual income of Vietnam veterans who saw heavy combat was $3,000 to $4,000 below those who did not, and in some cases "the differential was higher among veterans of the same age and educational level."[8] Similar research by the Ralph Bunch Center of New York University concluded that, of the 41 percent of New York City's 150,000 Viet Nam veterans who were experiencing serious financial or employment problems, the unemployment rate of those who saw heavy combat in Viet Nam was three times that of those who saw only light combat.[9] A recent study of over 2,000 twin pairs, one of whom served in Viet Nam and other who did not, found that veterans of combat in Viet Nam were nine times more likely than non-theater veterans to exhibit a dysfunctional response to events that fell "outside the range of usual human experience" which ultimately was labeled post–traumatic stress disorder (PTSD).[10]

Combat-related stress had been observed in veterans of the Second World War and the Korean War.[11] Its origins and manifestation in Viet Nam veterans, however, proved unique. It centered upon the veterans' pathological need to continually revisit painful memories "of what they did, what they saw and what they remember about their combat experience in Viet Nam," which they then sought to expunge through intoxication or the replication of wartime survival-driven behavior.[12] Such behavior, often violent, paranoid and always intensely antisocial in civilian life, when combined with the failure of family ties and public institutions to meet the challenge of the disorder's multifaceted symptoms, deprived these veterans of timely support and inhibited appropriate treatment. The lack of early intervention led to a worsening of their condition that further alienated them from their friends, families, and treatment facilities.[13]

The role of war trauma in inhibiting the transition of Viet Nam veterans to normal civilian life was disguised by the manner in which it differed from combat trauma that had been called "shell shock" and "combat fatigue" in earlier conflicts. Such behavior was associated with increased combat stress in the field, but it decreased rapidly when the patient was removed from the immediate causes of that stress. On the other hand, the Viet Nam War had produced only a few cases of war-related neuroses in battle, but led to an increasing number of such cases where combat stress impeded post-war readjustment. In 1988, the Centers for Disease Control, which under-reported combat stress, nonetheless described the persistence of delayed stress episodes in Viet Nam veterans as "the single most significant finding in [its] survey of the health effects of the general Viet Nam experience."[14]

The disabling effects of what came to be known as PTSD helped push many Viet Nam veterans into low-paying jobs.[15] The opportunities of all Viet Nam veterans were further limited by unprecedented structural changes in the American economy which led to a lower demand for low-skilled jobs, cutbacks in social programs and a shortage of low-income housing. They were also forced to negotiate the post-war job market with a government benefits package much smaller than that provided veterans of the Second World War.[16]

As a result, thousands of Viet Nam veterans slipped into unemployment, under-employment and homelessness. The federal government has estimated that more than 250,000 veterans are homeless on any given night and that twice that number will be homeless at some time during the year. Both the federal government and veterans' groups believe that approximately half of all homeless veterans served in Viet Nam. They also believe that the majority of homeless Viet Nam veterans are likely to be among the 500,000 Viet Nam veterans who have experienced PTSD to some degree.[17]

The most recent and reliable study of war trauma confirms that there is a close connection between combat stress in Viet Nam and homelessness "back in the world." Even though this study's population sample excluded any then currently homeless Viet Nam veterans with PTSD, a full 35 percent of those veterans interviewed who were diagnosed as PTSD-positive reported that they had been vagrant or homeless at one time, as opposed to little more than 6 percent of those who were PTSD-negative.[18] Other evidence suggests that some level of combat-related trauma is characteristic of the vast majority of homeless Viet Nam veterans. Homeless Viet Nam veterans interviewed in Atlanta, Boston, Los Angeles and Washington for a 1994 film documenting their condition invariably proved to be victims of combat trauma. Most of these men and women held jobs after their return from the war. They felt alienated from all save other homeless veterans and, believing the V.A. did not respect them, they resisted attempts by their families and friends to get them to seek public assistance. Their status, appearance and conduct closely resembled the protagonist in Larry Heinemann's *Paco's Story*.[19] Like Paco, these combat veterans' bodies are scarred by the wounds of war and they are living on the margin of existence. Their lives are locked in a recurring cycle of insecurity and self-reinforcing dysfunctional attempts to gain control. They work when they can; that is, when their mental and motor skills are not eroded by flashbacks, survivor guilt, and sudden anxiety, and their sanity is not threatened by dead comrades-turned-demons which often only alcohol can keep at bay. They live in a world of hurt that they believe few who have not been there themselves can understand, and in this they are right.[20]

There was never any doubt among Viet Nam veterans' advocacy groups that combat-related physical and psychological trauma, compounded by a lack of social support and by reduced economic opportunity, were the major causes of homelessness among those who had served in Southeast Asia. However, their efforts to draw attention to these links and solicit aid from the nation which sent these men and women into battle were obstructed by the very agency charged with their care, the Veterans Administration. Not only was the V.A. dilatory in acknowledging that Viet Nam veterans had special needs, but, once these needs were recognized, it was slow to address them and resistant to innovative treatment and aid strategies developed by the veterans themselves. The failure of leading V.A. officials and the presidential administrations they served to aggressively pursue solutions to the plight of the least fortunate of America's Viet Nam warriors is tragic, but it is also readily intelligible when seen against the background of the V.A.'s institutional history and postwar domestic politics.

While the general unpreparedness of the V.A. for the influx of Viet Nam veterans is a matter of record, it is less well known that the V.A. was particularly unready to act as advocate for those with war-related trauma or those who experienced chronic homelessness. According to pioneering veteran sociologist Wilbur J. Scott, the need to address the health problems of the aging American veterans of the first half century of total war had converted the V.A. into an institution preoccupied with geriatric medicine. The arrival of younger veterans requiring "treatment, rehabilitation, and compensation of war-related injuries and diseases ... produced tremendous strains in a health care system by now accustomed to addressing the needs of older veterans with ailments unrelated to war."[21]

The status quo at the V.A. was upset by Viet Nam veterans in other ways. Disillusioned by a war "whose chief lesson was to never believe their government again,"[22] these veterans, particularly those PTSD victims slipping in and out of vagrancy, tested the patience of Second World War–vintage V.A. doctors and counselors.[23] In many cases the latter were offended by the younger veterans' often poor appearance and uncooperative behavior and could not identify with their low opinions of themselves and their country. Sadly, as the V.A. now admits, race, class and gender played a role in the delivery of services to Viet Nam veterans. Both homelessness and PTSD were disproportionately high among African Americans and Hispanics; low-income whites also had more than their share. The rate of PTSD among women veterans remains controversial, but was nonetheless significant.[24] The V.A. concedes that well-off whites received far better care than less affluent and nonwhite veterans, while female veterans may well have received the lowest standard of care.[25]

The V.A. was also unprepared to deal with the cluster of problems— high rates of divorce, alcoholism, and unemployment—that Viet Nam veterans were experiencing, and quickly became frustrated by their inability to address these veterans' PTSD–related anxiety and depression through traditional therapies.[26] Such frustration, when combined with the clinicians' cultural and professional prejudices, easily translated into the treatment of Viet Nam veterans as second class citizens, the belittling of their problems and the withholding of vital early social and medical intervention.[27]

Had V.A. personnel been armed with better diagnostic tools, the aberrant behavior of these veterans might have more closely engaged their attention and solicited greater sympathy. The V.A. was, however, wedded to the second edition of the *Diagnostic and Statistical Manual for War Neurosis* (DSM-II) prepared for it by the American Psychiatric Association. According to Scott, for reasons possibly more closely related to a concern for the financial liabilities of the V.A. than the health of its patients, DSM-II abandoned the first edition's identification of gross stress reaction, which referenced the dire and long-term effects of extreme environmental stress in wartime. It also ignored contemporary research into the persistence of such effects in those with no prior history of mental illness.[28]

Since DSM-II provided no nomenclature or specific entries for war-related psychiatric disorders, V.A. medical personnel generally assumed that even veterans who were troubled by, or repeatedly talked about, their war experiences suffered from neuroses or psychoses whose cause lay outside the realm of combat. In time, though numerous studies established that it had little relevance in cases involving combat trauma, clinicians exhibited an "irrational insistence on the primacy of predisposition theory: the view that pretrauma personality characteristics—defects, flaws, and weaknesses—are the primary or most variable in the production of PTSD."[29] Worse, "for the sake of clinical purity," early studies of combat stress avoided cases complicated by alcoholism or drug abuse. The failure to consider that these behavior patterns played a major role in attempts by veterans to deal with PTSD not only impeded effective treatment, but deprived the V.A. of the means to gauge the impact of PTSD–related alcoholism on veterans' employment prospects and potential for homelessness.[30] Often the cost of the V.A.'s early approach to PTSD was much higher. Chief V.A. psychiatrist Arthur S. Blank has argued that the non-diagnosis of PTSD or the deferral of its early treatment could be measured in lives lost or lives impaired beyond number; literally in this case, because the physicians and staff that could number them would be vulnerable "to lawsuits and other adverse reactions."[31]

In the 1970s, antiwar veteran groups, as critical of the V.A. as they were of the other agencies of the executive branch of government, successfully sought relief from the V.A.'s lack of responsiveness by seeking help from two antiwar psychiatrists, Robert Lifton and Chaim Shatan. These therapists were already critical of the lack of war trauma elements in DSM-II and had been sensitized to the issue by their participation in private veteran-designed and -run "rap" groups. It was Shatan who first formally identified the elements of delayed massive trauma, a diagnostic label later changed to post–traumatic stress disorder when it was incorporated into the third edition of the American Psychiatric Association's manual and accepted by the V.A. in 1980.[32] The medical profession and the V.A. were thus given a means of assessing the condition not merely of Viet Nam veterans or the homeless among them, but all of those who exhibited dysfunctional responses to human disfigurement, brutality and death, particularly when events impeded the expression of grief associated with the traumatic events.[33] According to Arthur Blank, it was only after the adoption of the PTSD diagnosis that the V.A.'s approach to the problems of these veterans ceased to be as dysfunctional as some of the clients it sought to serve.[34]

Unfortunately, the V.A. did not as an institution rush to embrace PTSD as a diagnostic tool, nor did it soon consider it as a factor in homelessness among Viet Nam veterans.[35] Despite the V.A.'s intransigence, individual V.A. doctors and treatment facilities began to collect military histories of veterans and developed effective assistance programs. Their efforts, however, were viewed with hostility by their colleagues and won the enmity of the V.A. which acted to shut down experimental PTSD treatment units in the 1970s.[36] A few non–V.A. federal programs experimented with education, job-training, housing assistance and mental health and substance abuse counseling. In 1972, when the Department of Education lent support to Viet Nam veteran Arthur

Barham's Veterans Upward Bound program in Atlanta, it helped create one of the first and most successful of all veterans' reentry programs.[37] However, attempts by Barham and others to convince the V.A. to create PTSD treatment centers and shelters for homeless Viet Nam veterans proved futile. All major progress in these allied directions was destined to be made through the efforts of veterans themselves.

During their campaign to gain recognition for PTSD in the early 1970s, Lifton and Shatan enlisted the aid of congressional critics of the war such as Senator Alan Cranston (D–Calif.) to pass legislation mandating the establishment of veterans' centers within the V.A. that would better identify and treat the special needs of Viet Nam veterans. Cranston's legislative vehicle carried too much liberal antiwar political freight to win swift approval. It was, moreover, stridently opposed by the two largest veterans' organizations, the American Legion and the Veterans of Foreign Wars. These groups were then on poor terms with Viet Nam veterans, whom older veterans often stigmatized as having been among "those guys over there losing the war."[38] Lobbyists for the Veterans of Foreign Wars and American Legion also feared, wrongly as it proved, that this legislation would shift to Viet Nam veterans' resources that were then being provided to their major constituency: veterans of the Second World War and Korean War.[39]

The passage of Cranston's legislation came only on its fifth try in 1979, but its ultimate impact was heightened by the means chosen by President Carter's new chief at the V.A., Max Clelland, to implement it. Clelland, whose concern for the welfare of fellow Viet Nam veterans has already been noted, developed a separately funded and separately sited national system of Veterans Outreach Centers, or Vet Centers. These centers, often operating out of storefronts, were staffed by Viet Nam veterans on the theory, quickly validated by experience, that the delivery of PTSD counseling services would be more effective if its caregivers could say, "I am not the government, I am a vet."[40] The therapy regimen pursued at these centers was based on the impromptu veteran-to-veteran "rap" group sessions observed in the early 1970s by Lifton and Shatan. This therapeutic approach quickly proved its worth in aiding veterans to express and often resolve their feelings about their war service and their readjustment problems. More important, in their first two years, these clinics served thousands of veterans who would have never entered mainstream V.A. facilities.[41]

The Vet Center system, which numbered 137 in 1981, quickly made a broader impact on the health of veterans. In the mid–1980s, the centers joined with over 50 parallel state and privately financed veterans-helping-veterans facilities in the pursuit of a holistic approach to veterans' problems. No longer would a veteran's problems with alcohol be considered separate from his or her homeless state or PTSD, and no longer would jobs and housing be provided to veterans without regard to their mental or physical health.[42]

Unfortunately, no sooner was the Veteran Outreach Center system established and a new approach to the delivery of services to veterans adopted than a concerted effort was made to terminate them. What the political process had given the veteran, it soon threatened to take away.

The end of the war heralded a period of national introspection and debate heightened by the Watergate crisis and the perceived weakness of the Ford and Carter administrations. While American liberals used this time to engage in political fratricide, conservatives developed a new political program that was designed to heal the wounded American psyche and capture it for the conservative cause. This program, by the 1980s called the Reagan-Bush agenda, or neoconservatism, was built around a drive for moral and military rearmament. It elevated America's defeat in Viet Nam to the level of a glorious failure attributable to weaknesses in the body politic brought about by America's surrender to welfare-state values. What America needed was more guns and less butter, both to resume the anticommunist crusade abandoned in Viet Nam and to promote a sense of individual responsibility necessary for the revival of the national will.

Presidents Ronald Reagan and George Bush repeatedly expressed respect for the sacrifices of soldiers in Viet Nam, but their administrations had little to offer the veterans of that conflict in terms of government services. Neoconservative domestic policy, keyed to undoing the alleged free spending of liberals on domestic programs, specifically targeted for elimination of the least cost-effective social welfare programs because they dealt with relatively small numbers of people on the margin of American society. Several of the targeted programs were of significance for combating homelessness among veterans.

In 1981, Reagan's budget director, David Stockman, initiated an attack on the funding for the only program specifically addressing the needs of Viet Nam veterans: Clelland's Veteran Outreach Centers, which represented only $12 million out of the V.A.'s $22 billion budget. Stockman was determined to eliminate the entire program and, in other hands, this effort continued until the last days of the Bush administration. The Reagan administration also withheld funds from a Small Business Administration pilot program for Viet Nam veterans. Its attempts to trim V.A. spending sent that agency into a crisis, and included an effort to take 13,000 hospital beds out of service without reporting the reduction.[43] It opposed a bill that provided on-the-job and vocational training to disabled veterans who had been unemployed for 15 of the previous 20 weeks, a step critics said would exacerbate "the Viet Nam veteran's problem of being the last hired and first fired."[44] Further, the Reagan administration sharply curtailed a home-loan insurance program, an action that "adversely affected veterans with low incomes."[45]

The Bush administration continued these policies and strove to underfund or understaff veterans' programs whenever possible. For example, a program intended to treat thousands of mentally ill veterans in each city it served was limited to two counselors per city.[46] While the V.A. enjoyed Cabinet-level status under the Bush administration, the latter's view of its new role was indicated by the appointment of Edward J. Derwinski as secretary of veterans' affairs. Derwinski's qualifications for the post were questionable and he demonstrated little concern for veterans' affairs beyond reducing V.A. services and costs. He lost the confidence of women and Hispanic veterans by referring to the female members of his staff as "Little Miss Coffee Makers" and to the latter ethnic group as "wetbacks." He was removed from office as a result of the public outcry that followed his tactless broaching of the Bush administration's intention to open veterans' hospitals to non-veterans. This step was opposed by veterans who feared that the already poor service they received would worsen if they were forced to compete for care against other patients.[47]

Viet Nam veterans on the margin of homelessness also suffered from the Reagan administration's effort to reduce civilian and service personnel on welfare. Roy P. Benavidez, 80 percent disabled by wounds received during an action which won him a Medal of Honor in Viet Nam, had been praised for his gallantry by President Reagan in 1981. However, a review of the social security disability payment system sought by the Reagan administration later stripped Benavidez of his disability payments and forced him to undergo three medical examinations in an attempt to have the payments restored. Benavidez made his situation known to the press "more for my buddies than for me ... if they can do this to me, what will they do to the others? It's like someone's trying to make fun of you."[48]

Max Clelland, reentering the political fray in an attempt to save the Outreach system, shared Benavidez's sense of outrage and betrayal. He argued that for candidate Reagan to call the Viet Nam War a "noble cause" and then do away with the most effective services available to its veterans was "going to deepen the sense of frustration and sense of alienation on the part of Viet Nam veterans."[49]

Presidents Reagan and Bush did not deliberately seek to humiliate any veteran or inflict hardship upon homeless Viet Nam veterans. They were, however, determined to assist these Americans by means that were consistent with the values of self-help and volunteerism that formed the centerpiece of their political philosophy. One such means was their sponsorship of private veteran support groups led by successful veteran businessmen who would rely on their own resources—not the government's—to provide job training and counseling to troubled veterans. This program, part of a larger effort called the Private Sector Initiative, was called the Viet Nam Veterans Leadership Program. It attracted many able directors including John Wheeler, a Viet Nam veteran who had been involved in the creation of the national Viet Nam Veterans Memorial and served as a special counsel to the chairman of the Securities and Exchange Commission.

The Viet Nam Veterans Leadership Program's locally based committees accomplished much. Yet, organizations such as these, whose strengths lay in referrals to alcohol treatment centers and the creation of seminars on how to start a small business or obtain a loan, were less adept at assisting veterans who suffered multiple health problems or were haunted by nightmares, riddled with survivor guilt and living under freeway overpasses. Some Viet Nam Veterans Leadership Program leaders came to resent the fact that the White House failed to maintain the federal grants that helped initiate their job-training programs, and some, such as Bill Elmore of the St. Louis Leadership program, hoped for a broader federally supported national effort. They also began pressuring the federal government to do a better job of informing veterans of the publicly financed programs to which they were entitled.[50]

Wheeler soon found that the Reagan and Bush administrations had not used the funds freed up by veteran-volunteer programs to improve the V.A.'s delivery of veterans services. By 1991, the V.A.'s performance in this regard was so poor that, in Wheeler's opinion, if Gulf War casualties had been as high as expected, the wounded would have "suffer[ed] the same conditions in veterans hospitals that brought so much pain in the Viet Nam era: underbudgeting, too few nurses, overburdened doctors, red tape, and a feeling of abandonment by their country."[51]

President Bush was undeterred by such criticism. His skill and determination to stay the course charted by the neoconservative agenda were reflected in his decision to identify state or privately supported Viet Nam veteran homeless shelters as "points of light." These invariably Viet Nam veteran–run rehabilitation centers and shelters had certainly earned the president's recognition as cost-effective non-federal programs. Holistic shelter and rehabilitation programs in Atlanta, New York, St. Louis, San Diego, San Francisco and at Ken Smith's well-publicized Boston-based New England Shelter for Homeless Veterans had achieved remarkable success in turning around the lives of even those veterans who had spent years on the street or shuttling from one V.A.–run center and hospital to another.[52] The New England Shelter's job and housing programs claimed a success rate of 95 percent for its barracks-like therapeutic environment, while its Viet Nam Veterans Workshop succeeded in creating a national model for an integrated-services approach to the needs of homeless veterans.[53]

Yet, while these institutions were proud of the honor bestowed upon them by the president, Bush's apparent attempt to use them for political purposes was met with derision from their financially hard-pressed state and private managers and sponsors. The leaders of the New York Veterans Shelter, mentioned in the president's State of the Union Address in March 1991, were bitter that they had struggled for almost a decade without federal assistance and could easily double the number of veterans the shelter served if it could get a hand, rather than a handshake, from Washington.[54] Ken Smith, whose speech at the 1992 Republican National Convention on the plight of homeless veterans was well-received, had this response to the president's naming of his shelter as the "142nd point of light."

> I've been open here [in Boston] three years, four months and twelve days, and I still haven't received a dime from the V.A. .... You'd think by now they'd get it that this is a deal for them, that we do for $11,000 per man what they don't do for three times as much. You'd think that they'd understand that it is more cost effective to make tax payers out of [the veterans in his program] than to send 'em back to hellholes and filthy shelters. Instead, they throw billions away over there, while some days I get in the car and scream, "How you gonna pay the gas bill, Smith."[55]

While the Reagan and Bush administrations' ideologically driven approach was rejected as inadequate and inefficient by its chosen exemplars, their efforts to strengthen the nation's moral fiber and revive its fiscal health by reducing the numbers of those on the federal dole was strongly endorsed by their allies in the media, such as *Forbes* magazine, and by conservative activists. These allies argued that American veterans had received a homecoming parade in 1982 and a memorial in the Mall and that, therefore, these veterans no longer had any reason to feel forgotten or put upon. They also sought to discredit advocates for troubled and homeless Viet Nam veterans by emphasizing how many Viet Nam veterans had made a successful transition to normal life or by intimating that many of those seeking public assistance were malingerers who were seeking to "hide behind the shield of having served in Viet Nam."[56] Some conservative Viet Nam veterans, like New York state assemblyman John L. Behan (R–Long Island) joined in these attacks because "we didn't like the image [troubled Vietnam veterans] were casting."[57] Efforts were also made to explain the recent gains in federal spending on veterans as the result of misplaced national pity successfully exploited by a garden variety special interest group merely seeking to protect its turf. Veteran advocates attempted to respond to these charges by referencing independently conducted analyses which demonstrated that homelessness among Viet Nam veterans was related to their war service, not willful misconduct. As to the charge of turf-guarding, they asked Americans to accept that homeless combat veterans had "a different kind of claim to what they're owed by society."[58] These appeals would help turn the hearts and minds of critics like Behan, but could make little headway among those whose deliberate purpose was not to inform, but to blunt calls for increases in veterans' benefits that might help derail the neoconservative drive to reduce the scope and cost of the federal government.

There was no doubt on which side of the debate over homelessness among Viet Nam veterans the V.A. bureaucracy would be found. The V.A. had never been comfortable with data indicating that alcoholism and homelessness were PTSD–related, nor had it overcome its initial prejudices against the ungrateful and suspicious behavior Viet Nam veterans directed at it. The V.A. was also fiercely opposed to programs like the Vet Center system that operated outside its direct control and failed to conform to V.A. institutional standards and rules. Many V.A. officials resented the diversion of resources to programs for the homeless.[59] It is thus not surprising that, when faced with a political atmosphere hostile to its most troublesome clients and forced to make deep cuts in its own budget, the leadership of the V.A. embraced the neoconservative approach of its political masters. They drastically reduced the number of V.A. benefits counselors and made little effort to streamline benefit application forms or eligibility requirements.[60] For a time, they refused treatment and even benefit checks to veterans who could not supply a fixed address.[61] When, in the mid–1980s, under the impact of delayed stress syndrome, "a vast number of Viet Nam vets in their middle thirties suddenly broke down, leaving behind them, in their free fall into isolate madness, mortgages and jobs and heartbroken families ... the V.A. denounced them as drunks and scammers, quashing their appeals for benefits."[62]

As might be expected given its own bureaucratic agenda, the V.A. also lent its full support to David Stockman's efforts to end the funding of the Veteran Outreach Centers. Ironically, under different political circumstances, the V.A. would later boast of this program's effectiveness and seek to introduce into its own facilities the veteran-guided integrated-treatment approach to the related problems of PTSD, alcoholism, unemployment and homelessness pioneered by these centers.[63] In the early to late 1980s, however, the V.A. tried to shut the Vet Centers down, and told many veterans who turned to the V.A. itself for PTSD counseling that "There is no cure for PTSD," or "We can't help you, your [condition] is too severe for us."[64]

The V.A. often justified such actions on the basis of studies generated by its own hopelessly compromised research staff. The latter tried to be loyal to the institution it served without doing violence to the highest standards of scientific truth. Its tortured efforts to accomplish this task were illuminated by the work of psychiatrist Robert Rosenheck, one of the V.A.'s leading experts on PTSD and homelessness. Rosenheck personally believed that it was "a moral outrage that people who served in a war should ... find themselves homeless," but he told reporters and a mystified congressional committee that "it isn't significantly true that war caused homelessness ... other factors—substance abuse or mental problems, the lack of family and other support in the first year after discharge—led more directly to homelessness than did any wartime experience."[65] Rosenheck's subtle point was that PTSD–related homelessness was often not directly connected to the horrors of war, but to the therapeutic means and socioeconomic opportunities available to an individual forced to confront them. However, the V.A. employed Rosenheck's arguments not to enlighten Congress or the public about PTSD, but to defend its long-held position that PTSD and PTSD–related homelessness were not directly combat or war-related, and hence not the V.A.'s responsibility. Rather than concede, as Rosenheck would, that combat trauma was still a contributing factor to homelessness, or take responsibility for failing to provide the vital early support Rosenheck identified, the V.A. sought to blame the victim.

The V.A. also tried to avoid responsibility for the increasing number of homeless veterans the Veteran Outreach Center clinics were identifying and referring to the V.A. for further assistance. The V.A. was proud of the success of the growing number of mental illness/substance abuse programs and domiciliary facilities, even though these programs, like the equally successful Vet Centers, had been forced upon it by public concern over what most Americans saw as a crisis in veterans' health and housing. Yet, its institutional range of vision was so narrow that it failed to develop any means of informing homeless veterans of the availability of these services and beds, 20 percent of which were empty. In 1989, the V.A. had to admit that all 30 beds set aside for homeless veterans in the Westwood, California, V.A. hospital remained empty for months because of the V.A.'s failure to develop effective communication with the homeless community.[66] Nor did the V.A. ensure that such facilities were associated with the requisite rehabilitation programs. Both issues troubled Viet Nam veteran advocacy groups. Mainstream V.A. outreach programs were essential because the majority of veterans with adjustment problems were combat veterans with PTSD. Their illness, whose symptoms included alienation and denial, together with their often disastrous initial encounters with less than supportive doctors and workers at the V.A., normally kept these veterans away from treatment centers, a strong rebuttal of the neoconservative movement's charge that most homeless veterans were abusing V.A. benefits. Outside experts in the field argued that even those veterans who were well-off and appeared readjusted "often need some type of counseling, but will not seek it because they won't openly identify themselves as Viet Nam vets."[67] Without integrated treatment programs, moreover, facilities for homeless Viet Nam veterans were not only ineffective, but fiscally irresponsible. As Michael Leaveck of the Viet Nam Veterans of America argued:

> Homelessness is the symptom, not the problem, and domiciliary beds are an expensive way to treat that symptom. You can feed people, change their linens, and put a roof over their heads, but unless you do counseling and rehabilitation, you aren't addressing the real problem. There are few homeless veterans who are job ready and need nothing more than a place to live.[68]

The V.A. was aware of these truths. Even its severest critics believed that, when properly funded and fully exploiting dedicated and sincere V.A. field personnel, V.A. facilities were capable of delivering quality care and making formidable improvements in the extension of their services.[69] Unfortunately, mired in old patterns of thinking and continually hampered by lack of funds, the V.A. neither rushed to accept advice such as Leaveck's nor stepped up its own outreach effort. For example, studies conducted between 1985 and 1987 indicated that fewer than 20 percent of Boston's homeless veterans were receiving any V.A. benefits, while fewer than 2 percent of homeless veterans in Los Angeles were receiving V.A. medical benefits. A survey of the three shelters in the Washington, D.C., area known to cater to homeless veterans showed they had never been contacted by the V.A.[70]

When, in the mid-1980s, the V.A. was forced to admit that it did not know, and had never developed any means of knowing, either the number of homeless veterans or the number among the homeless that might be eligible for federal benefit programs, the Reagan administration blamed the problem on state and local agencies, which were accused of removing "people from mental health and other institutions without providing supervision afterward."[71] In effect, the V.A. was to be absolved of its failure to seek out homeless veterans because state and local authorities—due in part to budget cuts mandated by local neoconservative-supported tax revolts—were dumping the disabled into the streets and abandoning any effort to monitor them. The chief problem inherent in this argument was that, under similar pressure from the White House, the V.A. was guilty of precisely the same practices.[72]

Eventually, even President Reagan's own chief of the V.A., West Point graduate Harry N. Walters, found himself unable to endorse the administration's continuing attempt to redraw the unwritten contract that bound the nation to provide for those who had risked their lives in its defense. Walters broke with the administration when, in December 1986, it accelerated its effort to shift veterans' care to the private sector and imposed deeper reductions in spending on veterans. When ordered by the Office of Management and Budget (OMB) not to attend a meeting of a congressional committee at which these cuts would be considered, presumably out of fear he might give testimony opposing the administration's stance, Walters made public a letter to the OMB in which he stated his opinion that the planned economies would "reduc[e] the quality of medical care" provided by the V.A.[73] Walters then resigned his post. Veterans' groups tried to exploit Walters' resignation as a rallying cry, but their efforts did not prompt remedial action.[74] The following year, Walters' successor, Thomas K. Turnage, declared that the problem of homeless veterans was simply beyond the reach of one department of government and that the V.A. could be most effective by accepting referrals from the same hard-pressed state agencies and local groups whose performance it had earlier criticized as unequal to this task.[75]

The National Coalition for the Homeless and the Viet Nam Veterans of America agreed with the V.A.'s leadership that the problem of homeless veterans was beyond the resources of a single agency. They also believed, however, that the agency responsible for the welfare of veterans should at least have an outreach program for homeless veterans equal to that of the Department of Labor. That agency, concerned about the number of veterans who were "so battered, so frightened ... that they are loath to come out and access the system," created an inexpensive pilot program in ten cities that would send former homeless veterans turned counselors "scouring street corners and shelters for destitute veterans."[76] This program quickly grew into one of the most effective weapons in the battle against homelessness among veterans.[77] In April 1987 the two veterans' groups brought suit in federal court to force the V.A. to meet or exceed the standard of service adopted by the Labor Department.[78] The lawsuit proved to be a watershed, not merely because it helped push the V.A. into launching its own outreach programs, but also because it was pursued with the support of the American Legion and the Veterans of Foreign Wars. These traditional veterans' groups and the maverick Viet Nam Veterans Association had finally been brought together by changing demographics within the older organizations and their collective frustration with the V.A.'s lack of responsiveness to their concerns.

This concordat proved timely. It allowed all three groups to present a united front before Congress when that body met in 1990 to formally address the problem of homelessness among veterans. In the face of their united testimony as to the seriousness of the problem, Congress not only rejected the cuts in veterans' spending recommended by the Reagan and Bush administrations, including those that would have terminated the Vet Center system, but recommended an expansion of veterans' services. As a result, not only was the number of Vet Centers vastly increased, but two new programs were developed whose unparalleled success was later conceded by the V.A.: the Homeless Chronically Ill and Domiciliary Care for Homeless Veterans programs.

The collective testimony of veterans' advocacy groups also had an impact upon the March 1990 hearings of the House Committee on Veterans' Affairs. These hearings gave these groups an opportunity to recommend federal support for cost-effective locally run veterans' shelters and innovative approaches to unifying housing and rehabilitation programs. They also had an opportunity to stress the need for linkages between private and government bodies at all levels. These hearings also permitted veterans' groups to reach out in a small but significant way to the V.A. Paul S. Egan, a staunch Viet Nam Veterans of America critic of the V.A., testified at these hearings that, while the V.A. had initially "exacerbated" and proved "slow to respond" to the problem of homelessness among veterans, it was improving and had done about as well as could be expected when pushed by Congress and given sufficient funding.[79] Coming from Egan, this was a large olive branch. It proved useful, for the V.A. hierarchy was undergoing its own demographic changing of the guard. Management at the V.A. was passing into the hands of Viet Nam veterans who had long wished to change the V.A.'s course in the direction sought by its Viet Nam veteran critics, but lacked the power to do so.[80] Such bridge-building paid large dividends with the arrival shortly thereafter of new political leaders who had pledged to improve the delivery of services to the homeless and in particular the homeless veterans.

President Clinton owes his elevation to the presidency at least in part to a backlash against the social policies of his two immediate predecessors. This backlash may have been rooted in a desire for a kinder, gentler nation than presidents Reagan or Bush had been able to deliver, though it is just as likely to have grown out of a conviction that a Center-Left Democrat with a record of responsible spending on social programs was just what the country needed in a future then darkened by doubts about the strength of the American economy. In any case, the new president, who made "I feel your pain" a much satirized but effective homily, proved sincerely committed to helping the least fortunate in society. His administration quickly began planning a national strategy for addressing the homeless in America and won praise from veterans' groups by making homelessness among veterans a priority. Much of that praise rightly has fallen upon Clinton's secretary of veterans affairs, Jesse Brown.

Brown, like the last Democrat to head the V.A. (Clelland), is a disabled Viet Nam veteran. Unlike Clelland, who left office before the connection between PTSD and homelessness had been made and homelessness itself became an issue, Brown was highly sensitized to these issues from the outset. He had witnessed one of his own Marine comrades, a veteran of heavy combat, fall victim to PTSD–related homelessness. Yet, in his pursuit of his president's directive to plot a course leading to the elimination of homelessness among veterans, Brown demonstrated an appreciation of the elusiveness of that goal and the high cost of reaching it. At a 1994 summit called to better coordinate the V.A. actions and those of veterans' groups—the first of its kind—Brown noted that, though the V.A. had at his direction almost doubled the money spent on homeless veterans, it had not visibly reduced their number. He warily observed that to get just 10,000 homeless veterans off the street the V.A. spends $40 million of its $36 billion annual budget. While he has repeated the V.A.'s time-worn refrain that "no government agency can solve this problem alone," he has not found it easy to enlist others. While he has placed a V.A. representative in the Department of Housing and Urban Development and that department has conceded that "today the number of homeless Viet Nam veterans are greater than the number of military personnel who died in Viet Nam," it has yet to designate any of its $1.2 billion homelessness warchest (compared to the V.A.'s $70 million) for veterans' housing projects.[81] Brown has yet to respond to veterans who argue that homeless veteran programs should receive their fair share of federal spending on homelessness; i.e. if the government determines that one-third of the homeless population are veterans, veterans' homeless programs should receive one-third of the funds spent to alleviate this condition.[82]

Brown's caution and his inability to move fiscal mountains is not surprising given Clinton's limited mandate for social services, which favors reform over additional spending. While this posture has frustrated some veterans' groups, Brown has delighted the entire veteran community by giving his full support to two cost-effective measures this community had long championed: a national coordinated outreach effort to identify and assist homeless veterans and federal funding for local government and private vets-helping-vets programs. Richard Fitzpatrick, executive director of the National Coalition for the Homeless, has remarked that for the V.A. to create an alliance with state and local private groups "is a phenomenal breakthrough.... It's a major first step." Fitzpatrick would no doubt place in the same category the V.A.'s first-ever cash awards, $5.5 million in 1993, to nongovernmental homeless veteran projects.[83]

Whether Brown will be able to make further progress in these and other directions remains problematical given the continued volatility of American domestic politics and the need for fiscal restraint. Yet his determination to effect a sea change in his agency was illuminated by his response to the politics of Gulf War veterans' affairs. While conservative critics tried to dismiss Gulf War Syndrome as merely another veterans' con game,[84] Brown is setting the vilest ghost of the Viet Nam–era to rest by attempting to ensure that no Gulf War veteran will be denied medical assistance because his or her symptoms lay beyond the ken of existing V.A. diagnostic manuals.[85] Brown has also taken steps to address the needs of the unexpectedly large number of otherwise distressed and homeless Gulf War veterans.[86]

The new priority given to outreach programs within the V.A. has raised the morale of V.A. personnel, who now have both the knowledge and the resources necessary to deliver more effective counsel and treatment to their clients than ever before. The dispersal of funds to community-based, veteran-run institutions and more humane and innovative thinking at the V.A. have also boosted the spirits of the staff of veterans' advocacy organizations such as the Viet Nam Veterans of America. The latter, long critical of the V.A.'s doctrinaire approach to the problems of veterans, derives great satisfaction from the knowledge that it was largely though the efforts of Viet Nam veterans that respect for what they sacrificed in Southeast Asia was restored, that a monument to that sacrifice was built, that a nation's obligations to the less fortunate among them was honored, and that the means for honoring that obligation were found.[87]

Today, American veterans tour the battlefields of Viet Nam. Major General Richard Secord, a former Special Operations (Ranger) coordinator in Viet Nam, brokers energy contracts with the same petroleum and oil officials he used to target for elimination. The United States government has a diplomatic presence in Viet Nam and the process of accounting for Americans missing in action in Southeast Asia has never run smoother. Americans have cast majorities of ballots for Vice President Dan Quayle and President Clinton, both of whom had to overcome criticism about their avoidance of military service in Viet Nam. Memorial Day celebrations referencing the Viet Nam War increasingly promote understanding rather than serve as opportunities for politically inspired breast-beating. The only battle of the war still raging is for the sanity and well-being of homeless Viet Nam veterans, too many of whom continue to suffer from wounds received in combat operations whose names are remembered by few of their noncombatant peers and are largely unknown by the succeeding generation of Americans. For over twenty years these veterans have fought some of the same enemies they fought in Viet Nam—national leaders with agendas distant from the battleground, an insensitive bureaucracy and an American public largely disengaged from the realities of their fight. They still face the possibility that another turn of the political wheel may deny them the victory recently promised by an ebullient but increasingly embattled president. In the clamor over future budget shortfalls or ideologically driven debates over welfare and health reform, that victory can still pass to those who claim that America's Viet Nam veterans have no reason for complaint and that the country now faces a multitude of problems more pressing than homelessness. It thus remains to be seen if these longest serving "winter soldiers" will be brought in from the cold.[88] Until they are, or the last of them dies neglected and forgotten, it will be impossible to say that the process of healing from the war, and hence the process of reconciliation, is complete.

Notes

1. "Homeless Ex-Marine Yields After Protest at Historic Fort," *New York Times,* 31 Aug. 1988, late ed., sec. 1:14. See also "A Vietnamese Confronts Homeless Vietnam Veterans," by Duc Nguyen, National Public Radio, *All Things Considered,* WABE, Atlanta, 23 May 1994.

2. Marc Leepson, "Lionized Viet Vets in the Cold," article in the *Washington Star,* 20 March 1981: A20, reprinted in Cong. Rec., 97th Congress, v. 127, part 5, no. 5670. Since retiring as the chief administrator of the Veterans Administration, Clelland, a triplegic, has served as Georgia's secretary of state.

3. Ross S. Yarrow, "Homeless Veterans: A Nation's Disgrace," *The Christian Science Monitor,* 10 March 1987: 16; and Mark Patinkin, "A Death on America Street," *Atlanta Journal and Constitution,* 2 July 1993, late ed.: A11.

4. See "Corporal Thach, First Confirmed NV.A. Kill," David Connolly, *Lost in America* (Woodbridge, CT.: Vietnam Generation and Burning Cities Press, 1994): 212.

5. John Wheeler, "Shaped By The War in Vietnam," *New York Times,* 22 June 1983, late ed., sec. 1:27.

6. See W. D. Ehrhart, "Review of Jonathan Shay, *Achilles in Vietnam: Combat Trauma and the Undoing of Character* (New York: Atheneum, 1994)," in *Vietnam Generation* 6.1–2 (1994): 195. Ehrhart has correctly challenged the effectiveness of too narrow a clinical definition of a combat veteran. He asks, "Certainly a rifleman who participated in the battle of the Ia Drang Valley ... is a combat veteran, but what about the artilleryman on a firebase that came under ground assault once in the six months he spent there? What about the truck driver whose convoy received sniper fire...? Can a soldier who is not a 'combat veteran,' who didn't have a commander betray 'what's right' or lose a special friend or go berserk suffer from PTSD?" The answer is yes, in terms of both the scholarly approach and clinical definitions employed in this essay.

7. Centers for Disease Control Viet Nam Experience Study, "Health Status of Vietnam Veterans, I. Psychosocial Characteristics," *Journal of the American Medical Association* 259 (1988): 2701–2707; William E. Schlenger et al., "The Prevalence of Post–Traumatic Stress Disorder in the Vietnam Generation," *Journal of Traumatic Stress* 5.3 (1992): 333–363. See also Kathy Sawyer, "Heavy-Combat Veterans Paying Toll," *Washington Post,* 24 July 1985: A3.

8. Albert B. Singerman and John F. Somer, "Yes, It Is Worse for Vietnam Combat Vets," letter, *New York Times,* 25 March 1986, late ed.: A30. The results of this survey can be found in *Environmental Research* 47.2 (1988): 109–211.

9. "Vietnam Veterans Give Ex-Comrades a Hand Up," *New York Times,* 11 Aug. 1985, late ed., sec.1:38.

10. Jack Goldberg, et al., "A Twin Study of the Effects of the Vietnam War on Post-Traumatic Stress Behavior," *The Journal of the American Medical Association* 263 (1990): 1227–1232.

11. Bessel van der Kolk and Onno van der Hart, "Pierre Janet and the Breakdown of Adoption in Psychological Trauma," *American Journal of Psychiatry* 146 (1989): 1530–1540; and David Gelman, "Reliving the Painful Past," *Newsweek,* 13 June 1994: 20.

12. Robert Rosenheck, "Malignant Post-Vietnam Stress Syndrome," *The American Journal of Orthopsychiatry* 55 (1985): 167–176.

13. Herbert Hendin, "Psychotherapy for Vietnam Veterans with Post-Traumatic Stress Disorders," *American Journal of Psychotherapy* 37 (1983): 87; Robert Long et al., "Chronicity: Adjustment Differences of Vietnam Combat Veterans Differing in Rates of Psychiatric Hospitalization," *Journal of Clinical Psychology* 45 (1989): 745–753; David P. Niles, "War Trauma and Post–Traumatic Stress Disorder," *American Family Physician* 44 (1991): 1663–1669.

14. For the controversy over the Centers for Disease Control study, see "Vietnam's Psychological Toll," *Science* 241 (1988): 159–160 and John Loyer, Andrew Carney and Terry Fearon, "For Vietnam Veterans, the War Refuses to End," letter, *New York Times,* 10 April 1986, late ed.: A30.

15. Sharon Cohany, "Employment and Unemployment Among Vietnam-Era Veterans," *Monthly Labor Review* 113.4 (1990): 22–29.

16. Paul S. Egan, "The G.I. Bills: Apples and Oranges," letter, *Washington Post,* 14 Sept. 1993: A20.

17. Judith Waldrop, "27 Million Heroes," *American Demographics* 5.11 (1993): 4.

18. Richard A. Kukla, et al., *Trauma and the Vietnam Generation: Report of the Findings from the National Vietnam Veterans Readjustment Study* (New York, Brunner/Mazel, 1990): 143; Richard Kukla, et al., *The National Vietnam Veterans Readjustment Study: Tables of Findings and Technical Appendices* (New York: Brunner/Mazel, 1990), Table VIII-18-1.

19. Larry Heinemann, *Paco's Story* (New York: Farrar, Straus and Giroux, 1986).

20. James Forsher, Lon Holmberg and Marc Jason Gilbert, *Lost Warriors* (film) (Forsher/Holmberg Productions, 1994).

21. Wilbur Scott, "PTSD and Agent Orange: Implications for a Sociology of Veterans Issues," *Armed Forces and Society* (1992): 596. See also Wilbur Scott, "PTSD in DSM-III: A Case in the Politics of Diagnosis and Disease," *Social Problems* 37 (1990): 294–307.

22. William Ehrhart, interview, *Vietnam: A Television History, Episode 13: Legacies,* videocassette, prod. by Richard Ellision, WGBH Educational Foundation, Boston, 1985.

23. Many homeless Viet Nam veterans encounter V.A. medical personnel only after having attempted suicide or after having been taken to a V.A. center, often by law enforcement personnel. Such rude arrivals and awakenings may provoke antagonism in disoriented veterans and further erode respect for them in the minds of hospital staff. See Sonnenberg, et al., pp. 241–242.

24. Schlenger, 333–363; Walter E. Penk, et al., "Ethnicity: Post-Traumatic Stress Disorder (PTSD) Differences Among Black, White and Hispanic Veterans Who Differ in Degrees of Exposure to Combat in Vietnam," *Journal of Clinical Psychiatry* 45 (1989): 729–

735; and Linda M. Van Devanter, "The Unknown Warriors: Implications of the Experiences of Women in Vietnam," in William E. Kelly, ed., *Post-Traumatic Stress Disorder and the War Veteran Patient* (New York: Brunner/Mazel, 1985).

25. Arthur Barham, interview, August 9, 1994. Statistician Robert Rosenheck both shocked and earned praise from the audience at the 1994 V.A. summit conference on homelessness when he broached this long-suppressed issue. For an account of these remarks, see Joseph Cerquone, "Brother Can You Share $1.13 Billion? The V.A. Summit on Homelessness Among Veterans," in *VVA Veteran* 14.4 (1994): 20.

26. See Steven M. Southwick, Rachel Yehuda, and Earl Geller, Jr., "Characterization of Depression in War-Related Post-Traumatic Stress Disorder," *American Journal of Psychiatry* 148 (1991): 179–183. This study noted that "the nature of depression in PTSD differs from that in major depressive disorder" (179).

27. Ken Smith, quoted in Patricia Edmonds, *USA Today*, 28–31 May 1993: 1.

28. Scott, *PTSD and Agent Orange*, 596.

29. Arthur S. Blank, "Irrational Reactions to Post-Traumatic Stress Disorder and Viet Nam Veterans," Stephen M. Sonnenberg, Arthur S. Blank, Jr. and John Tabot, eds., *The Trauma of War: Stress and Recovery in Vietnam Veterans* (Washington, D.C.: American Psychiatric Press, 1985): 81–82. See also David Foy, et al., "Premilitary, Military and Postmilitary Factors in the Development of Post-Traumatic Stress Disorder," in *Behavior Therapist* 10.1 (1987): 3–9.

30. Scott, *PTSD*, 298; Hendin, 87.

31. Blank, 75–76.

32. American Psychiatric Association, *Diagnostic and Statistical Manual of Mental Disorders* (Washington, D.C.: American Psychiatric Association, 1980): 236.

33. Scott, *PTSD and Agent Orange*, 598.

34. Blank, 73–74.

35. Max Clelland, interview by telephone, 5 August 1994. See also James Thompson, "Strangers at Home: Vietnam Veterans since the War," *British Journal of Psychology* 65 (1992): 556.

36. Blank, 75.

37. Arthur Barham, interview, Aug. 9, 1994.

38. Laurie Goldstein, "Among Homeless Former Servicemen, War Evokes Cynicism, Pain and Pride," *Washington Post*, 31 January 1991: A3, A11.

39. Scott, *PTSD and Agent Orange*, 598–599.

40. Bob Adukoski, quoted in "Among Homeless Former Servicemen, War Evokes Cynicism, Pain and Pride," *Washington Post*, 31 Jan. 1991: A3.

41. Leepson, A20.

42. Arthur Barham, interview, 8 Aug. 1994.

43. Ben A. Franklin, "Panel Is Told V.A. Faces Deep Crisis," *New York Times*, 8 Sept. 1988, late ed., sec. 1:21.

44. John P. Murtha (D–Penn.), quoted in "Congressman Presses for Bill," *New York Times*, 29 May 1983, late ed., sec. 1:25.

45. Andree Brooks, "Effects of New Cutbacks," *New York Times*, 16 Feb. 1986, late ed., sec. 8:1.

46. United States Congress, House, *Hearings Before the Subcommittee on Housing and Memorial Affairs of the Committee of Veterans' Affairs*, 101 Cong., 2nd sess., Washington. GPO, 1990: 110.

47 *New York Times*, 18 Sept. 1990, late ed., A23; and *New York Times*, 27 Sept. 1992, late ed., sec. 1:17.

48. "Veteran Fighting Denial of Benefits," *New York Times*, 29 May 1983, late ed., sec. 1:25.

49. Leepson, A20.

50. Jason DeParle, "Aid for Homeless Focuses on Veterans," *New York Times*, 11 Nov. 1991: A8; and Diane Stepp, "Vet Saluted for Opening Doors," *Atlanta Journal and Constitution*, 21 July 1994, North Fulton Extra ed., J1.

51. John Wheeler, "Toting Up the Cost of the Gulf War," editorial, *The Atlanta Constitution*, 23 Feb. 1991: A19.

52. Paul Solotaroff, "Exile on Main Street," *Rolling Stone*, 24 June 1993: 66.

53. See Vietnam Veterans Workshop, Boston, *The Project to Shelter Homeless Veterans: Call to Action* (Boston: Vietnam Veterans Workshop, 1993).

54. Tom Lewis, "Honoring a Contract with Veterans," letter, *Washington Post*, 20 Mar. 1981: A22.

55. Solotaroff, 68.

56. Eric T. Dean, Jr., "The Unforgotten Vietnam Vet," letter, *New York Times*, 18 April 1991, late ed.: A25; Joseph R. Kurtz, Jr., letter, "Vietnam Veterans' Nonstop Con Game," *New York Times*, 10 March 1986, late ed., sec. 1:1; and Dyan Machan, "Nam Returnees Make Good," *Forbes*, 11 July 1988: 136. The article in *Forbes*, which inaccurately compared "shell shock" to PTSD, appears to have been part of a concerted campaign to defeat a veterans' spending bill then before congress.

57. John Behan, quoted in Jane Gross, "Veterans of Vietnam Gaining New Aid in Fighting Addiction," *New York Times*, 26 Dec. 1985: B6.

58. Singerman, A30; and Kim Hopper, quoted in Jason DeParle, "Aid for Homeless Focuses on Veterans," *New York Times*, 11 Nov. 1991, late ed.: A8.

59. Cerquone, 20.

60. United States Congress, 104.

61. United States Congress, 104, 110.

62. Solotaroff, 64.

63. United States Congress, 8-9.

64. Solotaroff, 68.

65. Robert Rosenheck, quoted in Patricia Edmonds, "Plight of the Homeless a Disgrace," *USA Today*, 28–31 May 1993: 1; and Robert Rosenheck, quoted in United States Congress, 18.

66. Louis Sahagun, "V.A. Hospital Assailed on Care for Homeless Vets," *Los Angeles Times*, 26 May 1989: A4.

67. Singerman and Somer, A30.

68. Michael Leaveck, quoted in Tamar Lewin, "Nation's Homeless Veterans Battle a New Foe: Defeatism," *New York Times*, 30 Dec. 1987, late ed.: A1.

69. United States Congress, 111; and James A. Magill, quoted in United States Congress, 104.

70. Lewin, A10; and Jim Schachter, "V.A. Being Pressed to Aid Legions of Homeless Veterans," *Los Angeles Times*, 7 March 1987: A24.

71. Spencer Rich, "Thousands of Homeless Deprived of U.S. Help," *Washington Post*, 29 Dec. 1984: A8.

72. Paul S. Egan, quoted in United States Congress, 110.

73. Harry N. Walters, quoted in Robert Pear, "U.S. Health Care for Veterans Cut in Budget Debate," *New York Times*, 27 Dec. 1985, late ed.: 1A.

74. Ben A. Franklin, "Director of Veterans Administration Steps Down," *New York Times*, 24 Jan. 1986, late ed.: A19.

75. Thomas K. Turnage, quoted in Jim Schachter, "V.A. Being Pressed to Aid Legions of Homeless Veterans," *Los Angeles Times*, 7 March 1987: A24.

76. Daniel R. Cloutier, quoted in Schachter, A24.

77. Arthur Barham, interview, 8 Aug. 1994.

78. Schacter, A24.

79. Paul S. Egan, quoted in United States Congress, 45 and 113.

80. William Crandell, interview, 5 Aug. 1994 and Phil Budahn, interview, 5 Aug. 1994.

81. Department of Housing and Urban Development, *Federal Plan to Break the Cycle of Homelessness* (Washington D.C., Department of Housing and Urban Development, 1994): 50.

82. Cerquone, 19.

83. Richard Fitzpatrick, quoted in Patricia Edmonds, *USA Today*, 25 Feb. 1994: 3.

84. James Brady, "Is Someone Being Conned?," editorial, *Advertising Age*, 26 April 1994: 30.

85. "House OKs Priority Treatment for Gulf War Veterans," *Congressional Quarterly* (1993): 3278; and Susan F. Willard, "The Gulf War Syndrome: The Unseen Enemy Lingers," *VFW*, March 1994: 24–26.

86. Patricia Edmonds, "After the War: Parade to Shelters," *USA Today*, 1 June 1993: 1.

87. Brad Crandell, interview, 5 Aug. 1994.

88. William Crandell, "What Did America Learn from the Winter Soldier Investigation?" in *The Viet Nam Generation* 5.1-4: 143. Crandell reminds us that Tom Paine could have been writing about Viet Nam veterans when, in his first *Crisis* paper, he wrote these familiar words: "These are the times that try men's souls. The summer soldier and the sunshine patriot will, in this crisis, shrink from the service of his country; but he that stands for it *now*, deserves the love and thanks of man and woman."

7. Managing the Elusive Veteran: Blank Page, Tripwire, or Interstate Nomad

TOBEY C. HERZOG

"He had realized he wanted to live. But how? How to live with the legacies of war, with his loss of faith, his guilt and nightmares?"

Philip Caputo, *Indian Country*

This quote from Caputo's aftermath novel raises a fundamental question for veterans: How do they live with, or reconcile, the legacies of their Viet Nam experience? The question has spawned a whole cottage industry as authors, literary critics, artists, dramatists, historians, psychologists, government officials, and sociologists, just to name a few, have been quick to suggest answers. But this quote also suggests a less explored but equally important corollary question: How does America live comfortably with the legacies of this war—especially with the veterans? Furthermore, within a literary context, the question becomes, How do authors and readers respond to characters who are veterans? An episode on television's *Northern Exposure* illustrates the pitfalls involved in coming to terms with these veterans. As Maurice— superpatriot, ex–Marine, and retired astronaut—tries to force a homeless man to leave Ciceley, Alaska, he discovers that the individual is a Vietnam veteran. Suddenly, Maurice's attitude toward the man changes as Maurice attempts to assuage his own sudden guilt by pulling out a wad of bills and an array of stereotypes to deal with the cause of this vet's sorry state: "Was it drugs, unemployment, PTSD?" Maurice confidently asks. As one might anticipate on this often bizarre but insightful show, the vet responds in an unpredictable way, one that emphasizes his humanity and individuality: a recent experience with a UFO has caused him to leave his job in a small town in Illinois for what he labels a "change of venue."

This exchange between Maurice and the veteran suggests in an odd way what this article is all about: Americans attempting to reconcile with trau-

113

matized Vietnam veterans' construct images of these individuals to fit myths, stereotypes, reality, or social, political, ideological, and literary agendas. In short, American society, authors, and readers try to manage, or control, these often troubling elusive figures by labeling them and assigning them simplistic and convenient roles. These responses and their outcomes, as well as the veterans' own ways of coping with their Vietnam experiences, are represented by three images—the blank page, the tripwire, and the interstate nomad— which are at the core of Philip Caputo's *Indian Country* and Larry Heinemann's *Paco's Story*.

In thinking of these various efforts to manage the Vietnam veteran, I am reminded of Chance Gardiner, the central character in Jerzy Kosinski's early '70s novel *Being There*, a satire about the effects of television on its viewers. Nurtured and educated solely by television, Chance, in his early thirties, lacks a character of his own. He responds to life simply by imitating what he has seen on television. But more significant is the way politicians, business people, the media, authors, and sophisticated society respond to Chance. True to his code name "Blank Page," supplied by the Soviet KGB, Chance becomes all things to all people. To satisfy their own agendas and to feel comfortable with this elusive individual, these people simply create their own character for Chance; they figuratively fill in the blank page labeled "Chance" with imagined characteristics ranging from those of an economic theorist, to an expert on the Soviet Union, to a potential vice presidential candidate.

The blank page metaphor is, I think, one appropriate way of understanding America's general efforts to live with elusive Vietnam veterans. Over the years, many of these veterans have remained blank pages for the rest of American society, the media, and even other veterans. These individuals or groups then fill in the page labeled "Vietnam Veteran" to entertain the public, to validate personal perceptions of these veterans, to fit widely held stereotypes, to promote ideologies, to assuage guilt, or to dismiss them from the American agenda (tear up the page). As a result, the labels and roles given to these veterans are myriad, conflicting, ever-changing, and often simplistic. For example, early in the war, 1965–1967, returning veterans were widely viewed as war heroes who had fought nobly to satisfy America's Cold War obsession with stemming the tide of communist aggression in Southeast Asia. From 1968 on, as domestic opposition to the war grew and Tet and My Lai shocked middle-class America, veterans "came to symbolize everything that was wrong with the war ... corrupted, tarnished, and ruined innocents" (Dean 61). After the fall of Saigon in 1975, hawks viewed the vets as losers, and a significant segment of American society labeled them dopers, baby killers, and psychotics. Later, in 1982, according to Harry Haines, the dedication of the Vietnam Veterans Memorial marked the beginning of various media's attempts to "reintegrate" the veterans as "timeless heroes" who had fought in an "inexplicable cause" (96). And more recently, in 1988, Vietnam veteran

William K. Lane, speaking for the self-styled normal, well-adjusted veterans, called for an end to media stereotypes of Vietnam veterans as "whining, acting nutty, or looking for a free ride" (24). But the labeling and appropriating continue today as different groups (Hollywood screenwriters, psychologists, liberals, conservatives, revisionist historians, literary critics, sociologists, authors, readers, and veterans themselves) take their turns at semantically, socially, and psychologically managing the elusive Vietnam veteran to fit various agendas or to assuage America's guilt or confusion.

The result of these attempts at filling in the blank page is a collage of conflicting images and labels (all things to all people): Vietnam veterans as "sick" vets, criminals, drug abusers, agents of violence, paraplegics, guilt-laden sufferers of PVS, violent individuals in the throes of PTSD, victims of Agent Orange, mythic figures, archetypes, trauma survivors, veterans similar to or different from veterans of other wars, African Americans, Hispanics, whites, women, antiwar protesters, crybabies, forgotten patriots, good soldiers, heroes, and well-adjusted citizens. The list goes on and on. Uniting these diverse categories is what Foucault would describe as America's preoccupation with the Vietnam veteran so he or she can be "managed, inserted into systems of utility, regulated for the greater good of all, made to function according to an optimum" (quoted in Bibby, 159). Perhaps the ultimate symbol of this management might be found in the Vietnam Veterans Memorial in Washington, D.C. Without question this impressive and moving memorial, whose presence is the result of veterans' own efforts to have it erected, has done much to heal the psychic trauma of the war for both veterans and the American public. But unintentionally the black granite with its 58,000-plus names has evolved into a another convenient way for some segments of American society to manage emotionally and intellectually the war and its participants. For some people, these names and dates of American deaths in Viet Nam confine the war and its fallout to this physical space. The inscriptions also give form and meaning to this formless war by reconstructing a definite beginning, middle, and end to the war and by presenting the American soldiers as heroes dying in a just cause.

On a literary level, the procedures and outcomes for this social, psychological, and historical management may, perhaps, be suggested by two additional images to fill in the blank page of the veteran. One image is familiar, the other relatively obscure. Both are associated with PTSD, which congressional studies suggest afflicts 479,000 of America's 3.5 million Vietnam veterans (Witteman 77); both represent veterans' physical and psychological responses to living with Vietnam's aftermath, and both further reinforce the perception of these veterans as conundrums. The first, that of the tripwire veteran, is an image of withdrawal into a defined protected space and is associated with real tripwire veterans who have isolated themselves from society. As noted in numerous news articles and even a Broadway play (Lanford

Wilson's 1993 drama *Redwood Curtain)*, these veterans are living in remote areas, such as the wilds of Alaska, the jungles of Hawaii, the backwoods of Maine, the sequoia forest of Northern California, or the deep woods of Washington's Olympic Peninsula. In an article on the tripwire veterans of the Olympic Peninsula, Larry Heinemann describes them in the following way:

> In Viet Nam, a tripwire was sometimes attached to noisemakers a good distance from the encampment—an early warning device.... If you think "early warning device," the tripwire metaphor clicks. Think of the tripwire as the distance that many Vietnam veterans seem to maintain ["Just Don't Fit" 56].

The other more obscure and complex image, that of the interstate nomad, is associated with cross-country drifters. As far as I can determine, use of this image first occurs in two passages in Caputo's *Indian Country* where veteran Chris Starkmann twice fantasizes about escaping the war's fallout by wandering America's interstate highways:

> ...He could move from one town to the next, eating in fast-food restaurants, sleeping in chain motels, an Interstate nomad, a citizen of the fringes, unnoticed, unremembered, unknown [87].

> Often, he renewed his fantasy of becoming an Interstate nomad, surviving on hamburgers and tacos. Interstate 95, Interstate 10, Interstate 65—there were dozens of them, a concrete trailwork forty thousand miles long, a country unto itself, a domain of strangers [339].

Both of these metaphors—the tripwire and the interstate nomad—symbolize troubled veterans' quests for isolation and anonymity, but on another level, within the Vietnam aftermath novels *Indian Country* and *Paco's Story*, these two images highlight authors', readers', and society's ability or inability to fill in the blank page, to manage these veterans, and to relegate them to a comfortable place in the American psyche. Sometimes this process works; at other times the process of social, psychological, and literary management fails—and for good reason. Let's look more closely at these two literary representations in Caputo's and Heinemann's novels.

For both Caputo and readers of *Indian Country*, filling in the blank page for Chris Starkmann, Vietnam veteran, is relatively easy and thus undercuts the overall emotional impact of this novel. Starkmann becomes an all-too-familiar figure within the media and literary landscape of the Vietnam aftermath. He has been traumatized by his participation in the war, by his resulting strained relationship with his father (a minister and antiwar activist), and by a mental breakdown while serving in Viet Nam. But Chris, as readers learn late in the novel, also carries with him a deep, dark secret from the war and a heavy dose of guilt: Chris was unintentionally responsible for the death of his boyhood friend during a chaotic battle. Ten years after his return from the war, he desperately seeks his father's forgiveness and his country's acceptance in the form of a welcome home: "Welcome home, son. Say it, damn you" (263). As a result of carrying this psychic baggage ["Though he was done with the war, it was not done with him, the war had started again" (112)], Chris exhibits a textbook case of Post–Traumatic Stress Disorder. In fact, it's interesting to catalogue just how many of the classic symptoms Caputo is able to work into Chris's behavior: survivor guilt, flashbacks to the battlefield, nostalgia for Viet Nam, hallucinations in the form of conversations with dead friends, paranoia, nightmares, bizarre behavior, violent actions against others, a wariness of people, depression, alcohol abuse, sleep disorders, nervousness, strained relationships with his wife and children, an obsessive quest for order in his life, and an overriding desire for isolation from people.

Late in the novel, this obsession with keeping people at a distance and with mastering his environment takes Chris into the world of the tripwire veteran and distinguishes him from other veterans suffering from PTSD. The unemployed timber cruiser brings the physical landscape of Viet Nam to his house and forty acres located in an isolated area of Michigan's Upper Peninsula. He turns his property into a physical and psychological sanctuary—a Viet Nam base camp complete with barbed wire ringing the perimeter, foxholes, a reinforced gate at the entrance to the property, a garage converted into a command bunker, perimeter patrols, and imaginary conversations with his dead combat buddies from the war. Such a sanctuary recreates the real tripwire vets' "hard camps" in the Olympic Peninsula as described by Heinemann: "One man said he knew of five places around the state of Washington where groups of veterans and their families lived in 'hard camps' tricked out with bunkers, tunnels, barbed-wire perimeters that had been booby-trapped, and cleared fields of fire" ("'Just Don't Fit'," 57). But before Chris can commit suicide in this sanctuary, he is brought under control—returned to mainstream society through a combination of his wife's love and understanding, a V.A. psychologist's insight into Chris's problems, and Chris's own efforts to heal himself.

The end of Chris's successful quest to find a spiritual *home*, symbolically the last word in the book, marks a convenient and somewhat unsatisfactory finish to Caputo's and readers' efforts to fill in the blank page for this veteran and to group him with others. By the end of the novel, Caputo leaves readers with a comfortable character type. Such a description may seem odd for a veteran whose behavior and psychological demons have been so bizarre and disturbing throughout the novel. But Chris's actions fall into widely documented categories of behavior for Vietnam veterans. Thus, the perspective of Chris's character is permanently fixed, a tripwire veteran suffering from a named and documented disorder: "There were ... thousands of veterans suffering from something he [the psychologist] called Post-Traumatic Stress Disorder, which he described as a delayed reaction to terrible experiences that had happened five, ten, even fifteen years in the past" (321).

As a result, like Chris's wife when she hears the diagnosis, readers also take comfort in this diagnosis: "To be able to identify it [Chris's behavior] lessened its power to frighten her" (321). Furthermore, within the novel, Chris has become less menacing to society. As a tripwire veteran erecting physical barriers to keep society out, he has also literally and figuratively fenced himself in by following quite closely the familiar behavior of tripwire veterans suffering from PTSD. By physically confining himself to his sanctuary, he has allowed society to manage him "for the greater good of all" and perhaps to dismiss his aberrant behavior because it has a name. Captured physically, psychologically, and semantically, he is not free to haunt society. Therefore, this elusive veteran has been stalked, tagged, and managed. For readers, he represents the post–Vietnam Memorial view of the traumatized veteran as hero, simply because his role is defined, he is reconnected with society (if only through a label), and his life becomes a lesson for others. He's not roaming the literal and metaphysical interstate as he once fantasized. Reconciliation has occurred. Readers can put the war and Chris Starkmann out of their minds, or at least into a convenient category of understanding and character type.

Shifting this scrutiny of America's social and literary control of the elusive veteran to Larry Heinemann's 1986 aftermath novel, *Paco's Story*, we move from a fixed perspective of Chris Starkmann as a tripwire veteran to conflicting perspectives of the enigmatic Vietnam veteran Paco Sullivan as an interstate nomad. Like Starkmann, Sullivan has survived a traumatic tour of duty with the Army—the only survivor from Alpha Company at the massacre at Firebase Harriette. Also, Paco, like Chris, is on a quest to escape his psychological demons as he seeks a physical and spiritual home: "He wants to discover a livable peace, as if he's come ... upon a comfortable cabin" (174). He, too, keeps people at a physical and emotional distance. But here the similarities with Starkmann end. Paco is a mystery, a veteran who resists easy classification and management by society, the author, and readers. As the more enigmatic of the two literal and figurative interstate nomads appearing in this novel (but never specifically labeled as such), Paco roams America's landscape and collective conscience. He hides within society rather than away from it. Existing in an anonymity that both haunts and threatens society and readers, Paco travels across the country via an "interstate bus" (40). Heinemann's novel, which describes one of Paco's brief stops in the small anywhere town of Boone, evokes shifting perspectives of this Vietnam veteran from townspeople and readers as they unsuccessfully fill in the blank page of Paco Sullivan, interstate nomad.

The least interesting, most conspicuous, and most easily categorized of these two interstate nomads is Jesse, a drifter who arrives one day at the Texas Lunch where Paco washes dishes. During Jesse's few hours in Boone, this veteran, who has heard about the massacre at Firebase Harriette, talks openly (in between glances at the nearby interstate) about his tour of duty, media coverage of the war, a proposed Vietnam Veterans Memorial, and his interstate travels: "I've thumbed my ass from one end of this continent to the other" (150). With his brash statements, comic hyperbole, outspoken anti-establishment feelings, Jesse is a quasi–interstate nomad who easily falls into the category of the disaffected, cynical veteran on a never-ending journey "looking for a place to cool out" (155). Jesse's final piece of advice to Paco, his fellow veteran and nomad, is about hitchhiking: "Stick to the interstates. Local roads are for yokels and rookies and yobboes" (160).

In contrast, Heinemann intentionally avoids giving readers the comfort of categorizing Paco the way readers confidently fill in the blank page for Jesse and the way Caputo allows other characters and readers to fill in the blank page for Starkmann. Instead, Paco remains for readers, other characters, and even Heinemann a curiosity and mystery throughout the book. He is not the romanticized troubled veteran—diagnosed, cured, and restored to society. Rather, he is the pre–Vietnam Memorial veteran, the true interstate nomad who resists precise characterization and remains physically within society but psychologically outside. What readers don't know about Paco is just as significant as what they do know. What they do know is that he initially fits the mold of the classic *silent* drifter-hero right out of a Hollywood western movie. He arrives in Boone because he has run out of money. His appearance is marked by his slight build, numerous physical scars, a pronounced limp, an ever-present black hickory cane, and the familiar 1,000-meter stare of someone who has experienced heavy combat. Responding to the wearisome question of "Why do you have that cane?" he tersely replies, "wounded in the war." Unlike the loquacious Jesse, Paco, for the most part, keeps his thoughts and personal information to himself. And because readers receive only limited information about Paco from the narrator, a ghost from Paco's combat unit, readers remain as uncomfortable with Paco as the residents of Boone. But readers' discomfort and their difficulty in filling the blank page for this interstate nomad are distinguishing features of Heinemann's novel and make this work successful as a powerful and complex portrait of the elusive veteran.

Initially, readers' sympathies firmly reside with Paco as the townspeople express their cruel and stereotyped perspectives of Paco, in particular, and Vietnam veterans, in general. Responses of Boone's inhabitants, old and young, include ignorance ("What war was that?" [75]); derision ("slug" [115] and "gimpy deadbeat" [65]); distrust ("a body hears too many stories as to how they [veterans] go acting so peculiar" [84]); contempt ("Them Vietnam boys sure do think you owe them something, don't they?" [85]); and even sexual fantasies ("she would lay her head on his [Paco's] shoulder and stroke the scars of his belly" [101]). Furthermore, the ghost of Alpha Company does his best to present Paco in a sympathetic light. He focuses on Paco's war-related scars covering his body and on the permanent pain from his wounds, which require an endless cycle of anti-depressants and muscle relaxants to help him endure his waking hours and sleep at night. Also, according to the narrator, Paco stoically accepts his fate ("but Paco, for all his trouble, has never asked, Why me?" [136] and is glad to be alive ("But I'll tell you something else: I'm just glad to be here'" [163]).

With all this evidence, readers nearing the end of the novel may believe that, like the citizens of Boone, they have filled in the blank page for this Vietnam veteran. Perhaps he can be comfortably labeled the good soldier victimized by the war. Traumatized by his combat experiences and treated shabbily by an ungrateful country, he stoically endures—another familiar version of the Vietnam veteran as hero. But Paco is elusive. He cannot be so easily managed and inserted into more conventional categories for veterans. Revelations by the narrator, as well as the actual filled-in blank page of another character's diary, shake readers' constructs of Paco.

The first piece of conflicting information jolts readers like an unexpected mortar round. It contains an apocalyptic heart-of-darkness experience involving Paco's participation in the rape and brutalization of a "hard-core" V.C. girl who had participated in the ambush of an American night listening-post. As described by the ghost, also a participant, this episode is the conventional atrocity scene found in various forms in so many narratives. But the ghost's narrative, shockingly detailed and matter-of-factly related, is one of the most disturbing and frightening in all the Vietnam narratives. It reveals the evil side of humans out of control and sinking into a brutish state. Also disconcerting is the fact that Paco, the good soldier, is a willing participant in the abhorrent act. Furthermore, a few pages later, the narrator reveals more information about Paco that undercuts the sympathetic view of Paco as a victim of violence and trauma and suggests that he may be an agent of his own depressing fate. We learn about Paco's job in Alpha Company as the fearless and expert "booby-trap" man who after going off alone to set up his various "mechanical ambushes" would be able to "kill another man, unseen, and still sleep profoundly" (194). Or within the same brief war story, the ghost describes Paco's face-to-face encounter with one of his wounded, helpless victims that ends with Paco calmly taking his fillet knife and "first pricking the skin, then stabbing down firmly—like cutting into a hard, warm cheese" (195).

Finally, as perspectives of Paco continue to shift, Heinemann once more shakes readers' comfort level with Paco through another narrative twist, a character sketch of Paco from someone other than the ghost. A page from the diary of a young woman, Cathy, who has a room next to Paco's at the local boarding house, presents another view of Paco. Their relationship involving sexual fantasies and sexual mind games has been carried on from a distance without any human contact, as Cathy has relished the mental and sexual torment she has been causing Paco. Out of frustration, Paco sneaks into Cathy's room. While rifling through her clothes (a symbolic rape), he discovers a diary entry revealing Cathy's immaturity, sexual fantasies, and insensitivity. The diary also, however, portrays Paco in an unflattering way as this quasi-author describes the veteran's nightly rituals of cheap booze, pills, and erratic behavior:

> He gets up in the morning, dresses. Clean, dirty, it's all the same to him. Goes to work, doesn't talk much with anyone. He gets this set look on his face. Gives me the creeps. Unc says he wonders if the guy knows where he is half the time. He'll sneak back across the street in the afternoon and have himself a drink [206].

Finally, Cathy's filled-in page contains the disturbing comment "he's a dingy, dreary, smelly, shabby, *shabby*, little man" (205).

As the novel ends, a frustrated and disillusioned Paco, AWOL bag in hand, boards the interstate bus to leave Boone. At the same time, frustrated and disillusioned readers ponder the accumulated revelations about Paco. Whose portrait of Paco is accurate—the ghost's, Cathy's, the townspeople's? Is Paco the traumatized hero stoically attempting to live with his mental and physical wounds from the war? Or is he merely a pathetic, contemptible, or even dangerous figure whose 1,000-meter stare, drug use, alcohol abuse, anti-social behavior, and violent acts during the war justify the townspeople's ridicule and fear: "creeps like him [Paco] are best got rid of" (206)? What is the answer? In a book where overt political or social messages from the author are deliberately avoided and where the focus is on characters and their interaction, or lack of interaction, Paco Sullivan, Vietnam veteran and interstate nomad, remains a puzzle. At one moment he seems a tragic victim; at another an agent of his own fate. And Paco's taciturnity only adds to the confusion. Unlike the comfortable and simplistic ending to *Indian Country*, resolution of these conflicts in *Paco's Story* does not happen, and integration of this veteran into American society through classification and healing does not occur. Heinemann intentionally—a warning?—leaves unresolved society's and readers' relationships with this veteran. Paco remains spiritually outside society, unmanaged, uncontrolled, and unreconciled. For this reason, the novel disturbs readers because it does not reinforce conventional constructs of the Vietnam veteran. Readers are purposely left with questions and uneasiness as the mystery figure heads west on the interstate: "[he] is soon gone" (209), the last phrase in this novel. Paco, then, is the "homeless" and elusive interstate nomad. He still haunts America's highways, disturbing the collective psyche and thwarting efforts to control him "for the greater good of all" and to assuage America's guilt about the war and its survivors. Paco can be neither managed nor dismissed. As Heinemann intended, Paco remains an elusive, complex individual rather than a simple, comfortable type. Perhaps his interstate wanderings will eventually even take him to Ciceley, Alaska, for a "change of venue" where he also will make Maurice uncomfortable.

Works Cited

Bibby, Michael. "'Where Is Vietnam?' Antiwar Poetry and the Canon." *College English* 55 (1993): 158–78.

Caputo, Philip. *Indian Country*. 1987. New York: Bantam, 1988.

Dean, Eric. "The Myth of the Troubled and Scorned Vietnam Veteran." *Journal of American Studies* 26 (1992): 59–74.

Haines, Harry. "They Were Called and They Went: The Political Rehabilitation of the Vietnam Veteran." *From Hanoi to Hollywood: The Vietnam War in American Film*. Eds. Linda Dittmar and Gene Michaud. New Brunswick, N.J.: Rutgers University Press, 1990. 81–100.

Heinemann, Larry. "'Just Don't Fit': Stalking the Elusive 'Tripwire' Veteran." *Harper's*, April 1985: 55–63.

_____. *Paco's Story*. 1986. New York: Penguin, 1987.

Kosinski, Jerzy N. *Being There*. New York: Harcourt Brace, 1971.

Lane, William K. Jr. "Vietnam Vets Without Hollywood, Without Tears." *The Wall Street Journal*, 26 July 1988: A24.

Witteman, Paula A. "Lost in America." *Time*, 11 Feb. 1991: 76–77.

8. "To Live in the Past Is to Walk in Darkness": Reconciliation in the Return Journey

CATHERINE CALLOWAY

Thinking that he had successfully placed his Vietnam War experiences in the past, William Broyles, Jr. visited the Vietnam Veterans Memorial during its 1982 dedication in Washington, D.C., only to discover "that other names weren't there—the names of the men and women we fought, our enemies" (12) and that "the war was still in [him], like a buried piece of shrapnel [that] works its way to the surfaces" (13). Broyles has not been alone in his act of self-discovery: Associated Press reporter Hugh A. Mulligan documents his return to Viet Nam twenty years after the war in two recent reports;[1] Morley Safer chronicles his 1989 journey to Southeast Asia in *Flashbacks: On Returning to Vietnam*; Neil Sheehan details his 1989 visits to both North and South Viet Nam with his wife in *After the War Was Over: Hanoi and Saigon*;[2] and in a recent *Newsweek* column Jack Estes recounts the visit that he made to Viet Nam with his wife and children to look for an old Vietnamese friend and to deal with his painful war memories (10). Another veteran, Roger Camp, a former Marine who served in Viet Nam in the late 1960s, has returned to Viet Nam to live indefinitely, advocating that a postwar trip to Southeast Asia can be "the best therapy" for veterans (Gray 1C, 10C). As the growing number of feature articles, personal memoirs, and other literary works indicates, only in the past decade or so have the effects of the Viet Nam war on its survivors been most penetratingly examined. Particularly relevant in society and literature today is the subject of the aftermath of the war, its lingering effects on both Viet Nam and the United States, and the attempts of both Vietnamese and Americans to reconcile the numerous aspects of their involvement in Southeast Asia's lengthy conflict.

In a 1971 essay, "When We Dead Awaken: Writing as Re-Vision," Adrienne Rich invents the term "re-vision" to describe "the act of looking back, of seeing with fresh eyes, of entering an old text from a new critical direction"

123

(18). While Rich uses this term in regard to a woman's sexual identity and self-knowledge (18), the concept can be applied to Viet Nam, the war, as well as to the literature that has resulted from that war. America's involvement in Southeast Asia is a text which Americans must continually approach anew and reevaluate from a fresh and present perspective. Like Rich's concept of looking at women in literature and life through "fresh eyes," Americans must also re-examine their roles in Viet Nam from new angles of vision, thus broadening the scope of the war experience. As Rich states, it "is for us more than a chapter in cultural history: it is an act of survival" (18).

Many veterans who served in Viet Nam only wanted to forget about the war when they first returned from Southeast Asia. For instance, Lynn Hampton, who served as a combat nurse in 1967, comments that when she returned from Southeast Asia, "Like most everyone else at the time, I pretty much locked the door on Vietnam and threw away the key" (207). However, Viet Nam has proven itself to be a door that will not stay locked. In fact, "I don't have control of Viet Nam; Viet Nam has control of me" has become a common phrase echoed by many who served in Viet Nam. The attempt to reconcile the experience of Vietnam has by no means been an easy one. The "smooth, orderly arc from war to peace" (184) that Paul Berlin, the protagonist of Tim O'Brien's novel, *Going After Cacciato*, desires is as elusive in fact as it is in fiction,[3] but the basic form for this journey remains the same. More and more frequently, the act of reconciliation takes the form of a journey—not only a psychological one, but also a literal trip to the very land where the war's ghosts and shadows have haunted both Americans and Vietnamese.

The writers of personal narratives and memoirs about the war reveal different reasons for making return trips, but whatever their reasons, their journeys ultimately contribute to the act of healing. In *Brothers in Arms: A Journey from War to Peace*, William Broyles, Jr. states that he returned to Viet Nam for several reasons: "to answer the question: 'What does it mean to go to war?' ... to find a man I never knew—my enemy ... and to find the pieces of myself I had left there, and to try to put the war behind me" (255). Broyles metaphorically acknowledges that facing only what the war meant to the American soldiers would not be adequate: "I had to reach farther. I had to reach out in that tunnel and try to touch that other man. To know myself I had to know my enemy" (13).

As a result of his return to Viet Nam, Broyles has come to accept the Vietnamese people as human beings like himself. For example, when he finally confronts an "old enemy" (142), a former North Vietnamese company commander named Hien, he is surprised to find that Hien is "a slight, polite man with brown eyes as gentle as a deer's" (142–143), and after talking with one Vietnamese widow, whose husband may well have been killed by Broyles' own platoon, Broyles sees the difference between the enemy as "an abstraction" (202) and "as a man with parents, a wife, children..." (202). When

Broyles views photographs of young North Vietnamese soldiers enjoying such typical activities as reading mail from loved ones, challenging each other at games, and playing musical instruments, he realizes that the Viet Cong were very similar to the American soldiers (237). Both the Viets and the Americans were "young men sent to war, trying to stay alive, savoring anything that reminded them of home" (Broyles 237). Moreover, in general the postwar Vietnamese do not seem to feel bitter or cynical toward Americans. Expecting to be greeted with "a mixture of curiosity and hostility" (114), Broyles is surprised to be treated hospitably:

> It was as if some giant switch had been thrown and everyone, from government ministers to peasants, suddenly stopped fighting Americans and began courting them. War? What war? We are friends, friends, friends... [114].

In fact, one Viet colonel, Pham Tuan, even desires to share a space "mission with Americans, with the sort of men he once took such joy in shooting down" (Broyles 51). Another Viet official makes a toast "To peace!" (102), informing Broyles that he is "the first [American] to come [to Viet Nam] as a friend" (102).

Another revelation to Broyles is the high cost of the war to the Vietnamese. According to one Viet official, 9 million unexploded "mines and bombs" have been located since the war, with thousands of people killed or wounded as a result (Broyles 155). In addition, Broyles notes the plight of the Amerasian children who are also victims, "a living link to the past" (169). "We Americans were gone," states Broyles, "but we had left behind a new generation neither American nor Viet—outsiders, wearing history on their faces" (169–170). He learns, too, that the subject of reconciliation is as important in Viet Nam as it is in America. After the war, the Communist Party had to persuade the South Viets, whose loved ones had been tortured and murdered by the Viet Cong, "that reconciliation [between the North and South] was right" (Broyles 180).

Perhaps one of the most startling discoveries that Broyles makes is that he and his enemies share a love of warfare. "War is the only utopian experience most of us ever have," Broyles writes (190); "Men love war because it is a game, a brutal, deadly game, the only game that counts. War is the thrill of a great challenge..." (191). Broyles acknowledges that whether he actually killed anyone or not does not really matter. What really counts is that he worked hard in his attempts to kill the enemy. Both Broyles and the Vietnamese love the beauty of war that can coexist with the dark side of themselves, the side that loves war, no matter how ugly or at what cost to human life (190). If one had to die in a war, then a firefight after dark, with its red and green tracers dotting the landscape, would have been a lovely environment to have died in (Broyles 194).

Larry Rottmann, another combat veteran, documents his journey to the former site of the war in two accounts, "A Hundred Happy Sparrows: An American Veteran Returns to Vietnam," a diary-like essay published in *Vietnam Generation* in 1989, and *Voices From the Ho Chi Minh Trail*, a collection of poems published in 1993 that reiterates the main ideas of the earlier essay. Like Broyles, Rottmann also had several purposes for returning to Viet Nam. Two decades after he left the war, Rottmann returned to Southeast Asia "as a university scholar in search of materials for [his] Vietnam Literature class, as a father who felt a growing responsibility for the children of Southeast Asia, and as a veteran still trying to find answers to many questions about the war, not the least of which is 'Why?'" (113). Although not all of his questions were immediately answered, "It was a journey during which [he] ultimately learned as much about [himself] as [he] did about Viet Nam" (Rottmann, "A Hundred" 115).

Rottmann's two accounts effectively contrast the differences between Viet Nam "then" and Viet Nam "now." In both the essay and the poetry, Rottmann indicates that he is surprised by the beauty of the tranquil Vietnamese countryside, now devoid of the harsh sounds of warfare. In "Noise," he writes,

> ...it's totally astonishing
> to be in a Viet Nam of peace and quiet.
> To hear everywhere not the horrible
> din of war,
> but natural sounds [*lines 17–21*].

> The songs of birds...
> the ripple of water...
> ...the lilt of raindrops;
> the tinkle of bicycle bells...
> the jesting of men; the banter of women;
> the laughter of children;
> the murmurs of prayer [*lines 22–28*, Voices 77].

Rottmann is surprised as well by the children who ask him "about Disneyland" ("A Hundred" 129) instead of American war atrocities; by the youth in general, who are optimistic and happy in spite of such postwar problems as unemployment, poor transportation, and inadequate educational and medical facilities; and by the clean, orderly towns and cities with their subtle, yet not so subtle, reminders of the war—flower pots fashioned from old bomb casings, culinary equipment made from aircraft aluminum, and, of course, people deformed and scarred from war injuries ("A Hundred" 137). The friendliness of most of the people encountered by Rottmann also astonishes him. In "This Time," he notes that

It is a good trip.
People smile and want to talk, instead of fleeing in fear.
They look me in the eye, man-to-man, woman-to-man.
Equals [*lines 14–17*, Voices *75*).

A turning point in Rottmann's journey is his visit to the mausoleum containing the body of Ho Chi Minh, a crucial experience that defines for him the purpose of his return to Viet Nam. "It is time," he says, "to actively start seeking the resolution I've been drawn back to Indochina for" ("A Hundred" 123). Like Broyles, Rottmann needs to meet his former enemy, whom he now views as "real people" ("A Hundred" 132), face-to-face: "I want to meet these folks. To hold them. Touch them. Smell their life and sweat. I want to know they are alive … I need to be reassured that we didn't kill or poison them all" ("A Hundred" 132–133). Before he leaves Viet Nam, Rottmann is ready to "re-vision" the war, to think "about what [he] might do in the future regarding Vietnam, rather than continuing to dwell so extensively—to live so exclusively—in that bitter and confusing period of the past" ("A Hundred" 138). In a poem appropriately entitled "Reconciliation," written after his return to the United States, Rottmann writes,

I've been too busy since I got back
to examine whether or not I've gained any valuable new perspectives.
But last night, for the first time ever,
I had a dream about Vietnam at peace [*lines 5–8*, Voices *119*].

The literary work by a combat veteran that deals most extensively with a postwar return to Viet Nam is Frederick Downs' *No Longer Enemies, Not Yet Friends*. A combat officer in Viet Nam in 1967, Downs made not one but five return trips to Southeast Asia between 1987 and 1989 for humanitarian reasons. His left arm missing as a result of the war, Downs was asked to return to Viet Nam with General John Vessey twenty years after his war experiences to open dialogue with the Vietnamese, to gather information about the POW/MIA situation, and to analyze "the conditions which affected the care and rehabilitation of the disabled in Viet Nam, particularly in the area of prosthetic fitting and fabrication" (105).

Like other veterans, Downs had mixed emotions about returning:

All my adult life has been affected by Viet Nam the country, and Vietnam the war. My wife asked me once, not too long after I had given a speech on combat leadership, if I would ever be able to let go of Vietnam. I was surprised at the question. I had never thought about it that way. I had often wondered about the question from the other side, though: Would Vietnam ever let go of me? [6].

At first Downs was not sure that he wanted to help the Vietnamese people, for whom he lacked respect. On the one hand, he states,

> I felt no love for the Vietnamese and thought of them as the enemy, the "dinks" I used to fight against who had killed and wounded so many of my friends.... To my way of thinking, the Vietnamese were evil ghouls who for years had continued to torment the families of our missing in action and prisoners of war.
> I had hated the Vietnamese for years [Downs 18].

Upon noticing the "large number of [Vietnamese] Hero cemeteries" (40), Downs felt pleasure: "They were proof that we had hurt them badly during the war" (40). On the other hand, he felt "strangely drawn to Viet Nam, and ... wanted to help the Vietnamese people" (Downs 20), asking himself, "Were these people really still my enemy?" (Downs 52).

During his five trips to Viet Nam, Downs had numerous opportunities to interact with the Viets and, in doing so, made a number of important discoveries. He learned to identify with the Viets whom he now viewed "as soldiers [rather] than as enemies" (Downs 92), to acknowledge the "personal dignity" and humanity of the disabled (Downs 164), to release his hatred, and to accept "them as a people" (Downs 223) whose suffering should not be ignored. After all, "the disableds' personal misery took precedence over the politics of the country" (Downs 245). For the first time Downs realized that villages were more "than a cluster of meaningless primitive mud and straw huts" (293). "I knew people lived in the 'hootches,'" he writes, "but I never thought of them as homes" (Downs 293). While in Viet Nam, he also noted the tremendous sacrifices incurred by the South during the war, when their homes and land were bombarded with "millions of artillery shells ... bombs, rockets, and bullets" and people were forced to relocate in "resettlement camps ... refugees within their own country" (Downs 301). Like Broyles, Downs learned that the Viets had their own difficulties with reconciliation when the war was over. As one Viet delegate told him,

> So many families were on different sides of the revolution that family and friends and neighbors were split. A neighbor who killed a man's son during the war, regardless of which side the other was on, could not have blood revenge taken out on him by the son's family. So there was a lot of work to be done in reconciling the differences between the two sides [Downs 290].

A particularly meaningful experience occurred when Downs entertained a member of the North delegation in his own home in Maryland, an event which forced both the American and the Viets "to turn away from the past and look toward the future" (317). When the Viet gentleman held Downs' colicky child and sang soothingly to her, Downs thought about how "as individuals" both he and the Viet "could become friends" (318). The importance of family in each country was realized by both Downs and his visitor. While in Downs' home, the North Viet man admitted that America did not fit the stereotype assigned to it by the Viets. "'I had been told,' he stated, [that] America was preoccupied with sex, had a high crime rate, was an unruly, violent country, and cared nothing for the family. I feel my visits with Americans in their homes have shown me the family is very important. American families truly seem to care for each other'" (Downs 347). Likewise, Downs learned that his guest cared deeply for his own family. When Downs listened to the man discuss the recent death of his own wife, Downs "was stunned to see tears well up in [the man's] eyes" (321). Downs was even more surprised to find that his guest's compassion extended to the American nation at large. When Downs took the man to see the Vietnam Veterans Memorial in Washington, D.C., his visitor, who had been a surgeon for the North during the war, later remarked, "You know, even though I never held a gun or shot at an American, I feel somehow responsible for those names on the wall" (334). Such a comment caused Downs to reevaluate his own previously uncharitable thoughts about the Viet hero cemeteries and helped him to realize that "the real tragedy [of Viet Nam] was that, despite everything that had occurred, neither the Americans nor the Vietnamese were happy with the end result" (390).

A return has been necessary for other people who served in the war, not just for the combat soldier. The many women who served have also found return journeys necessary. According to Kathryn Marshall, editor of *In the Combat Zone: Vivid Personal Recollections of the Vietnam War from the Women Who Served There*, several of the women that she interviewed eventually returned to Viet Nam. Debbie Wong, who went to Viet Nam as a civilian, returned to Viet Nam before the war was over (Marshall 24), and Marjorie Nelson, a doctor who treated Vietnamese civilians during the war, has made two return visits to Viet Nam (Marshall 157). Linda and Murray Hiebert, Mennonites who were teachers and administrative workers during the war, have returned to Viet Nam almost a dozen times (Marshall 115).

Two combat nurses, Lynn Hampton and Lynda Van Devanter, who have written book length accounts of their Viet Nam experiences, also felt the need to return. For Lynn Hampton, author of *The Fighting Strength*, visiting Viet Nam twenty years after her war experiences was a means of catching up to Viet Nam before it caught up to her. For years after her return to the United States, Hampton experienced a "'psychic numbing'" (217) and emotional desensitization and dreamed frequently of the war. In 1983 when her religious beliefs led her to volunteer "for medical teams to help the refugees in Central America" (226), Hampton felt that one of her purposes in life "was carrying the ministry of reconciliation" (226). This reconciliation eventually led her from El Salvador to Viet Nam in 1988, where, disguised as another veteran tourist, she secretly worked on the problem of American prisoners of war by writing messages on Vietnamese currency in the hope that some Viets would capitalize on the idea of a reward and provide valid information on the plight of missing American servicemen. Hampton's narrative, published three years later, ends with an account of her journey but offers no evidence as to whether or not her plan worked. However, she implies that merely having tried to help the POW situation provided her with a feeling of satisfaction and helped her to heal from the psychological wounds of her war experiences.

Lynda Van Devanter, a well-known nurse and veteran, also felt a need to return to Viet Nam.[4] In the epilogue of her acclaimed personal narrative, *Home Before Morning*, she recounts her journey back to Southeast Asia in 1982 as one of nine veterans whose purpose as a delegation was "to try to open dialogue with the Vietnamese" about three problems from the war: the effects of Agent Orange, the plight of Amerasian children still on Vietnamese soil, and the resolution of the issue of Americans missing in action after the war (361–362). Recalls Van Devanter, "our task was very different from the one we'd had so many years earlier. Then, we went as warriors. This time, we came in peace" (361). While nervous about the effects that the trip would have on her and her war memories, Van Devanter found her experience to be a positive one. Instead of finding the Viets to be hostile to the American delegation, the U.S. visitors were greeted warmly. Similarly, Van Devanter realized that she liked the Viets, whom she could suddenly recognize as "individuals" with a rich artistic culture and historical heritage instead of only "extensions of a war" (368). According to Van Devanter,

> I began to grasp a feeling for the people and the country that had never been available to me before. War destroys so many things, and one of the first to go is the ability to think of the enemy as human beings with a history and a future. If you do so, then it will not be possible to destroy them and their land. You must depersonalize someone to kill him, and that is what the war had done to all of us. We were now finally having the opportunity to see each other as humans. It was an important step for me [371].

When she realized that the Viets "were people, just like" the many American individuals in her life (373), Van Devanter could cry tears of relief and realize that the war was truly over for her. "It wasn't Vietnam that sucked," she states. "It was the war. I wanted to come back here to find something I had left, and I just found it. It was my youth, my innocence. I know now that I can never get them back, but I've touched them, and it's okay" (Van Devanter 374–375).

It is important for the American people to realize that a return to Southeast Asia is vital not only to the many who served there; it is also an integral part of the healing process for the Viet Kieu who left their own country during or after the war and emigrated to other parts of the world. In *When Heaven and Earth Changed Places*, Le Ly Hayslip alternates between narrating the story of her life in Viet Nam and her return journey to that country fifteen years later in 1986. For Hayslip the journey was necessary in order to discover the fate of the family, friends, and former neighbors she had left behind as well as that of the people in general. She considered her trip a duty and an obligation because the Viet culture stresses the importance of taking care of one's elders, and Hayslip had not seen her only surviving parent, her mother, for almost sixteen years. According to Hayslip, she returned to Southeast Asia not as a tourist, but as "a pilgrim. Like everyone, I must come back to start again" (*When Heaven* 307).

Like the American veterans who returned long after the war, Hayslip also noted "the vestiges of war" in Viet Nam: "graveyards ... monuments, orphanages, and the Tiny Y Te health clinic—a shell of a building with no permanent staff—for the maimed, diseased, and broken" (*When Heaven* 292). However, it did not take long for Hayslip to discover that the war had shifted from the battlefield to the marketplace where bargaining was not between "buyer and seller" but "predator and victim" (*When Heaven* 209), where customers and vendors argued "like snipers trading potshots in the jungle" (Hayslip, *When Heaven* 209). But the situation was somewhat paradoxical. Hayslip noted with alarm the dangers of materialism that could turn the people into greedy, corrupt, depraved, and alienated souls, particularly in the large cities. On the other hand, she realized that the bargaining concerned far more than money per se; it was "really an affirmation of their need for one another; a pledge of trust in the midst of suspicion, a lesson in how to survive as a community when that sense of community itself has been shattered" (Hayslip, *When Heaven* 209). Hayslip herself became less materialistic during her journey, although upon seeing the effects of war in her homeland, she realized that Viet Nam was very much "in need of the things that money can buy: food, medicine, warm clothes and shelter" (*When Heaven* 193).

The discovery that the war is not over for the people who still live in an atmosphere of suspicion and distrust startled Hayslip. When she finally reunited with family members, she soon sensed their fear even at being associated with her. "*My god,*" she writes, "*by coming here I've endangered them all! They're afraid of Communist informers—of their neighbors as well as the government!* ... Was this the purpose of my return after all these years—to bring more terror to the people I love?" (Hayslip, *When Heaven* 218–219). Hayslip knew that she placed her own life in jeopardy by returning to Viet Nam as she was on the Viet Cong death list when she emigrated to the United States, but she was not prepared for the rejection that she received from some of her own family members. Her brother would not even eat a piece of the candy she brought with her, and those relatives who did burned the wrappers immediately. Hayslip's mother, too, was standoffish at first and did not offer her daughter any affection.

The process of healing ultimately involved both Hayslip and her family. Hayslip not only improved her own relationship with the relatives that she left behind sixteen years before, but also helped to unite her mother with another daughter from whom she was estranged. Her mother stated, "See what you've taught me, Bay Ly? That you're never too old to forgive people; that it's never too late to patch the dike and save a little more of whatever life's left you" (Hayslip, *When Heaven* 337). Also noted by Hayslip's mother is that Hayslip's return had "completed [her] circle of growth" (*When Heaven* 314). Her mother told Hayslip, "'If you come back again, it will be part of another, new cycle—not the old one. Your past is now complete. The war for you is over. My destiny as your mother is fulfilled'" (*When Heaven* 314).

In her second narrative, *Child of War, Woman of Peace*, Hayslip tells of her life in the United States after the war, of subsequent visits to Viet Nam through 1991, and of new cycles that contribute to further healing. The father of her first child challenged her to a specific mission:

> "Em Ly, you must help people overcome the pain of the the war—to learn trust where they feel suspicion; to honor the past while letting go of it; to learn all these things so that they, in turn, may teach. Only this way can the circle of vengeance strangling us be changed into an ever expanding sphere of enlightenment" [Hayslip, *Child of War* 244].

Gradually Hayslip arranged for the construction of a clinic in Ky La by exporting clothing, medical supplies, and other aid to Viet Nam. "Since the Mother's Love clinic opened," she writes, "it has treated more than 16,500 patients and delivered 300 babies" (Hayslip, *Child of War* 364). A school and a medical clinic have been constructed at China Beach, where an additional rehabilitation center to aid the physically disabled and the homeless is also in progress. What Hayslip ultimately learned in her act of self-discovery is that it is all right to embrace more than one world. She learned that

> All my life I had been *caught in the middle*—between the South and the North, Americans and Vietnamese, greed and compassion, capitalism and communism, not quite peace and almost war. Now, instead of resisting that fate, I saw that *in between* was where I belonged [Hayslip, *Child of War* 329].

The last chapter of her book is appropriately titled "Two Halves Make a Whole."

The literary works of both Hayslip and these other writers demonstrate that the two halves, one representing the Americans and the other the Viets, must be joined in order for true reconciliation to take place. At the end of *Home Before Morning*, Van Devanter and a group of friends "gather ... in a garden" on Memorial Day, not in the United States, but in Viet Nam, where they form "a circle in the grass," pray for "the many hundreds of thousands who gave, by their blood, to the war," and pass each other a "branch of blossoms" (374). "Our silence," Van Devanter writes, "was unbroken, like our circle" (375). In order for the circle to continue unbroken, both nations must, as Adrienne Rich would term it, "re-vision" the war, to think seriously about the future and the new directions that the joint relationship must take. As Downs writes,

> Any soldier who has been in combat knows that there comes a time after the battle, when the smoke has blown away and the dust has settled, when you must lean down and give your foe a hand. For in that moment of generosity, the war is truly over [390].

We cannot reside in the past, for as Lynn Hampton so aptly states, "To live in the past is to walk in darkness" (221).

Notes

1. See Hugh A. Mulligan's "Reporter Tells Experiences During His Return to Vietnam," *The Jonesboro* [AR] *Sun*, 17 October 1993: 14B, and "Veterans Return to Vietnam for Some Very Personal Reasons," *The Jonesboro* [AR] *Sun*, 24 October 1993: 15A. Other news accounts of return journeys to Viet Nam include "The Friendship Force Is Seeking to Mend the Wound of Long War," *The Jonesboro* [AR] *Sun*, 21 November 1993: 14B; "U.S. Task Force Spends Holiday in Hanoi," *The Jonesboro* [AR] *Sun*, 26 November 1993: 6B; and George Esper's "Impressions of New Vietnam Given by Veteran Reporter," *The Jonesboro* [AR] *Sun*, 7 February 1994: 8b.

2. Unfortunately, space does not permit a lengthy discussion of Morley Safer's *Flashbacks: On Returning to Vietnam* (New York: Random House, 1990) and Neil Sheehan's *After the War Was Over* (New York: Vintage Books, 1992); however, these narratives are highly recommended as is Philip Caputo's *Means of Escape* (New York: HarperCollins, 1991).

3. A fictional account of a veteran who returns to Viet Nam can be found in Tim O'Brien's story "Field Trip," first published in *McCall's*, August 1990: 78–79 and later included in *The Things They Carried* (Boston: Houghton Mifflin/Seymour Lawrence, 1990).

4. Van Devanter's book is a seminal text in the literature of the Viet Nam war as its publication led many other women who had served in Viet Nam to step forth and tell their own, previously untold, stories. Important oral histories of women who were involved in the war include Keith Walker's *A Piece of My Heart: The Stories of Twenty-Six American Women Who Served in Vietnam* (New York: Ballantine, 1985) and Dan Freedman and Jacqueline Rhodes's *Nurses in Vietnam: The Forgotten Veterans* (Lubbock: Texas Monthly, 1987).

Works Cited

Broyles, William Jr. *Brothers in Arms: A Journey From War to Peace.* New York: Avon, 1986.
Downs, Frederick. *No Longer Enemies, Not Yet Friends: An American Soldier Returns to Vietnam.* New York: Pocket Books, 1991.
Estes, Jack. "Remembrance and Restoration." *Newsweek*, 30 May 1994: 10.
Gray, Stan. "Going Home to Vietnam." *The Jonesboro* [AR] *Sun*, 21 March 1993: 1C, 10C.
Hampton, Lynn. *The Fighting Strength: Memoirs of a Combat Nurse in Vietnam.* New York: Warner Books, 1990.

Hayslip, Le Ly. *Child of War, Woman of Peace.* New York: Anchor Books, 1993.

____. *When Heaven and Earth Changed Places.* New York: Plume, 1989.

Marshall, Kathryn, ed. *In the Combat Zone: Vivid Personal Recollections of the Vietnam War From the Women Who Served There.* New York: Penguin, 1987.

Mulligan, Hugh A. "Reporter Tells Experiences During His Return to Vietnam." *The Jonesboro* [AR] *Sun,* 17 October 1993, 14B.

____. "Veterans Return to Vietnam for Some Very Personal Reasons." *The Jonesboro* [AR] *Sun,* 24 October 1993, 15A.

O'Brien, Tim. *Going After Cacciato.* New York: Delta/Seymour Lawrence, 1978.

Rich, Adrienne. "When We Dead Awaken: Writing as Re-Vision." *College English* 34 (1972): 18–30.

Rottmann, Larry. *Voices from the Ho Chi Minh Trail: Poetry of America and Vietnam, 1965–1993.* Desert Hot Springs, California: Event Horizon Press, 1993.

Rottmann, Larry Lee. "A Hundred Happy Sparrows: An American Veteran Returns to Vietnam." *Vietnam Generation* 1.1 (1989): 113–140.

Van Devanter, Lynda. *Home Before Morning.* New York: Warner Books, 1983.

Homecoming, Seventeen Years Later

When I came home from overseas, from the nightmare,
I walked into my mother's house with a smile on my face,
Put down my duffel bag, and started crying.
"It's over now," she said; "You're safe. Stop crying."
And, military to the bone, I said "Yes ma'am" and stopped.
And then we did it again, an hour or two later:
"It's over now. You're safe. Stop crying."
"Yes ma'am." And then we did it again.

It all went away eventually—or did it?
A new life, a real home, civilian career and all.
I stand in the classroom talking about Shakespeare,
Telling war stories when the students ask,
Loving my students, trying to do for them
What I didn't or couldn't do for the ghosts ...

The ghosts?

Why has it all come back this year?
Why do the ghosts sit at my breakfast table with me,
Sharing my coffee, my morning paper, and my tears?
Why am I crying again after seventeen years?
"It's over now," I tell myself; "You're safe. Stop crying."
And, still military to the bone, I say "Yes ma'am" and stop.
And then I do it again.
Welcome home.

—PHOEBE S. SPINRAD

III.
LITERATURE OF
RECONCILIATION:
POETRY

9. Lessons Learned and Unlearned: The Aftermath Poetry of the War

DALE RITTERBUSCH

By consensus, the literature of war changed after the Battle of the Somme in July 1916. Rather than reflect the venerable old truths propagandistically expressed by higher authority, this new generation of war poets used their experience in the trenches to contradict the official view from above. The mission of such poets as Siegfried Sassoon and Wilfred Owen was to change our perceptions of war by writing anti-poetry that exposed the lies, the hypocrisy, the corrupt language of those shielding the public from the truth as the trench poets lived it through the monotony of daily slaughter. With the war over, their mission, if they survived, was largely completed. In contrast, the most significant Vietnam war poetry is still being written, in part because the war has stayed with the Vietnam poet longer—longer, in fact, than any previous war has stayed with its respective generation of writers. And although one talks of the tradition of war poetry in the twentieth century, the poetry of the First World War and the Second did not speak to the Vietnam veteran and poet. The sardonic humor of Sassoon, the photographic image of Owen, the distanced perspective of Jarrell, reflective of psychic numbing, told the Vietnam war poet little about his own war. With little or no audience at first, with no real writing models to follow, with not enough writing maturity, with hostility or indifference in the general public concerning the war, there was little for the poet to do but wait and write privately as the significance of Vietnam and its aftermath took hold and created this most substantial and distinctive body of poetry.

Perhaps the most distinctive element of Vietnam war literature is its persistence, its ability to engage both audience and writer long after the war has ended. In some measure the conference at the University of Notre Dame was a testament to that persistence. By providing insights not available earlier, or not approachable because of the confrontational perspectives embraced by nearly everyone at the time, the writer of this literature can still command an audience, in some quarters, and receive noteworthy attention. That Vietnam is a benchmark and that there are many lessons to be learned seems inescapable. However, although this literature is most often approached as an explanatory mechanism that answers the profound and compelling questions of the war, the question of continuing engagement by the war poets involves far more than a standard after-action report. "Unencumbered by history" (Barry 25), the Vietnam war poet is concerned more with the legacy, the lessons learned and unlearned, that are far more crucial than the history itself. Those readers who attempt to make sense out of the war, who want to reach an acceptable version of the truth not found in accounts by Kissinger and Westmoreland, can do so, but the literature of protest (against official policy), the literature of the historical record, remains the least consequential. It is the aftermath poetry that provides more compelling insights into the persistence of the myth of Vietnam and its far reaching effects upon our cultural identity. The cultural legacy of Vietnam is considerable, but its significance lies in the aftermath, not entirely in the facts of the war itself.

Although it is something of a cliché to say that the war simply did not end for so many writers, especially the poets, that they were unable to put the war behind them because of its far reaching effects and consequences, explanations for this persistence transcend the clichés; the explanations are complex and reveal a great deal about our social history as well as the nature of mythmaking and debunking that has consumed writers, filmmakers, and historians.

As a document of protest and a record of historical fact, the literature confirmed many objections voiced by critics of the war. But this was familiar territory in the history of war literature. Consider the platoon leader's perspective recorded by Philip Caputo in *A Rumor of War*. Caputo notes his embrace of the familiar Kennedy maxim, "Ask not what your country can do for you; ask what you can do for your country"; and he recalls the fervor with which he responded to the call to "bear any burden" in the pursuit of democratic freedoms. The speech was noble; Caputo later finds the cause was not. His rejection of the exalted language is similar to that of the trench poets who substituted an anti-poetic vocabulary. But Caputo's objection is specifically directed at the Vietnam war: Vietnam was not the right war at the right time, meaning that it was unfortunate for him that he had to serve in a war like Vietnam and not in the more heroic and just Second World War or perhaps the war in the Persian Gulf which he supported because U.S. interests were at stake. Thus his repudiation of war goes only as far as Vietnam.

Various poets may agree with Caputo, but a number of the best do not. Consider Bill Ehrhart's work which repudiates war as an instrument of U.S. policy, war as an extension of politics practiced daily in many parts of the world. Ehrhart condemns this policy generally, and specifically, in a number of poems. Proliferating throughout his work are references to Grenada, Panama, Nicaragua, Lebanon, the Persian Gulf and other places where the war in Viet Nam has been continued under another name. Ehrhart rejects the cloaking language used by officialdom in this passage from a love poem to his wife:

> Duty, honor, country:
> rubbish.
> I am a citizen only
> of your heart. You
> are the only land
> I'll ever love ["Patriotism," uncollected poem].

But this rejection is merely a repetition of the trench poets' experience and response. Seigfried Sassoon and the other World War I poets had come to similar conclusions considering the noble and exalted language of their political and military leaders. This is not an unusual circumstance in the twentieth century, and although we perhaps need daily reminders (consider Reagan's statement in the eighties that Vietnam was a "noble crusade"), still throughout much of this century, warnings concerning our gullibility, our susceptibility to the high-minded phrase defending the indefensible, have been expressed by the poets; Philip Larkin's admonition, "Never such innocence again," holds true for the age. Recognizing this shift in the old order of things, it was possible quite early in the war for soldiers to joke that they were engaged in the noble purpose of "keeping the world safe *from* democracy."

Is the Vietnam poetry that rebels against official doctrine, that refuses to accept the mission, invalid? Most certainly not, but it is familiar and predictable given our literary and political history. And no one can argue that the poetry that presents us with acute and fragmentary glimpses of the war, like a series of still photographs, is not an accurate description of the war more compelling and insightful than the distanced policy perspectives that pretend to give us the "big picture."

The poetry of protest, the poetry that exposes the "bright shining lie," has validity, of course. But in the tradition of Sassoon, Owen, and Rosenberg, it is not as revelatory as it would have been in 1916. The mission of Sassoon and Owen was to bring the message home that contradicted higher authority. One way to do that was to provide a photographic image in the poetry, an image that revealed the falsity of those censored photographs appearing in the daily newspapers. But, again, this had already been done as Randall Jarrell understood in his attempts at capturing the Second World War in his poetry. As opposed to Sassoon's graphic description of battlefield detail (as exemplified by references to "naked sodden buttocks" [105] and "Bulged, clotted heads" [105] littering the landscape) or Owen's depiction of a gas attack which contains the precise details of the chemical's effects on the lungs causing the soldier to drown in his own fluids (consider the "gargling," "froth-corrupted lungs" in "Dulce et Decorum Est" as evidence of this precise detail), Randall Jarrell creates some distance from the image, calling upon the reader's sensibility, imagination, and photographic record culled from all sorts of diverse sources. At the end of his most often anthologized poem, "The Death of the Ball Turret Gunner," the last line, "When I died they washed me out of the turret with a hose" (144), is imprecise, yet the reader sees every detail—internal organs disintegrated, blood splattered over the spidered Plexiglas turret, the slumped remains of what's left of the gunner. This is not detail recreated in the poem; it comes from the reader's intimate knowledge of the effects of modern war on the human form. So, the horrors of war are well known, and there is little difference between a body disintegrated by a five-nine in World War I and a body blown to pieces by a booby-trapped 105 round in Viet Nam.

But no Vietnam poet could turn to Sassoon or Jarrell for any assistance in writing about the war in Southeast Asia. Early attempts at recreating the war on the page to explain the lessons of Vietnam were largely unsuccessful, in part because the significance, the interpenetration of the war into the writer's own psyche and the psyche of his culture were not immediately apparent. Nor would they be for years after the war. The one exception to this would be John Balaban's *After Our War*, easily the most accomplished work completed at the time. In this work, Balaban already reveals the interpenetration of Vietnam into the far reaches of his life, unable to escape Vietnam as he works with diverse themes centered back home in the United States.

But for other poets it took years of continuous confrontation with the difficult questions posed by the war before a solid body of work was produced. And these poets have persisted, unable to disengage themselves or break off contact with the manifold and recurring complexities that still vex us to this present moment. The easiest explanation accounting for this persistence involves the concept of loss. Readers familiar with contemporary poetry recognize loss as a staple theme repeated from poet to poet almost to the point of cliché. And although some of the earlier Vietnam poetry verges on this cliché, the best extends this concept into complex explanations of the hold this war continues to have on our psychologies, individual and collective. So loss in the aftermath poetry is a given: the loss of a good friend and fellow soldier, the loss of innocence, both national and individual, the loss of our youthful sense of immortality, and the loss of ourselves—what we thought to be ourselves before the war taught us we weren't like that at all. And of course we lost our great American myth of the West, of the frontier. When Benjamin Franklin had us "extirpate" the "savages" "in order to make room for the cultivators of the earth" (112, 113), we civilized the land using the virtues of the saw and the ax—and the rifle—clearing the wilderness and creating a free democracy, or so we believed. But when we continued our march westward, continued our extirpation in Vietnam, we realized the barbarity of our virtues.

Vietnam taught us our limitations and taught us that we had outlived the usefulness of our myths. This is one of the primary lessons of Vietnam. And the poets insist on teaching us this lesson as opposed to those official records and histories constructed by such as Nixon, Kissinger, and Westmoreland who continued the lies and perpetuated the myth in their memoirs.

Evidence of the myth's debunking is found in the poetry's many references to the western hero in the movies: Actors like John Wayne, Gary Cooper, and Audie Murphy were interchangeable in their roles as western hero and soldier. There was little difference between clearing the beaches of Normandy or clearing a frontier town of the bad guys who prevented the establishment of democratic ideals and principles. "Indian country" was in effect the New Frontier.

If in some measure the poetry debunks the myth, it is with a great deal of painful introspection; there is little insolence or joy in exploding the hypocrisy or the degeneration of the ideal. If our myths bind us together, if our myths create a shared experience that defines our culture, then we must deconstruct or debunk these myths with care. And what do we substitute? If John Wayne is facing in the wrong direction at the end of the film *The Green Berets*, what process, literary or otherwise, can redirect our cultural energies and reconstruct a viable myth that redefines our culture?

Of course we could still continue to believe in the frontier myth and in our manifest destiny to stabilize the world and make it safe for democracy. But the poets who fought in Vietnam know that the myth had become corrupted and that its degenerative process had done its work on them; it was simply not true, and had no compelling hold any longer. For some it is possible to hold these contrary ideas together—the myth with its remarkable generative powers and its antithesis, the destruction that results from living out the myth: Both may be contained within the same psychology. It is this internal war that is at the heart of another lesson learned in Vietnam. The sophisticated socialization process has inculcated the myth deep within the poet's psychology; indeed, he has embraced the myth for a good part of his life. But the poet is torn between the myth and his knowledge that it is false and destructive. He remembers his belief in the rightness of his course, his mission, but his new knowledge refutes the frontier mentality and causes him to reconsider his place in his own culture, causes him to reevaluate the nature of his own identity. Often then, because of this knowledge, he appears as an outsider, a deviant who deserves social castigation. As an outcast he can neither be comfortable with his new belief or his disbelief in the old order of things.

There is a continuing war between the myth and the process of debunking. *The Deer Hunter* and *Apocalypse Now* necessitated *Rambo* and the Chuck

Norris *Missing in Action* films. We are resistant to any process that tears down our mythical constructs. Of course the bad poetry, what Ehrhart calls the "napalm and dead babies" poetry, contributes to the perpetuation of the myth by constructing an aberration that can be discounted or dismissed; it is not reflective of our national character and is subject to easy denial and refutation.

Renouncing armed resistance (in much the same way as Shane attempts to do in the classic Western film) is difficult; the military training often comes back, at least for a moment, when confronted with the facts of injustice or hypocrisy. Weaponless, the poet has only his words with which to combat the continuing war. In fact, it is a measure of their decency that writers like Ehrhart or Balaban confront the futility of overcoming the entrenched powers that continue the war in other quarters. Their writing demystifies our history, our essential systems of political and cultural beliefs. And virtually no one applauds the process by which those fundamental beliefs held most dear are revealed as specious and destructive.

Ehrhart's prose poem "What War Does" records a litany of images "tattooed" on the combatant's "soul," images that may, in part, have been the cause of the more than 50,000 suicides among Vietnam veterans since the war officially ended. Confronted with these images, these recollections, and the knowledge that little has changed, that the lessons have not been learned, Ehrhart goes back and (like Shane who puts on his guns once again to help the homesteaders) aggressively explains what it would take to effect a change in the moral course of our history:

> I have told you one lie. If I thought you would understand, I would push your face down into that cesspool and put my foot on the back of your neck and hold you there until you die of the stink and the shit and the blood in your lungs. I would not hesitate to suffocate you in the filth you refuse to see. It's what you deserve. You with your willful ignorance. You with your gentle lives. If I thought it would help.
> Pray that I never do [*Distance* 41].

Measured against the ethics and the moral imperatives of so much of his work, this poem may seem out of place, an atavistic impulse that reveals a failure to live by the precepts that inform his identity as a writer and bearer of transformative truths. But Ehrhart is too honest to keep these darkest returns from us; worse than the war itself is this self-knowledge that a return to the past once repudiated and disavowed is possible, even probable, given the right circumstances.

The poem "Not Your Problem" does the same thing, asking the reader to "Avoid this place" because of the disturbing lessons to be learned. Set just about anywhere the war is still being waged, but most concretely tied to Central America, the poem presents this foreboding premonition of change:

> Here being poor is a crime
> unless we are also quiet;

almost everyone is poor,
and we can hear a bullet
being chambered a mile away.
We will change all this.

You won't want to be here
when we do [*Laughs* 64].

Such poems are not intended to elegiacally record the terrible effects of war, but reveal instead how it is virtually impossible to escape our history and live fulfilled by the best we have to offer our wives, our children, our families, the world we must turn to for sustenance and healing when the larger world rejects the lessons we have learned.

The aftermath poetry, unlike the films and many of the novels, is an instrument of moral discourse. Set apart from various political arguments voiced in much of the earlier poetry, this work is affirmative and offers a different set of values, both cultural and personal, in place of the corrupted values that still find currency in much topical discourse from higher authority. The earlier arguments expressed by such poets as Denise Levertov and Robert Bly, arguments similarly voiced by such writers as Mary McCarthy and Susan Sontag, rejected mainstream American value structures and embraced an idealized and romantic vision of the world, reflective of some communal spirit and a calling back to the past, but a past that had been collectively sanitized. The generation of Vietnam poets that has continued to write recognizes the debasing effects of war on both sides, leaving even the heroes as anti-heroes, villains or worse. Barbarous acts are a condition of war, and no one can lay claim to a superior moral authority. Hence Vietnam is a symbol of the continued disintegration of moral imperatives. When Noam Chomsky denies the genocide of the Khmer Rouge, when the United States aids the KR by funneling materiel through Thailand and China, we may begin to trace the legacy of Vietnam and see it as symbol, and as symbol the poets have contributed an uncompromising ethical dimension. While many writers refused to recognize that they had been duped (Sydney Schanberg is the exception), many of the soldier-poets decried the genocide in Cambodia and were among the few voices confronting this most disturbing legacy of the Vietnam War. And unlike fiction writers who have often felt it necessary to add another layer of cover or camouflage to a landscape characterized by triple canopy jungle, the poets have attempted to strip away layer after layer until the experience has been confronted and laid bare.

Even the best of our mainstream poets, careerists at heart, have avoided the lessons of Vietnam in favor of poems that reflect our cultural prejudices concerning mixing poetry and politics. Gerald McCarthy's poem "The Sound of Guns" examines not merely this cultural prejudice, but the bias voiced by the most influential writers of our time:

> At the University in town
> tight-lipped men tell me the war in Vietnam is over,
> that my poems should deal with other things:
> earth, fire, water, air [*Darkness* 180].

And so, despite such restrictions, such compromises and accommodations, a few poets have continued to write, have persisted doggedly, "carrying the darkness," contributing the complexities of their moral vision.

Of course it will be objected that such discourse is not the proper province of poetry, that, as Poe suggested, poetry should be concerned with aesthetics, not the inculcation of moral principles. But, except in the worst and most didactic examples, the poetry does not preach, does not pretend to a moral superiority. It provides contradictory evidence inside the framework of "moral chaos," reveals the hold the old myth still possesses, reflects the dynamic that still, in various moments, controls and consumes the poet's psychic energies. There is in much of the aftermath poetry a sense of combativeness as much as there is the response of passive resistance.

In the second part of McCarthy's poem he continues:

> Seven winters have slipped away,
> the war still follows me.
> Never in anything have I found
> a way to throw off the dead [*Darkness* 181].

Yet it has proven fairly easy for other more mainstream poets to do this, and, perhaps in any other time, McCarthy, Komunyakaa, Ehrhart and the others might have preferred to do likewise. But they have been honest enough not to make such compromises. Consider the resistance: At various readings, poetry conferences, and workshops, it has not been unusual for this body of work and the Vietnam poets themselves to be castigated; various feminists have dismissed this work as the province of male aggression—what men do to one another and have done throughout history; these critics seek an alternative orientation, one that ignores the actuality of our history. And similar to Eugene McCarthy's denunciation of James Dickey as a "violent man," male writers and critics have rejected this body of poetry as evidence of male-generated violence that is symptomatic of an evil that must be conquered in our culture and our poetry. The Vietnam War is therefore not a proper subject of poetry, nor are its lessons of any value, aesthetically or otherwise.

Would Gerald McCarthy have written a different body of poetry if it were not for Vietnam? Assuredly, but it would be dishonest now to attempt any such disengagement and deny the far reaching penetrations of the war on his and our psychologies. In his poetry he wishes he could go back before that time, and, like other veterans, he inescapably confronts this every day of his life. "The Hooded Legion" records this in the following lines:

What did we dream of
the summer before we went away?
What leaf did not go silver
in the last light?
What hand did not turn us aside? [Shoetown 27].

From the beginning, John Balaban's work has shown the interpenetration of Vietnam into the far reaches of his life. Even the reprinting of several poems from one volume to the next reflects this interpenetration; from past to present, from deepest memory to recollection, the poems still resonate, call to us again and again. Interspersed in the volume *After Our War* are poems that go back and forth between Vietnam and Pennsylvania or Virginia. The landscapes of both continents are transmuted and meld into one another. The terrors of Vietnam are the "commonplaces" also of the American landscape as he explains in his poem "Some Commonplaces of the Times." And Similarly in "Hand-Painted Birthday Card: Abandoned Farmhouse," we see that "simple rains water equally / the accidental beauties, the incidental / horrors..." (War 75).

The more formal lyrics of Balaban put Vietnam in a historical context that is as far ranging as the geographical one. His return to Viet Nam in 1985 and the poetry that resulted from that return further established the context and continued interpenetration of the war. The extended lesson obtains as in "Mr. Giai's Poem," where Balaban, Ehrhart and Weigl meet with this veteran of wars against the "Japanese, Americans, and French"; Mr. Giai's son has just been killed in Kampuchea, and so, after his forty years of combat, very little has changed.

Time and geography: Both are interpenetrated by the war. In the poem "On a Photograph of Schoolchildren Wearing Gas Masks. Rheims. World War I.," Balaban carries the sameness of war forward from 1916 successively with snapshots, poetic images, and reflections through 1940, 1945, 1954, and 1965. Our consciences are clear despite the lessons, the hard evidence presented again and again, despite assaults on our image of ourselves, who we are, what we pretend to be.

In *Blue Mountain* the poem "Hitch-Hiking and Listening to My CB Walkie-Talkie" brings the sameness of the war home in a series of eavesdropping instances of violence; the last stanza reads: "Late at night, when radio waves skip across States,/ you can hear ricochets from Maine to LA" (8). This is the call home from Viet Nam, and the poet finds a terrible sameness. As Balaban says in "Riding Westward," "You know that something's not quite right," and it hits the veteran, the poet, every day of his life in a confrontation with evidence that the war will not go away. Balaban's task is not merely to record these instances of violence common to our culture, but to offer alternative visions based on the experience of Vietnam. One of those alternatives is voiced in the poem "Words for My Daughter." This title poem brings the reader forward from the not-so innocent experience of childhood, through Vietnam, to finally a compelling lesson he wants his daughter to learn: "I want you to know the worst and be free from it./ I want you to know the worst and still find good" (*Daughter* 12). This is the lesson found in much of the aftermath poetry, a lesson we have so far failed to learn.

Yusef Komunyakaa came to this late; as he says, it was fourteen years before he could confront Vietnam. But apart from the compelling poems in *Dien Cai Dau*, most of which recollect past experience and then in a remarkable act of transmutation, transcend the significance of the experience and evoke images of "symbolic perception," there are poems in *Magic City* recalling childhood experiences while growing up in Louisiana that presage the dynamics of Vietnam. "The Steel Plate" tells the story of "Mister Dan" who "Came back from World War II/ With a steel plate in his head" (22). He dies later, "Blackjacked" by the police, and his story stays with Komunyakaa, reified by his own experience in Viet Nam. Komunyakaa's poem "Believing in Iron" reveals an involvement with war that could not have been foreseen by a young boy collecting scrap iron that is subsequently turned into a "warship or bomber" (46). Although he says he dreamed of the reworking of this metal and envisioned its wartime use, it is the time spent in Viet Nam that causes Komunyakaa to tie the elements of history together and discern the connections that caused his eventual involvement in the war. Unlike Robert Graves who disavowed his war poetry, perhaps paralleled by Michael Casey who seems to have done the same, Komunyakaa has waited until his war could be satisfactorily worked into art—a difficult task given the "moral chaos" and the confusion of values that govern and mediate both personal history and complicated questions of aesthetics.

In the preface to his collection of essays, *In the Shadow of Vietnam*, Ehrhart explains that he never set out to be a Vietnam War poet; the role was largely thrust upon him. In part this role has entailed making the poem accessible to a larger audience by eliminating the use of military jargon and the concomitant elements of a stylized military language. Other techniques have been used to extend the range of the poems, but still, Vietnam often resists such attempts at inclusiveness. Our cultural identity is still resistant to learning the appropriate lessons, and the prejudices, the stereotypes, the adherences to outmoded mythologies abound. After the publication of *Carrying the Darkness*, I talked to him about the role of the poet so long after the war had ended. He believed misrepresentation in other quarters required the voice of the poet to explain the war, to set things straight. I argued for a different audience, more restricted, more private. After all, the war had become about as familiar to some audiences as the Peloponnesian War or Caesar's conquering of Gaul. His poem, "Song for Leela, Bobby and Me," as the title suggests, has a private and select audience; it is for Robert Ross, killed in Vietnam, and it contains perhaps the strongest closure of all of Bill's poems. The last stanza reads:

I still have that photo of you
standing by the bunker door, smiling shyly,
rifle, helmet, cigarette, green uniform
you hadn't been there long enough to fade
somewhere in an album I don't have
to look at anymore. I already know
you just keep getting younger. In the middle
of this poem, my daughter woke up crying.
I lay down beside her, softly singing;
soon she drifted back to sleep.
But I kept singing anyway.
I wanted you to hear [*Laughs* 82].

This poem need never go beyond the audience of Leela and Bobby and Bill Ehrhart. That small and special audience is sufficient. Yet, if the larger audience is lost, the tragedy of the war will be compounded. And so, years from now, when Vietnam gets lost in history, when it becomes indistinguishable from so many other conflagrations, we must insure that Ehrhart's voice, this poem, will still call out resonant with its transcendence.

There may be no revision of revisionist interpretations possible in the poetry; there may be no credible substitution of an equally dynamic myth for the one discredited by our history, but there is the compelling voice of the aftermath poetry teaching us what perhaps we should have known all along, the lessons we have failed to learn, the voice, like Ehrhart's, saying privately to all of us, "I wanted you to hear."

Works Cited

Balaban, John. *After Our War*. Pittsburgh: University of Pittsburgh Press, 1974.
____. *Blue Mountain*. Greensboro, NC: Unicorn, 1982.
____. *Words for My Daughter*. Port Townsend, WA: Copper Canyon, 1991.
Barry, Jan. *In the Footsteps of Genghis Khan*. In W.D. Ehrhart, ed., *Carrying the Darkness*. Lubbock: Texas Tech University Press, 1989.
Ehrhart, W.D. *The Distance We Travel*. Easthampton, MA: Adastra Press, 1993.
____. *Just for Laughs*. Silver Spring, MD: Burning Cities Press, 1990.
____. *Patriotism*, an uncollected poem. In ART:MAG, Series I, 1-M, 1984.
Franklin, Benjamin. *Autobiography and Other Writings*, ed. Russell B. Nye. Boston: Houghton Mifflin, 1958.
Jarrell, Randall. *The Complete Poems*. New York: Farrar, Straus & Giroux, 1969.
Komunyakaa, Yusef. *Magic City*. Hanover, NH: Wesleyan University Press, 1992.
McCarthy, Gerald. *Shoetown*. Bristol, IN: Cloverdale, 1992.
____. *The Sound Of Guns*. In W.D. Ehrhart, ed., *Carrying the Darkness*. Lubbock: Texas Tech University Press, 1989.
Sassoon, Seigfried. *The War Poems*. London: Faber and Faber, 1983.

10. Reconciliation and Women's Poetry

VINCE GOTERA

A couple of months before President Clinton lifted the U.S. trade embargo against Vietnam, *Newsweek*'s "JFK Cover-UP" issue—a fascinating title if you're a conspiracy buff—contained two interesting items vis-à-vis the Vietnam war: first, a picture of the unveiling of the Vietnam Women's Memorial on Veterans Day, 1993, and second, "The War Without End," an article by retired Army colonel David Hackworth. Both items center on the theme of reconciliation—an unavoidable topic, especially after the lifting of the long-standing embargo. Hackworth's article is a "going back in country" piece, describing his meeting with "soldiers and commanders who had fought against [his] battalion," a meeting he calls "a kind of reconciliation" (45). The Women's Memorial photo, strangely enough, is an illustration for an article on President Clinton's Asia-Pacific Economic Cooperation summit in Seattle. The implications are telling: Hackworth's language underlines his perceptions of the "maleness" of that war—"now we were just old soldiers out for what seemed like a Sunday picnic [and we] discussed tactics and operations like young lieutenants at infantry school" (45); the Women's Memorial photo did not even deserve a notice in its own right but rather served merely as an index of the continuing presence of the war in U.S. policy toward Asia. If we were Martians and all we had were this article and this photograph, we might conclude that Vietnam/U.S. reconciliation has very little to do with the women who served in that war.

In the context of American poetry about the Vietnam war, we find certain similarities vis-à-vis reconciliation. In a recent interview, veteran poet Bruce Weigl[1] said, "All my efforts now are towards normalization [with Viet Nam].... Our government won't do it, so the writers are doing it" (Schroeder 193). Weigl has returned to Viet Nam more than once for this purpose, accompanied by other poets—W.D. Ehrhart, John Balaban, Yusef Komunyakaa, Larry Rottmann. The interesting thing to note is that the poets named here are all men; are women poets making similar moves to reconcile Viet Nam and the United States?

I will focus on two collections of poetry; *Shallow Graves: Two Women and Vietnam,* by Wendy Wilder Larsen and Tran Thi Nga, and *Visions of War, Dreams of Peace: Writings of Women in the Vietnam War,* edited by Lynda Van Devanter and Joan A. Furey. In contrast with analogous compilations of poetry by male Vietnam veterans, such as *Winning Hearts and Minds* or *Demilitarized Zones,* these women's collections lean more toward reconciliation by including a significant number of poems by Viet and Viet Kieu writers. And yet within these poems, we still see in a large number of the non–Vietnamese writers a certain kind of isolationism or, at best, naïveté about their Viet counterparts. Proportionally, there are more of the Viet and Viet Kieu women poets represented in these texts who reach toward the theme of reconciliation. These texts may therefore suggest in microcosm the issues, controversies and concerns which have plagued reconciliation and normalization between the United States and Viet Nam for many years.

In his introduction to *Visions of War, Dreams of Peace,* W.D. Ehrhart outlines the problematics of the literary history of American women's poetry about the war before the publication of *Shallow Graves:*

> In 1972, when the remarkable and seminal anthology *Winning Hearts and Minds* … was published, it contained only two poems by women, only one of whom had actually been in Vietnam. In 1976, when the companion anthology *Demilitarized Zones* … was published, it contained only five poems by women, none of whom had been in Vietnam. In 1985, when *Carrying the Darkness* … was published, it contained, again, only five poems by women, and again, none of them had been in Vietnam (Van Devanter and Furey xvii).

It may be important to add that in these three ("men's") books, there is only one poem by a Viet writer (Barry and Ehrhart 95).

When *Shallow Graves*—a collection of poems by two women, an American and a Viet—was published in 1986, reviewers primarily noted the book's utility as oral history and rarely referred to the quality of the poetry; one reviewer in fact asserted, "although the poems make *Shallow Graves* appear as fiction or literature, it is a brilliant study for any historian" (*Virginia Quarterly Review* 135). One face of history is literary, as in another reviewer's reference to "*truyen,* or verse novels … a uniquely Vietnamese form," noting that "the poetic structure of *Shallow Graves*—the book works as a kind of verse novel—links it to the thousand-year literary history of Vietnam" (Lotozo 12).[2] Approaching the poetry *as* poetry, a third reviewer's commentary focused on Larsen more than Tran Thi Nga: "Larsen's poetry [is] transparent and understated and punctuated with flashes of irony and wonder" whereas Tran Thi Nga's "shrewd and remarkable story … would probably work better as prose" (Eder 3, 11). Although I personally find that Tran Thi Nga's poems stand exceedingly well on their own as poems, I must admit that there is reason for this third reviewer's skepticism: Tran Thi Nga's narrative was originally an oral history which she narrated to Larsen, who taped it and then, as Larsen explains in her foreword to *Shallow Graves*, "I transformed her memories into narrative verse trying to stay as close to her voice as possible."

Reconciliation is clearly a central focus for Larsen, as the writer/editor of these poems, and we glimpse this in the book's architecture: first 102 pages of Larsen's story, then 171 pages of Tran Thi Nga's story, and a closing 4-page coda (in Larsen's voice) with the two women meeting "in the American Museum of Natural History" to view the Vietnam exhibit in the "Hall of Asian Peoples." Larsen's final stanza imagines solidarity between herself and Tran Thi Nga ("I picture us, Ba Larsen and Madame Nga, / arm in arm walking .... We carry no flags and we make a sad song")—an image of reconciliation where two individuals represent in microcosm the mutual mourning of their nations, without overt nationalism. But Larsen has missed the import of what Tran Thi Nga says in the previous stanza—"'I think your country wants to forget about mine'" (278)—so that Tran Thi Nga has already disclaimed and disarmed Larsen's approaching image of the two of them "arm in arm walking."

Although Larsen seems well intentioned, the poems of her section reveal a certain kind of obtuseness about her own experience in Vietnam. She observes her seamstress, "Chi Ai," eating "plain rice, / nothing on it," and notes how "She'd swish the last kernel / from her bowl / with cold brown tea." Remembering her mother's admonition about "the starving children of China," Larsen can only recall "the bottom of [her cereal] dish, / Beatrix Potter's Peter Rabbit, / the prize for finishing" (37). Of course, the poem is self-deprecating, with Larsen parodying her own dangerous innocence, but the important point here is that Larsen as a poet can see only the foreignness of Chi Ai, and by extension, the starving Chinese children of her childhood. What Larsen doesn't grasp is the ineffable importance of rice to the Vietnamese; in her memoir *When Heaven and Earth Changed Places*[3] Le Ly Hayslip recalls how "a peasant seeing lightning will crouch under the table and look for lost grains in order to escape the next bolt," noting that "Good rice was considered god's gemstone—*hot ngoc troi*—and was cared for accordingly on pain of divine punishment" (9). Indeed, Chi Ai may *be* as hungry as "starving Chinese children," but the point is that Larsen projects this condition herself, not realizing the hallowed place of rice in the Vietnamese cultural universe. We are reminded of Edward Said's notion of "Orientalism" in which the Orient is seen by the Westerner as "a place of romance, exotic beings, haunting memories and landscapes, remarkable experiences" representing the Westerner's "deepest and most recurring images of the Other" (1). Larsen's stance regarding the seamstress Chi Ai is one of "*positional* superiority," to use Said's term, "which puts the Westerner in a whole series of possible relationships with the Orient without ever losing him the relative upper hand" (7). In poem after poem, Larsen retains this sense of superiority although she may be quite ingenuous about her wish for reconciliation, and part of this is the "positional" upper hand she has as the "writer-in-charge"; as Larsen admits in the book's foreword, "I feel like the performer of Tran Thi Nga's story as well as my own." Larsen's naïveté about her own positional superiority ultimately undermines any potential for reconciliation.

The most revealing poem is "The Noodle Cart," in which Larsen, knowing her journalist husband is due to be sent back to the United States, asks Tran Thi Nga, who has been her guide to Vietnam, to "help [her] find a noodle cart." In three quick lines, Larsen narrates Tran's search: "she had to talk a family out of theirs. / The son was all in favor, but not the father / who was dead against selling the family business." The unacknowledged irony of this poem is that Larsen includes the following lines right after the phrase "selling the family business":

> Now the noodle cart stands
> on my brother's porch in California
> stocked with little green bottles of Perrier water
> Mr. and Mrs. T's Bloody Mary Mix [95].

She deconstructs her own position by her acknowledgment of the triviality of the noodle cart's present purpose in the face of the destruction of a "family business." Tran Thi Nga's poem by the same title narrates the story from her side of the transaction; she uses 35 lines to narrate her search, which turns out to be a harrowing odyssey, until finally "the son told [her] to sneak back in the evening and take the cart," so that Tran Thi Nga becomes herself embroiled in what is ultimately a shady deal. Larsen, "my boss's wife," as the poet calls her, says only "It's perfect" (220–221)—in utter negation of the personal and familial disruptions which have occurred. That Larsen is unaware of what George Uba has called the "subversiveness" (68) of Tran Thi Nga's poem is demonstrated by her inclusion of both texts in *Shallow Graves*.[4]

In sharp contrast to Larsen's writing, Tran Thi Nga's poems discover an amazing array of marvels, portraying a remarkable woman whose life mirrors the tremendous hardships and survivals of the country of Viet Nam: her difficult exile to South Viet Nam after the 1954 Geneva accords, her marriage to a Chinese general (recapitulating Viet Nam's conflicted relations with China for millennia), the splintering of her family during the American war, her eventual (second) exile to the United States, and the deleterious effects of assimilation on her children's connection with Vietnamese culture. Delivered in an understated and matter-of-fact manner, Tran Thi Nga's poems characterize her as a meticulous and unswerving observer:

> One day when I opened the gate
> for Father to go out,
> there were corpses collapsed against the wall. I fainted.

> Father offered soldiers money to remove the corpses.
> Sometimes they took bodies that were still alive.
> People would call from the carts,
> "Don't take me. Don't take me.
> I'm not dead yet" [156–57].

Although the young Tran faints (so that conceivably she does not hear those horrific pleas), the mature Tran, as poet, does not shy away from giving these people the respect and dignity they deserve by representing them nakedly, without comment. Keen observation also allows her to paint beauty without overly ornamenting it:

> I remember in mountain lakes
> the protected fish
> black, pink, silver—
> their mouths breaking the surface
> of the still water
> to eat the popped corn we threw.

This poem closes with a catalog of apt, strategic details: "the spring peach blossoms / green willows in my courtyard / the warm summer rain / giant chrysanthemums in autumn" (173).

Reconciliation for Tran Thi Nga is problematic because she sees the United States as a cultural wilderness: in a poem where her children refuse to celebrate Tet, the lunar New Year celebration—"What for? / So we can sit around the table / and stare at each other'"—the poet admits, "Inside I was sad / feeling myself on a desert / knowing my customs will die with me" (264). Tran Thi Nga begins to feel that *she* is herself losing touch with these customs. After her mother's death—a death she doesn't hear about until a month has elapsed—she and her family visit a Buddhist temple that is "Just a red two-stories house with pine trees in the front / a parking lot in the back"; she prays somewhat hesitantly that "we children / ... had followed the ancient traditions so her spirit would rest with Father's in Paradise" (273). The influence of her father is a significant force, and for Tran Thi Nga, reconciliation is defined by a note her father wrote in 1945 during her first exile:

> "If Buddha is good," he wrote,
> "Pray for him to unify us.
> One day we will be together again
> in one country" [270].

Since her children have settled into America, I would suggest that the notion of "unification" for Tran Thi Nga is no longer so simple as being in "one country"—that is, a reunified Viet Nam—but rather that she would wish that some reconciliation could occur between her two countries—Viet Nam and the United States—so that her family's unification could occur "across the world from one another" (273). Nevertheless she wisely understands the remoteness of this possibility, as when she tells Larsen, "'I think your country wants to forget about mine'" (278).

When *Visions of War, Dreams of Peace* appeared in 1991, the importance of the book was drowned out by the national hoopla surrounding the Gulf War. Its central message, that American women *did* serve in the Vietnam war ("just as they have in every U.S. war" [Ehrhart in Van Devanter and Furey xviii]), was muted by media emphasis on the integration of women within the American troops of Desert Shield and Desert Storm. The few reviewers of the book emphasized this essential message; more importantly, with regard to reconciliation, Daniela Gioseffi noted that "the editors of this collection have been sensitive enough to include several Vietnamese poets" (19), both famous and not famous, three Vietnamese and three Vietnamese American. The ratio may not be as egalitarian as Tran Thi Nga's and Larsen's, roughly one-sixth since there are forty poets overall, but the point is that the Vietnamese and Vietnamese Americans *are* represented.

Several of the non–Vietnamese poets exhibit an "orientalist" perspective, to refer again to Said. Kathleen Trew's poem "Mamasan," for example, paints an unflattering portrait of a Vietnamese woman, using such negative imagery as "endless chatter," "blackened teeth," "waddling off," and "bowed legs." Although it is important to note that this poem is dated 1970 and to admit that the poet is still enmeshed in war and its exigencies, what we are given nevertheless is nothing less than an exclusionary stereotype. Even though the poem is dedicated "For Ms. Dung," implying friendship across a cultural divide, the poet nevertheless sees the Mama[-]san's world as inextricably separated and diverse from her own: the Vietnamese woman "filters out of our world / Back to hers" (23). Other poems focus on the incredibility of Viet Nam as a place, its perceived incongruities, its "Oppressive Heat—/The Malignant Stench," as Penny Kettlewell describes it (64), and so on. The majority of the poems by non–Vietnamese poets—most of them nurses—contend with the horrors of continual attendance with death. Norma J. Griffiths recalls, "I never / pulled someone's hair / for fear it would be in my hand, / with the scalp and skull attached" (112). In her poem "Hello, David," Dusty writes, "I am the last person / you will touch. / I am the last person / who will love you. / ... David—who will give me something / for my pain?" (44). These poems (and poets) are therefore very much in the vein of the majority of Vietnam-veteran writing: an emphasis on journalistic objectivity modulated by one's subjective reactions, bordering particularly on the surreal as a projection of the perceived alienness of Viet Nam in the viewpoint of young, inexperienced Americans. When the poems are not actively "orientalizing" Viet Nam, they are not exactly moving toward U.S./Viet Nam reconciliation either; on the other hand, if we expand our definitions, these poems are about nothing *but* reconciliation (albeit a strictly domestic brand): reconnecting with one's younger self in the war, reconciling one's memories, both horrific and beautiful, and reconciling with an American in whose collective unconscious "the very phrase 'woman veteran' ... seems almost a contradiction in terms," as Ehrhart put it (xvii).

Of the six poems by Viet or Viet Kieu, two are quite clearly about U.S./Viet Nam reconciliation. "The Vietnamese Mother" by Huong Tram— "a well known Vietnamese poet," according to the editors (212)—is a narrative poem which describes a "Vietnamese mother receiv[ing] a letter / From her beloved child" who had seen an American soldier die with "his last sigh [saying] / 'Oh Mama!'" After seven years, she receives another letter in which a companion of her son describes his death: "'Oh Mama!' he cried before he died / Bathed in moonlight." Her reaction is to include the enemy in her mourning:

> Again and again she cries
> For her lost son
> And for an unknown American mother
> Who lost her beloved child [41].

Vietnamese American Nguyen Ngoc Xuan's poem "My Letter to the Wall— November 1989" attempts to speak for all Vietnamese women who were involved in some way with Americans during the war:

> I'm the one who was wounded by your shrapnel.
> I'm the one you gave your life for.
> I'm the one who stole your wallet.
> I'm the one you sometimes didn't pay for the night.

The repeated phrase "I'm the one" builds up to a realization of possessing "knowledge and wisdom because you touched my life" and eventually settles into a kind of reciprocal identity or community between the living and the dead: "I'm the one who is part of you / And you are part of me." The speaker (or perhaps we might say a whole sisterhood of Vietnamese speakers) admits to forgiveness: "I'm the one who wants you to be happy and satisfied. / Because I'm alive and I can feel" (156–57). In both Huong Tram's and Nguyen Ngoc Xuan's poems, there is a sense of magnanimity consistently balanced with an open-eyed perspective about war's realities—its losses and its gains.

By no means do I wish, however, to downplay completely the reconciliatory aspects in the non–Vietnamese poets. Certainly, Grace Paley, in her poem "Two Villages," attempts to humanize Vietnamese who doggedly keep statistics about American attacks: "rockets 522 / attacks 1201 / big bombs 6998 / ... Mr. Tuong of the Fatherland Front / has a little book / in it he keeps the facts / carefully added" (24). The more exemplary case is Lady Borton, who consistently focuses on individual Vietnamese characters through objective and humanistic observation: the boy from Quang Ngai with "One hand ... partly usable, / the fingers of the other, / soldered to his wrist. / Napalm" (13), or the young girl, "Vo Thi Truong," who tends her mother's IV bottles and urine bottles in "the hospital's paraplegic ward," but nevertheless retains her vivacious youth—"She wriggles out, / runs over and hugs my legs, / giggling" (21–22). If we look again at ratios (although obviously we don't have a statistically valid sample here), we have here two poets who dramatize the possibility of Viet Nam/U.S. reconciliation out of thirty-four non–Vietnamese writers as opposed to two out of six Vietnamese.

When I first considered discussing these Vietnamese and especially Vietnamese American poets, one question that I thought would be germane is Trinh Minh-ha's conception of, in her terms, the Third World woman writer's "three conflicting identities. Writer of color? Woman writer? Or woman of color?" (6). These irreconcilable distinctions revolve around reception and its effect on the writer's conception of herself—that is, the way her identity is reinscribed by social expectation and then further reinscribed by her own writerly self and activity, in a kind of participatory, recursive dance. In the case of Tran Thi Nga, I don't sense an anxiety about this insofar as writing itself is concerned; the conflict for her seems to reside in acculturation, in the inroads made by American society into her identity as a Vietnamese. Tran Thi Nga's identity as a writer is cushioned by the buffer zone of Larsen's presence, as editor, as American, and finally, as a woman. Similarly, the Vietnamese and Vietnamese American writers in *Visions of War, Dreams of Peace* also do not apparently undergo Trinh Minh-ha's conflict either because they are comfortably ensconced within Confucian constructions of woman as daughter, wife, and mother, or because they are already comfortable with their reception as writers, particularly vis-à-vis a Vietnamese audience, or they do not see themselves as writers in a professional sense—and this third stance would seem to be true of several of the non–Vietnamese writers as well, if we are to believe Van Devanter's and Furey's assertion that "Some of the works contained in this anthology may not be what is referred to as great literature, but first writings rarely are" (xxiii).

The revealing application of Trinh Minh-ha's notion of "conflicting identities" may be seen however if we change the word "color" to "veteran"; the triple bind thus becomes: veteran writer? woman writer? woman veteran? Several poems deal with this trichotomy. Lily Lee Adams' brief epigrammatic poem "Being a Vet Is Like Losing a Baby" brings the dilemma into focus, equating the two experiences of woman and veteran, hinting that to be both constitutes double jeopardy (123). When Sara J. McVicker writes, "If one more guy / asks me if I was in Saigon / or DaNang / I think I'll scream. / Or maybe pop him in the nose" (130), she dramatizes how a woman can accept and assume the traditionally male action, falling back on "veteran-ness": "That's what male vets do to get rid of their frustrations" (130). The salient point is that both the Vietnamese and non–Vietnamese poets acknowledge at some level their conflictual self-making and from this shared acknowledgment we can infer the potential of community. My original suggestion, that these Vietnamese and non–Vietnamese writers may recapitulate the dual stances which Vietnamese and Americans take on the normalization of relations between the United States and Viet Nam, is probably too simplistic, given these poems and their complex attitudes toward reconciliation. Through these writers' common experience of Trinh Minh-ha's idea of conflicted identities residing within the writerly self, however, we can imagine these women writers' rapprochement, a harbinger of the possibility therefore of reconciliation between (our) two nations.

Notes

1. Bruce Weigl's efforts to foster reconciliation and normalization betwen Viet Nam and the United States culminated in the 1994 publication of the anthology *Poems from Captured Documents*, which Weigl coedited and cotranslated with Thanh T. Nguyen. In his introduction to the book, Weigl writes:

> Thanh T. Nguyen and I hope that these translations will serve as a bridge to … understanding, and that by making available these intimate and deeply human glimpses from the lives of North Vietnamese and National Liberation Front soldiers during the American war, we will encourage and facilitate some kind of reconciliation—if not a political one, then an emotional and psychological one [vii].

The poems are presented both in Vietnamese and in English on facing pages, thus maximizing the audience to which the book can broadcast its reconciliatory message.

2. Besides literary history, Eileen Lotozo also concerns herself with "herstory" and its struggle with standard (masculinist) history; Lotozo suggests that in general women's "voices re-member our torn history; they recollect, restore, re-story," and that *Shallow Graves* in particular "reinstates women in Vietnam—a landscape from which they are continually dismissed by the standard histories and popularizations of the war" (12).

3. Le Ly Hayslip is another Viet Kieu woman writer who actively supports reconciliation between the United States and Viet Nam. In the prologue to *When Heaven and Earth Changed Places*, Hayslip dedicates her book to "all those who fought for their country, wherever it may be. It is dedicated, too, to those who did not fight—but suffered, wept, raged, bled, and died just the same" (xiv). The exhaustive inclusiveness of this listing signals Hayslip's driving passion for reconciliation. Her passion is underlined by her founding of the East Meets West Foundation in 1987 "to heal the wounds of war and break the circle of vengeance that perpetuates suffering in the name of justice around the world" (367).

4. I am indebted to George Uba for his insightful article "Friend and Foe: De-Collaborating Wendy Wilder Larsen and Tran Thi Nga's *Shallow Graves*," which helped to shape and sharpen my thinking on the theme of reconciliation in women's poetry of the Vietnam War. Uba's subject is "the perils of cross-cultural collaborations" (63), and his main point is that *Shallow Graves* is ultimately "an object lesson in the differences that continue to vex rather than facilitate efforts at cultural rapprochement, differences that continue to separate rather than join peoples and cultures but whose full recognition is vital if such rapprochement is ever to have any meaning at all" (69).

Works Cited

Abrams, Linsey. "Vietnam, East and West," review of *Shallow Graves* by Wendy Wilder Larsen and Tran Thi Nga. *New York Times Book Review*, 15 June 1986: 14.

Barry, Jan, and W. D. Ehrhart, eds. *Demilitarized Zones: Veterans After Vietnam*. Perkasie, Pa.: East River Anthology, 1976.

Eder, Richard. Review of *Shallow Graves* by Wendy Wilder Larsen and Tran Thi Nga. *Los Angeles Times Book Review*, 20 April 1986: 3+.

Ehrhart, W.D., ed. *Carrying the Darkness: American Indochina—The Poetry of the Vietnam War*. New York: Avon, 1985. Reprinted as *Carrying the Darkness: The Poetry of the Vietnam War*. Lubbock: Texas Tech University Press, 1988.

Gioseffi, Daniela. "Women in the Light of Fire," review of *Visions of War, Dreams of Peace*, edited by Lynda Van Devanter and Joan A. Furey. *American Book Review* 13.6 (Feb.-March 1992): 19+.

Grefrath, Richard W. Review of *Shallow Graves* by Wendy Wilder Larsen and Tran Thi Nga. *Library Journal* 111 (15 April 1986): 75.

Hackworth, David M. "The War Without End." *Newsweek*, 22 Nov. 1993: 44–48.

Hayslip, Le Ly, with Jay Wurts. *When Heaven and Earth Changed Places: A Vietnamese Woman's Journey from War to Peace*. New York: Doubleday, 1989.

Holliday, Bob. "The Years They Lived Dangerously," review of *Shallow Graves* by Wendy Wilder Larsen and Tran Thi Nga. *Book World* 16 (11 May 1986): 7.

Larsen, Wendy Wilder, and Tran Thi Nga. *Shallow Graves: Two Women and Vietnam*. New York: Harper and Row, 1987.

Lehman, David. Review of *Shallow Graves* by Wendy Wilder Larsen and Tran Thi Nga. *Newsweek*, 7 July 1986: 60A.

Lotozo, Eileen. "Tragedy into Poetry," review of *Shallow Graves* by Wendy Wilder Larsen and Tran Thi Nga and *Fragments from the Fire: The Triangle Shirtwaist Company Fire of March 25, 1911* by Chris Llewellyn. *Women's Review of Books*, June 1987: 12–13.

Monaghan, Pat. Review of *Visions of War, Dreams of Peace*, edited by Lynda Van Devanter and Joan A. Furey. *Booklist* 87 (15 May 1991): 1775.

Nguyen, Thanh T., and Bruce Weigl, ed. and trans. *Poems from Captured Documents*. Amherst: University of Massachusetts Press, 1994.

Primm, Sandy. Review of *Visions of War, Dreams of Peace*, edited by Lynda Van Devanter and Joan A. Furey. *Viet Nam Generation Newsletter* 3.3 (Nov. 1991): 78.

Ratner, Rochelle. Review of *Visions of War, Dreams of Peace*, edited by Lynda Van Devanter and Joan A. Furey. *Library Journal* 116 (1 May 1991): 79.

Review of *Shallow Graves* by Wendy Wilder Larsen and Tran Tri Nga. *Kirkus Reviews*, 15 March 1986: 448–49.

Review of *Shallow Graves* by Wendy Wilder Larsen and Tran Tri Nga. *Kliatt Young Adult Paperback Book Guide*, September 1987: 31.

Review of *Shallow Graves* by Wendy Wilder Larsen and Tran Tri Nga. *Time*, 2 June 1986: 26.

Review of *Shallow Graves* by Wendy Wilder Larsen and Tran Tri Nga. *Virginia Quarterly Review* 62 (Autumn 1986): 135.

Review of *Visions of War, Dreams of Peace: Writings of Women in the Vietnam War.* by Lynda Van Devanter and Joan A. Furey. *Kliatt Young Adult Paperback Book Guide*, September 1991: 35.

Rottmann, Larry, Jan Barry and Basil T. Paquet, eds. *Winning Hearts and Minds: War Poems by Vietnam Veterans*. Brooklyn: 1st Casualty Press; New York: McGraw-Hill, 1972.

Said, Edward. *Orientalism*. New York: Pantheon-Random, 1978.

Trinh T. Minh-Ha. *Woman, Native, Other: Writing Postcoloniality and Feminism*. Bloomington: Indiana University Press, 1989.

Uba, George, "Friend and Foe: De-Collaborating Wendy Wilder Larsen and Tran Thi Nga's

Shallow Graves: Two Women and Vietnam." Journal of American Culture 16 (Fall 1993): 63–70.

Van Devanter, Lynda, and Joan A. Furey, eds. *Visions of War, Dreams of Peace: Writings of Women in the Vietnam War.* New York: Warner, 1991.

Weigl, Bruce. "Bruce Weigl: 'Poetry Grabbed Me by the Throat.'" In Schroeder, Eric James, *Vietnam, We've All Been There: Interviews with American Writers.* Westport, CT: Praeger, 1992. 181–95.

11. "What Shall We Give Our Children?" Fatherhood Poems by Veterans

LORRIE SMITH

> For perhaps we are like stones; our own history and the history of the world embedded in us, we hold a sorrow deep within and cannot weep until that history is sung.
> —Susan Griffin, *A Chorus of Stones*

It is not surprising that the most moving voice of conscience to come out of the war in Bosnia so far belongs to a child, and that Zlata Filipović's diary should inevitably—even if inaccurately—recall an earlier child-witness, Anne Frank. Nothing illuminates war's unnatural horror more powerfully than the suffering and death of children. The literature of the Vietnam War—particularly its poetry—is haunted by nightmare images of the war's most innocent victims. Robert Bly's "Teeth Mother Naked at Last," a furious protest poem written during the war, ends with a harrowing scream designed to elicit civilian shame and rage and force the reader to compare her own safe children to those in Viet Nam. No doubt exploiting public familiarity with one of the war's most famous photographs—a naked girl running towards the camera aflame with napalm—Bly's poem anticipates the anguish, grief, and trauma that accompany the real memory of such images in many veterans' postwar poems:

> But if one of those children came near that we have set on fire,
> came toward you like a gray barn, waking,
> you would howl like a wind tunnel in a hurricane,
> you would tear at your shirt with blue hands,
> you would drive over your own child's wagon trying to back up,
> the pupils of your eyes would go wild—
>
> If a child came by burning, you would dance on a lawn,
> trying to leap into the air, digging into your cheeks,
> you would ram your head against the wall of your bedroom
> like a bull penned too long in his moody pen—

161

> If one of those children came toward me with both hands
> in the air, fire rising along both elbows,
> I would suddenly go back to my animal brain,
> I would drop on all fours screaming,
> my vocal chords would turn blue, so would yours,
> it would be two days before I could play with my own children again [174].

Many years later, alluding to the same photograph, veteran Bruce Weigl calls up a similar image; here, Bly's conditional "if" becomes immediate flashback within an ironically titled poem, "Song of Napalm": "I close my eyes and see the girl / running from her village, napalm / stuck to her dress like jelly, / her hands reaching for the no one / who waits in waves of heat before her" (*Napalm* 33). Weigl's poem not only relives this atrocity for us, but testifies to the impossibility of forgetting it, wishing it away, or ignoring it. Though he doesn't retreat to his "animal brain" and he does find words to express his grief, the speaker's continuing trauma is evident:

> The lie works only as long as it takes to speak
> and the girl runs only as far
> as the napalm allows
> until her burning tendons and crackling
> muscles draw her up
> into that final position
> burning bodies so perfectly assume. Nothing
> can change that, she is burned behind my eyes
> and not your good love and not the rain-swept air
> and not the jungle-green
> pasture unfolding before us can deny it [*Napalm*, 34–35].

In searching for a way to live with postwar trauma in a culture bent on forgetting the war, veterans have written about many sources of catharsis and healing: nature, camaraderie, political activism, erotic love, family acceptance, return trips to Viet Nam, poetry itself. But one of the most helpful possibilities for recovery, and perhaps even redemption, comes through fatherhood, as in Weigl's "Small Song for Andrew," where the sleeping child "is more beautiful / Than the light / Before the light has touched anything." Such moments of grace may offer respite for individual writers, but the many poems of fatherhood by veterans suggest something larger at work, as well—a transformation of the very culture that justifies sending young men to war and dropping napalm on children. While raising children is construed in our culture as a highly personal activity, many of these writers insist that it is also a profoundly social commitment to our shared future, one entailing conscious ethical and political choices. Veteran poets seem to recognize, as Susan Griffin puts it, that "the histories of families cannot be separated from the histories of nations. To divide them is part of our denial" (11). Thus, much writing by veterans resonates with the moral imperative at the end of W.D. Ehrhart's "To Those Who

Have Gone Home Tired": "What answers will you find / What armor will protect you / when your children ask you / Why?" (*Mercy* 61).

Traditionally, the experience of parenthood and the emotions it releases have been viewed as women's subjects. Yet Lynda Van Devanter's collection of poems by women veterans of the Vietnam war, *Visions of War, Dreams of Peace*, includes just a few poems addressed to or about a child, and one, Marilyn McMahon's poignant "Knowing," about the choice not to have children after Dioxin exposure.* More frequently, the soldiers nurses tended are mourned as hurt or dead children, which, indeed, they were. In contrast, recent poems by male veterans locate fatherhood as a central point of reference in their ongoing poetic project to discover, in Weigl's words, "what saves us." Partly, this reflects a cultural shift; many fathers in the Vietnam generation seem willing to "mother" their children—that is, to relinquish at least some patriarchal habits in favor of more culturally feminine expressions of tenderness, nurturing, vulnerability, and reciprocity. But the experience of fatherhood for veteran writers carries particularly loaded significance and complexity, for it means confronting painful memories like those in the poems above and accepting their complicity—however ambivalent—in the war which caused such suffering. In addition, fatherhood brings many writers face to face with the loss of their own childhoods cut abruptly short by the war.

One way to view the Vietnam War is as a grotesque form of child abuse, abandonment, and betrayal by parents who repressed and lied about their own earlier traumas of World War II and Korea. Fought by nineteen-year-olds conscripted and commanded by older, often inept officers, the war epitomized the generation gap that so defined the sixties in America. Robert Bly describes a kind of generational grief and "erosion of male confidence" which he blames on "older men lying to younger men," and the "bad judgment of older men that resulted in damage to younger men or death of younger men" (165). John Balaban expresses similar anger towards the older generation in his search for new life after the war in "In Celebration of Spring":

> Our Asian war is over; others have begun.
> Our elders, who tried to mortgage lies,
> are disgraced, or dead, and already
> the brokers are picking their pockets
> for the keys and the credit cards.

Meanwhile, "the wounded walk about and wonder where to go." The poem finds hope in traditional sources—youth and the return of spring: "As she

---

**According to Van Devanter, a recent survey of Vietnam war nurses uncovered the startling fact that the number of women veterans who remain unmarried and who have no children is much larger than the numbers in the population at large—a demographic fact which seems to accord with this poetic absence. For a treatment of women's poetry of the war, see my article, "The Subject Makes a Difference: Poetry by Women Veterans of the Vietnam War."*

chases a Frisbee spinning in sunlight, / a girl's breasts bounce full and strong; / a boy's stomach, as he turns, is flat and strong." Though Balaban's own innocence may have been shattered, he vows to learn from his experiences and cultivate a hopeful world for the next generation:

> Swear by the locust, by dragonflies on ferns,
> by the minnow's flash, the tremble of a breast,
> by the new earth spongy under our feet:
> that as we grow old, we will not grow evil,
> that although our garden seeps with sewage,
> and our elders think it's up for auction—swear
> by this dazzle that does not wish to leave us—
> that we will be keepers of a garden, nonetheless [*Mercy* 16].

As veterans like Balaban, Ehrhart, and Weigl became fathers and naturally absorbed that experience into their poems, they uncovered whole new perspectives on the war which enable them to integrate private and public history. Their poems reveal two main movements hinged by the experience of fatherhood: back to their own childhoods and forward into the world in which they raise their children. Writing about their young children in relation to the war allows these poets to revisit some of their own childhood wounds so that, as Griffin puts it, "the unnatural heaviness of unspoken truth is dispersed" and cycles of repression are broken. Often, the child is a healing mediator between the painful past and the future. In many poems, feelings of parental protectiveness invoke memories of suffering children. The menacing intrusion of the past into the present, as in Weigl's "Song of Napalm," brings to the surface deeply troubling associations between Vietnamese children and their own. Finally, children represent, of course, hopeful new life. While childhood is a theme susceptible to cliché and sentimentality, veteran poets generally avoid these pitfalls by representing children as a gift of grace in a dangerous world poisoned by evil "sewage." None tries to recuperate an innocent, pre–Vietnam garden, nor are they fooled into thinking their children will ever be completely safe. But by realistically facing their own childhood and wartime traumas, these poets show a strong determination to break patterns of violence, neglect, and denial, to do things differently for their own children, and to assume responsibility for struggling against the forces that threaten all children.

Significantly, both Balaban and Ehrhart open recent volumes with poems remembering their own boyhoods in relation to the war. Ehrhart's title poem, "Just for Laughs," returns to a formative moment of childhood when the omnipotent ten-year-old "thought that I / would live forever, I could kill / whatever I pleased, I was all / that mattered." The poem then recalls incidents of boyhood cruelty towards animals and ends with confession and self-knowledge: "Years later, I volunteered for war, / still oblivious to what I'd done,

/ or what I was about to do, or why" (*Laughs* 13). The poem yields complex and suggestive meanings: the obvious narrative linking of childhood violence and war is clear; more obliquely, imagery such as "firecrackers / stuffed down throats of frogs and lit: / hop, hop, boom. A lot of laughs" echoes numerous war stories of torture, and the macabre vision of "baby watersnakes ... small wriggling slivers of the mother's flesh" crawling out of the gashes in her side evokes the horrific spectacle of battle-torn bodies. Read in the context of the volume's many tender poems about Ehrhart's daughter, this opening poem sets a chilling tone for the book. Moreover, it demolishes, through ironic self-critique, the most recalcitrant cultural myths linking manhood, war, heroism, and innocence. This poem's confessional theme and the speaker's complicity are later echoed in "Chasing Locomotives," which ends lamenting "It's little enough / my daughter has to keep her / from a world full of men / like me / who can't imagine any world / except the one they think / belongs to them" (*Laughs* 69).

A newer poem, "Guns," remembers another ten-year-old, this one the victim of Ehrhart, the eighteen-year-old soldier. The poem centers on a dialogue between the poet and his four-year-old daughter, who's now full of questions about "a world full of men" with guns. As he imagined in "To Those Who Have Gone Home Tired," long before he ever had a child himself, he is accountable to the next generation's "why":

> How explain a world where men
> kill other men deliberately
> and call it love of country?
>
> Just eighteen, I killed
> a ten-year-old. I didn't know.
> He spins across the marketplace
> all shattered chest, all eyes and arms.
> Do I tell her that? Not yet,

The poem both confesses its truths and defers them until the daughter can understand better, consciously countering the kind of repression that shaped his own "ignorant" youth and led him right from high school to the Marines:

> though one day I will have
> no choice except to tell her
> or to send her into the world
> wide-eyed and ignorant.
> The boy spins across the years
>
> till he lands in a heap
> in another war in another place
> where yet another generation
> is rudely about to discover
> what their fathers never told them. (*Distance* 42)

Like all parents, Ehrhart has to admit his impotence to stop larger cycles of history or to protect his daughter's innocence forever. He does, however, use his power as a witness and a survivor to take a stand against war, refusing to take part in the kind of betrayal and repression that led the frog-exploding, gun-lugging boy to Vietnam.

Such intrusions of wartime memories in connection with his daughter are disturbingly insistent in Ehrhart's newest book, *The Distance We Travel.* In what is possibly the angriest piece Ehrhart has ever written, a prose-poem entitled "What War Does," memory indelibly scars the present: "When you look at your daughter, you see the child dead in its mother's arms, its skin blue, its small body turning rigid. When you look at your wife, you see the mother keening softly, rocking the child as if to sleep, unaware of the armed men staring down at her, unaware of her own fatal wounds, lost in a mother's grief that nothing will ever set right" (40). By witnessing this pieta, a complete inversion of the many tender scenes with his own daughter in earlier poems, Ehrhart attacks complacent apathy and forces us, too, to "look and look till what you are seeing is burned into your retinas, until it is tattooed on your soul."

Unlike Ehrhart, John Balaban did not go to Vietnam as a warrior but as a healer and pacifist working as a conscientious objector with war-injured children, as his recent memoir, *Remembering Heaven's Face*, beautifully dramatizes. In his poetry and prose, Balaban continues to be a strong voice of conscience. An earlier poem, "After Our War," voiced a painful crisis of language signifying deeper spiritual losses: "Will the myriad world surrender new metaphor? / After our war, how will love speak?" (*Mercy* 14). Not only do images from his experience of the war impinge directly on his experience as a father in his newest volume, *Words for My Daughter*, but one suspects that the war itself is a big part of what instigates this book's quest to answer his earlier questions and to satisfy "the hunger for words pure as clear water / that will slake the pain of our parched tongues / and, splashed against our brows, shall let us see" (*Words* 25). If Balaban's dilemma is not solved completely, he does—by speaking poems to his daughter and dedicating the book to her—find a way for love to speak. Like "Just for Laughs," Balaban's title poem begins with a return to his own boyhood and a juxtaposed association with the war. He unflinchingly remembers his rough childhood in the projects in a series of violent vignettes: "Reds ... huge as a hippo" running from his drunk father's beating, Bobby Connelly attacking the milkman who raped his "alcoholic mother," a girl running down the street "with a dart in her back," a boy hanging from a tree by the neck. While Ehrhart confessed guilt for his gratuitous childhood violence and located it on a trail leading straight to Viet Nam, Balaban loves his playmates for surviving with "justice and valor and desperate loves / twisted in shapes of hammer and shard." He bequeaths these equivocal memories to his daughter not to evoke pity, but to suggest that such violence, however "twisted," is not the worst that can happen; he goes on to give witness to a scene of almost unutterable atrocity, as if by speaking it, he might ward off the worst for his own child:

> Worse for me is a cloud of memories
> still drifting off the South China sea,
> like the 9-year-old boy, naked and lacerated,
> thrashing in his pee on a steel operating table
> and yelling "*Dau, Dau,*" while I, trying to translate
> in the mayhem of Tet for surgeons who didn't know
> who this boy was or what happened to him, kept asking
> "Where? Where's the pain?" until a surgeon
> said, "Forget it. His ears are blown." (11)

Such a memory, like the burning girl in Weigl's "Song of Napalm" and the eruptions in Ehrhart's poems, can never be denied or imagined away. But it can be used to make judgments and bring personal memory into the sphere of the social and political: certain instances of suffering are worse than others and demand witness and response. The poem shifts, then, to remember a Halloween when a peaceful moment with his baby daughter was interrupted by a "tiny Green Beret" trick-or-treating. Balaban returns from a flashback in which he hears the "awful chorus of Soeur Anicet's orphans writhing in their cribs" to a present when fathers still mindlessly pass on a culture of militarism. The boy gets a Mars Bar; to the father "waiting outside in fatigues" he hisses, "'You shit' ... in a pose I know too well." The juxtaposition of childhood playmates, sleeping daughter, suffering Vietnamese children, and "midget" soldier comes together in the final stanza, where the father chants a prayer for deliverance and grants the child power to heal:

> I want you to know the worst and be free from it.
> I want you to know the worst and still find good.
> Day by day, as you play nearby or laugh
> with the ladies at Peoples Bank as we go around town
> and I find myself beaming like a fool,
> I suspect I am here less for your protection
> than you are here for mine, as if you were sent
> to call me back into our helpless tribe. (12)

So powerful is this regenerative gift of the child that Balaban returns to it in his memoir:

> But today is a sunny August afternoon in 1989. Later, when I have finished writing this part of my seance with remembrance, I will go downstairs to help my wife organize our daughter's birthday party. Our daughter is four. Hers is a world of play with screamy girlfriends under a bright sky and sheltering elms strung with paper lanterns, where locusts drone through the hot afternoon and katydids and crickets will sing throughout the night ... When

I watch her play, I am constantly awed by her beauty and perfect health. She has no idea how much the sight of her restores me, how often her gay little voice summons me out of the murmurs of the past into her happy world, how much rescue she has in her little hand as she pulls me around town [*Heaven's Face* 106].

Like Balaban, Bruce Weigl places memories of the Vietnam War in a context of spiritual crisis signified by blocked language and song. In his newest book, *What Saves Us*, he admits, less hopefully than Balaban, that "What used to save me / was my child's voice / singing at night in his bed / songs he'd learned at school." Such consolation is no longer available or effective, and Weigl takes as his epigraph lines from Siegfried Sassoon resisting easy resolution or unambiguous tones: "The song was wordless / The singing will never be done." Weigl's latest poems of memory dramatize a painful stasis recognizable in much of his work: "always of two minds, / singing the few songs / I know over and over, / their notes a gathering black in the sky." Like his earlier "Song of Napalm," "The Hand that Takes" ends not with childhood's innocent song but with an update of Blake's songs of experience:

> I heard a child's scream
> and the rockets
> crash through bamboo.
> From the mother's legs
> we are dropped into fire.
> There is not even time
> for the moon to turn away,
> or the words to be said
> and then mean nothing,
> or the fear to make men
> not kiss the dead. (40)

The ambiguity expressed by such double negatives is a signature of Weigl's work. Yet, as its explicitly religious title and cover (a medieval Madonna) suggest, Weigl's book is not without moments of grace and hope. Just as Ehrhart and Balaban find release in poetic language, Weigl suggests that the song of fallen history might be a force for atonement, healing, and salvation. In "The Impossible," an unnerving poem about "the man who made me suck his cock / when I was seven," the most horrifying experience might always be transformed: "In his hands he held my head like a lover. / Say it clearly and you make it beautiful, no matter what." Weigl's middle-aged search for "what saves us," like Balaban's and Ehrhart's, leads back to his own broken childhood and, inevitably, to the war that brought his childhood to such a violent end. Weigl's newest book contains a number of striking poems about his working class childhood strongly reminiscent of Philip Levine as well as the "chronic angers" of Robert Hayden's "Those Winter Sundays" and the rough love of Roethke's "My Papa's Waltz." As with Hayden, it is the grown man, now a father himself, who can belatedly but compassionately appreciate the father's "austere and lonely offices" of love. In "Why We are Forgiven," the father is larger-than-life, evoked through the textured particulars of poetic memory:

> and in my hungry brain
> a spirit recalls my father
> home from the mill in his white T-shirt
> like a god
> and the smell of the mill
>
> all over his body
> and the taste of his delicious sweat.
> Those evenings when he touched me,
> those lingering hours after work and beer
> when he reached down
> into the nowhere my fear invented
> I would come alive.
>
> I would be drunk with joy
> and in my small bed
> I heard the ore boats
> call from the river and the railcars
> couple in the roundhouse
> And the ringing hammer voices
> of the nightshift workers sing us free.

In "The Years Without Understanding," the father's violence is forgiven since, as in Balaban's poem and after Vietnam, it's not the worst that the poet remembers:

> And what you teach someone
> with a belt across his back
> is belts,
> or I missed the point of those beatings
> which were not so bad—
> the loud voice in the hallway, then the belt
> flashing
> then the kisses on his lap.

And in "Meditation at Pearl Street," Weigl remembers moments "in the quiet hours, / when the chronic angers were still / and the father's curses / did not slam down on the table / a rough love bound us in a feast / where all our hearts were opened." The reader might recall, with these poems, the equivocal sacraments of earlier Weigl poems. In "The Kiss," the father saves his son from a tornado and bestows a benedictory kiss as he boards a plane to Viet Nam, but also delivers the orders to go to war. In "Anna Grasa," the father greets the returning son with a "sign / made at the foundry: WEL-COME HOME BRUCE / in orange glow paint. / He rented spotlights, / I had to squint"; the shaken son must hide from "the terrible thing" behind his grandmother's dress. In the last poem of *What Saves Us*, "The Forms of Eleventh Avenue," what finally soothes the speaker traumatized by postwar depression and anxiety is this paradoxical inheritance retrieved from memories older than the war:

> What saved me
> were the Latin prayers
> come back from the years
> like desire,
> and the many mouths
> open in absolution,
> and the nakedness,
> the belt flashing,
> the fists from out of nowhere,
> the abandonment of love.

Accepting unavoidable ambiguity (he is both abandoned by his father and embraced in passionate abandon) enables Weigl, finally, to discover a meaningful point of continuity between his own childhood and his son Andrew's in "The Confusion of Planes We Must Wander in Sleep," which rewrites a primal scene of midnight intimacy:

> I stood naked in the corner as my mother
> changed the wet sheet and clucked her tongue though spoke
> as kindly as she could, my father stirring angrily
> in the bed across the hall. Lost, my legs sheened in piss,
> I stumbled, drugged with the grief
> children practice to survive. I was apart
> from the cold and heavy smell. I was not attached
> to the world though I followed my young and weary
> mother into the timeless dark, and tonight,
>
> I pull my own son's blankets back and speak to him:
> how nice a dry bed will be, how good to get up
> without a fuss and go. I lift him to stand,
> his penis a wand waving its way magically
> before us, and something makes sense for once in my head,
> the way that what we pass on is not always a gift,
> not always grace or strength or music, but sometimes
> a burden, and we have no choice but to live
> as hard as we can inside the storm of our years
> because even the weaknesses are a kind of beauty
> for the way they bind us into what love, finally, must be.

In this healing and transformative moment, Weigl chooses his mother's part rather than his father's—showing compassion rather than anger—and there is hope that his son will not grow up as he did numbed by grief and shame.

The phallus is not a rod of brute power but a magic wand from which flows clarified feeling and connection.

Ehrhart and Balaban, too, find moments of release and salvation in connection with their children, though all three poets, steeped in history, resist fairy tale endings. At the end of his book, Balaban returns from his archetypal journey through the western landscape where he witnessed "living metaphors" and where "no lies are told," bearing the gifts of renewed language and love for the next generation: "Child, I bring back the water's benediction ... . Love like water makes the canyons bloom" (70). His last poem echoes his first, the daughter who protected him now calling him once again "back into our helpless tribe": "When I scoop you up into a hug / you'll cry, 'Don't crush me *bones!*' / My tiny guide to a wiser life. / Little wren who calls me home" (71).

While such healing is registered in personal terms, a 1992 poem, "Viewing the New World Order," reopens the linguistic wound of "After Our War" in a masterful blend of private and collective history. Standing with a poet-friend at a resonantly historical point of origin, the ruins of Athens, Balaban is "awed by the lonely grace of stones fallen, stones still standing." From this site he surveys a world of unjust, politically motivated suffering and utters a fierce jeremiad castigating the triumph of corporate capitalism in "the New World Order my president would praise." The poem ends with a plea on behalf of his own daughter, but it assumes almost prophetic dimensions in speaking to a global future embodied by all children. He mimics the Greeks by invoking a muse and pouring libations, but has no assurance the chorus of stones will answer:

> *These old stones cry out for more.*
> Surviving centuries, sculpted here for all to see,
> the handsome youth, the maiden at the well, their inward smiles
> declare our need for beauty and laws like love
> for this tiny *polis* of a planet spinning wildly,
> for my daughter, snug, asleep in Pennsylvania, for
> Aleko who played in the Chernobyl cloud,
> whose father now stands near the Nike's rotting frieze,
> looking out upon the city jammed with cars. Georgi
> opens his flask of vodka, pours some on a stone
> before we drink our toasts to the new world order
> and to whatever must shall come to give us words.

Ehrhart's recovery, too, is qualified. Like Balaban's, his songs are almost always suffused by memories of the war and tinged by his realization that "There are things too evil for words, too evil for silence," and that "What I want for my daughter / she shall never have: / a world without war, a life / untouched by bigotry or hate, / a mind free to carry a thought / up to the light of pure possibility" (*Laughs* 38). Yet the final poem from his new book, *The Distance We Travel*, finds reconciliation that is both personal and political—even diplomatic—through the mediating life of his daughter. Returning to Viet Nam for the second time since the war, still a "strange American" with "no answers," he yearns to "gather the heart of this place / into himself, to make it forgive him." A moment of grace comes when he is brought into the circle of a Vietnamese family whose father, like the poet, was injured by "V.C." Ehrhart communicates by showing a picture of his daughter (spelled in the poem with Vietnamese phonetics) and the father, surrounded by his own children, responds: "'Li-La,' the father softly says, touching / the stranger's heart with his open hand." Such moments of unaccustomed mercy remind us that we do have choices about what we pass on:

> What shall we give our children?
> Paco's company blown to jungle junk
> by our own obsessions—or a graceless kiss,
> my weaponless hands, your smile [Laughs 84].

Doug Rawlings, a founding member of Veterans for Peace and a contributor to early collections of veterans' poetry, gives an unequivocal answer to Ehrhart's question in his unpublished volume, *Giving Silence: Poems for Our Children.* Underlying Rawlings' poems, like those of so many veteran poets, is the urge to use the lens of his experience in Viet Nam to envision a peaceful world for his children. A poem entitled "Giving Silence: for Josh and David Turning 13," charts new space for the sons to grow in—beyond Bly's blind rage at the fathers' betrayal, beyond the impasse of blocked language in Balaban, beyond the ambivalence of Weigl's wordless song, beyond the either/or choices Ehrhart lays out. Voiced by a "we" the poet has defined specifically as veterans who denounce war, Rawlings' poem celebrates his son's coming of age by defining a whole new way of being male:

> Yet we have known
> for years now
> that the silence
> of our fathers
> will not do
>
> And, yes, we have also known
> that words alone
> cannot become the sacred knives
> to bleed yourselves free
> of raging doubt
>
> So listen up
> to these words of silence:
>
> Open up your fists
>
> Watch women move
>
> Scorn uniforms
> Don't march
> Dance

If we are to break cycles of war and repression, we have no choice but to keep singing to our children, to speak honestly of our own traumas so they won't contribute to lies, secrets, and silence, to accept the burden and gift of love where we find them.

Works Cited

Balaban, John. *Remembering Heaven's Face: A Moral Witness in Vietnam.* New York: Touchstone, 1991.

____. "Viewing the New World Order." *Witness* 6:1 (1992): 9–11.

____. *Words for My Daughter.* Port Townsend: Copper Canyon Press, 1991.

Bly, Robert. "The Vietnam War and the Erosion of Male Confidence." In Reese Williams, ed. *Unwinding the Vietnam War: from War into Peace.* Seattle: Real Comet Press, 1987: 161–177.

Ehrhart, W.D. *The Distance We Travel.* Easthampton, MA: Adastra Press, 1993.

____. *Just for Laughs.* Silver Spring, MD: Vietnam Generation, Inc. and Burning Cities Press, 1990.

____, ed. *Unaccustomed Mercy: Soldier Poets of the Vietnam War.* Lubbock: Texas Tech University Press, 1989.

Griffin, Susan. *A Chorus of Stones: The Private Life of War.* New York: Doubleday, 1992.

Rawlings, Doug. "Giving Silence: for Josh and David Turning 13." *Journal of American Culture* 16:3 (Fall 1993): 117.

Smith, Lorrie. "The Subject Makes a Difference: Poetry by Women Veterans of the Vietnam War." *Journal of American Culture* 16:3 (Fall 1993): 71–79.

Van Devanter, Lynda, and Joan A. Furey, eds. *Visions of War, Dreams of Peace: Writings of Women in the Vietnam War.* New York: Warner Books, 1991.

Weigl, Bruce. *Song of Napalm.* New York: Atlantic Monthly Books, 1990.

____. *What Saves Us.* Chicago Tri-quarterly Press, 1992.

The Other Side of Blue

Today in the rain
the purple loosestrife waver
in the marsh's blue haze
and I remember a day when the rain
lifted and the streets of a city
wavered in the heat
a young boy who held out
a tin-backed mirror—you buy,
he said, I sell.
I bought the mirror
its back hammered out by hand
from discarded beer cans.
The glare from the highway
makes me blink and stare
and I see his face again
his eyes pleading
for the small colored bills,
their name like the French name
for the rain. The mirror is gone now
cracked and broken beneath the weight of years,
the boy's face has become
the face of a young girl
who worked the potato fields of upstate New York,
and asked me to take her away.
And her face becomes the face of the child
standing by a roadside in Salvador, or Bosnia,
or South Africa, all of those children
we watch in quick clips on the evening news;
like voyeurs, we avoid
the outstretched hands, the eyes
which speak the same language, ask
the same questions.
How long will it take until we learn
each child matters, each face
turned toward us
is a face in the mirror,
a reflection that will not go away.

—GERALD McCARTHY

IV.
LITERATURE OF RECONCILIATION: PROSE

12. American War Myths and Vietnam Veteran Narratives

JOSEPH T. COX

The myths found in American war narratives perform at least two functions: they set the boundaries within which the war's interpretation and the story of the soldier's personal experience may proceed, and they enforce the rhetoric of those interpretations by setting the terms of the narrative. The history of the production of these myths has always occurred in a complex cultural system defined by ideology, gender, class, race, value commitments (to name but a few variables), and their reception is similarly situated. When John Hellman analyzes the enduring trauma of Vietnam's "disruption of the American story" (221), he deconstructs a conglomerate American myth-history. But what of the things that hold at the center of war experience? What are we to make of the stories formed by the imagination, experience, and culture of combat veterans? Specifically, how do Vietnam veteran narratives stand in relation to the myth history of combat constructed by American veterans of earlier American wars? And what conclusions can we draw from these histories of constructed truth?

Like the recollective architecture of war memorials, war narratives reflect and recall struggles to the death over different values. As in our efforts to critically appreciate our war monuments, we must try to understand war narratives' social context, the effects on those that read them, and the context of their mythic symbolism.

In order to illustrate how American myth history influenced the Vietnam narrative, I will illustrate that narrative's relationship to earlier accounts of war through a comparison of the Vietnam Veterans Memorial's relationship to historically antecedent and neighboring monuments.* Just as any visit

*I gratefully acknowledge three articles which helped me "read" the Wall and the surrounding monuments: Todd Lindberg's "Of Arms, Men & Monuments" in Commentary, October 1984; Shirly Neilsen Blum's "The National Vietnam War Memorial" in Arts Magazine, December 1984; and especially Charles L. Griswold's "The Vietnam Memorial and the Washington Mall: Philosophical Thoughts on Political Iconography" in Critical Inquiry, Summer 1986.

to the Vietnam Veterans Memorial draws its significance from the Wall's proximity to and geometric differences from adjacent memorials, Vietnam narratives depend on the structure and substance of the earliest American war stories for their full significance. The truth of the narrative may have as much to do with the history of the myth as with the immediate experience recollected.

A visitor in search of the Vietnam Veterans Memorial takes a bearing from either the Washington or Lincoln Memorial. Dominating the horizon of the Mall on which the Vietnam Veterans Memorial rests, the Washington Memorial, although not a war monument, represents in part the idealized martial discipline of the nation's founder, and, although there is no trace of the man in the monument, it stands as an abstract, idealized human embodiment of the Republic. It is and suggests a towering presence. Since a visitor can climb to its top, the monument serves as an observation tower from which the average citizen can look down on his nation's capital and judge it from the heights of the myth of Washington's heroic idealism.

From the very beginning, America's central war myth has inscribed in the nation's cultural consciousness a celebration of abstract heroic idealism. The written record begins with the towering ego of Captain John Smith, a veteran of the crusades, where, he tells us, before massed armies, he killed three Turkish champions in single combat. Taken prisoner and made a slave, he killed his master and fought his way back to England. At Jamestown, the first permanent English colony in America, Smith's experience in survival proved valuable to his fellow colonists. Smith's accounts of conflict with native Americans argued that combat experience produced a special quality of character and was a special qualification for leadership. He urged his fellow colonialists to be "brave spirits that advanced themselves from poor soldiers to great captains, their posterity to great lords." In his romantic history, war is a life-affirming endeavor that allows the rugged individual to assume his natural role as leader in a new society. Thus, from its beginnings, America has been a place where war is both the proving ground of character and the best way to become "somebody."

The narratives of every American war reinterpret and reinforce this abstract heroic myth. During the War of 1812, Andrew Jackson, that war's personification of this heroic ideal, attributed his victory at New Orleans to his soldiers' "untutored courage." Henry Clay declared that the War of 1812 achieved "the firm establishment of the American character."

Nathaniel Hawthorne wrote of the war with Mexico that the "valor" that wins America's battles is "not trained in the hardihood of veterans, but a native and spontaneous fire," for "there is nothing in any other country similar to what we see in our own, when the blast of the trumpet at once converts men of peace into warriors" (66–67). Paul H. Buck reports how after the carnage of the Civil War, *The Road to Reunion* celebrated exclusively heroic ideals where men both North and South demonstrated exceptional character. "The history that the veterans told," Buck asserts, "was of a war in which valor countered valor, and each side devotedly served the right" (Buck 248).

The Spanish-American War Memorial depicts "The Hiker," a statue of a frontiersman turned soldier, and reaffirms the individual warrior myth of the solitary, resourceful, and consummate self-made man prepared to liberate the world.

At the end of World War I, three Marine veterans, Thomas Boyd, William March, and Laurence Stallings, take exception to the well-inscribed myth. They believed, as Stallings put it, that "truth lies at the bottom of a microscope." They wrote realistically of the horrific details of their combat experiences. The 1922 memorial to Ulysses S. Grant, located in front of the capitol and looking down the Mall to the Lincoln Memorial, has a group of statues on either side that depict such realistic, antiheroic details of war. One side depicts a cavalry charge and includes a falling trooper about to be trampled to death by his fellow soldiers, and the other is a sculpture of men and horses pulling a caisson into position. This post–World War I memorial to the physical strain of war is a self-conscious, realistic, anti-romantic anti-monument to the nation's long-standing notions of abstract individual heroism. Even the massive equestrian statue of Grant placidly surveying the Western horizon and the far-off graves of Arlington National Cemetery offers no heroic pose or resolution.

Just as the Grant Memorial works against a moral affirmation of the abstract individual heroic myth, so, too, does the Vietnam Veterans Memorial and most Vietnam veteran narratives. Yet, many veterans exploit the heroic myth tradition for self-promotion and self-justification: in *Soldier,* LTC (Ret) Anthony B. Herbert, Korea's most decorated soldier, portrays himself as a victim of a corrupt system in order to help explain his relief from battalion command in Vietnam; ex–SEAL Commander Richard Marcinko writes *Rogue Warrior* from the Petersburg Federal Correctional Institution; and we are all familiar with LTC (Ret) Oliver North's story.

In contrast, Vietnam veterans trying to explore the truth in their experiences generally structure their narratives around their disillusionment with the myth of abstract American heroism. At the beginning of his story, when Ron Kovic shakes hands with the Marine recruiter, he is "shaking hands with John Wayne and Audie Murphy" (74). When the first bullet hits him, he "felt good inside. Finally the war was with me and I had been shot by the enemy. I was getting out of the war and I was going to be a hero" (221). But the second slug smashed his spinal cord to pieces, and the rest of his story is his painful deconstruction of America's fundamental abstract war myth, one that history and his childhood had so deeply ingrained in his consciousness.

In *A Rumor of War,* Philip Caputo plays off this essential warrior myth and, like Kovic, sees himself on a knight errand from President Kennedy's Camelot Round Table. As a boy playing on the "muddy stream called Salt Creek," he had dreamed of the old frontier, "that savage, heroic time" and had wished he could "find in a commonplace time a chance to live heroically"(5). He slowly learns that bloodless make-believe gives way to combat madness, and "the splendid little war" to "death's grey land." The description of his disenchantment is a self-consciously constructed verbal anti-monument to the notions of abstract heroism represented in the history of the romantic warrior myth, a quarrel with the myth as much as an account of the truth.

In *Chickenhawk*, Robert Mason's record of failed ideals and a failed spirit, he confesses that, after his tour in Vietnam, he was caught and convicted of selling drugs. He doesn't have a clue as to how it happened. He is confused, not because he doesn't know right from wrong, but because as a child he "had dreams of levitation" (21), and he believed his helicopter heroism would lift him above the temptations of everyday life. His life doesn't follow the pattern of the mythic American hero, and he doesn't understand why.

In *If I Die in a Combat Zone*, Tim O'Brien, "who grew out of one war and into another," (11) asks, "Do nightmares have themes, do we awaken and analyze them and live our lives and advise others as a result? Can the foot soldier teach anything important about war, merely for having been there? I think not. He can tell war stories" (23). The messages are clear in all four narratives: the mythic pattern of American heroism doesn't hold, moral regeneration through violence is false, and notions of abstract, towering, native American heroism deserve no myth-sustaining verbal monuments.

Although war films such as *Rambo* and *Missing in Action* tap into this long established myth of American heroic exceptionalism in order to advance political agendas, to discredit the victors, and to make money, the majority of Vietnam veterans portray themselves as anti-heroes; their narratives consciously reject the fundamental heroic myth.

The second broad category of war myth that informs the Vietnam narrative is a collective sense of a divinely justified national purpose that is best represented on the Mall by the Lincoln memorial. Although not a war monument, it is a temple dedicated to the preservation of the Union through war. Lincoln, the nation's leader, healer, savior, and redeemer, sits like a hero-god. His solemnity, his Christlike overtones of sacrifice, his facing East—the mythic place of new beginnings—all suggest the importance of his and the Civil War's sacrifice to national unity and rebirth, and they reinforce an American faith in the myth of the moral imperative of war.

Just as so many Vietnam narratives rely on personal deconstruction of John Smith's heroic myth of combat, they also quarrel with the long established, originally Puritan, notions of war as moral duty and cleansing sacrifice. Puritan forefathers taught colonists to accept war as a terrible but necessary means of pursuing its unique mission in history; war was, Increase Mather explained, "God's dreadful judgment" for not pursuing "the blessed design of their fathers." It was a communal rite of spiritual cleansing necessary to making America pure enough to lead the new world order.

The American Revolution was the secular continuation of a unique experiment confirming God's promise of human and social perfectibility, a necessarily unpleasant first step toward a glorious millennium governed by human reason. The Civil War was God's cleansing punishment for a nation that allowed the sin of slavery to stain its noble promise; Civil War gore became baptismal blood "consecrating the birth of a new and greater nation" (Buck 248). In what has become a unique American moral calculus, war's suffering has a cleansing and providential significance to both religious and secular cultural-myth makers, who believe that the course of history depends on America for spiritual direction.

Ironically, the most disenfranchised group of American veterans attach transcendent national purpose to the war in Viet Nam. Wallace Terry, the author of *Bloods: An Oral History of the Vietnam War by Black Veterans*, believes that Martin Luther King's dream was realized on the battlefield in the early stages of the war, but nobody paid attention to it. Terry's anthology is a lament for the loss of what he believes should have been a larger lesson of national reconciliation. He expects black veteran narratives to "help complete the missing pages of the American experience" (xvi).

In *Brothers: Black Soldiers in the Nam,* a young paratrooper named Robert Sanders echoes Terry's faith in national renewal through war when he reflects:

> For the first time in my life, I saw total unity and harmony. In the states, even in the rear in Nam, blacks and whites fought each other. But in Nam, man, out in the field we were just a force of unity and harmony. We became just one person.... Sometimes it takes tragedy to bring people together. It really does. And I can't think of anything more tragic than that situation at that time [147–48].

On the other hand, Tim O'Brien rejects transcendent moral lessons in Viet Nam. His inability to reconcile the reality of the war with the nation's mythic war rhetoric prompts him to contemplate a flight to Vancouver and to confess to Army Chaplain Edwards, a character who, even in this factual account of war, emerges as a comic caricature of persistent national myth. Edwards explains O'Brien's moral dilemma in terms of "a simple principle. Faith. When you get down to it, faith is an ancient Christian principle.... The Spanish-American war wasn't some cold-blooded human decision. President McKinley waited and waited. He prayed to the Lord, asking for guidance, and the Lord finally told him to go to war" (55–56).

Contemplating this old myth during the days before he leaves Viet Nam, O'Brien finds it meaningless, and nothing he comes to experience there will change his mind. He concludes that you learn only "that war is not all bad; … some stories of valor are true; … you have to pick the times not to be afraid, but when you are afraid you must hide it to save respect and reputation" (198). The lessons are ones of humble personal courage, not grand national redemption.

On the other hand, despite General Westmoreland's self-conscious attempts to avoid myths of national mission, they still shape his story. He concludes hypothetically that history "may" judge the war as a "noble crusade," and he reports that, "It has also become evident that America's abandonment of the South Vietnamese people has had a sharp effect on national morale in the United States and on American prestige around the world. Can America be trusted? Do the American people have the courage and stamina to stand up to aggression?" (564). War boils down to an international "gunfight," and General Westmoreland asks if America will have the will to pull the trigger in the future.

For the most part, however, Vietnam veterans have deliberately exorcised national morality lessons from their accounts of combat in favor of O'Brien's lessons of personal courage. In his self-justifying narrative, *About Face; The Odyssey of an American Hero,* COL (ret) David Hackworth compares scars with a rugged VC prisoner and concludes that "The warrior-to-warrior exchange broke the ice. It was a common bond that transcended patriotism or nationalism or causes. We laid down our flags and allowed ourselves to be friends" (697).

At the end of his narrative, Philip Caputo makes a separate peace with the Viet Cong. "It wasn't the VC who were threatening to rob me of my liberty, but the United States government, in whose service I had enlisted. Well, I was through with that. I was finished with governments and their abstract causes, and I would never again allow myself to fall under the charms and spells of political witch doctors like John F. Kennedy" (315).

In the end what counts for most veterans are immediate relationships. In his narrative *The Killing Zone,* dedicated to the men of Delta One-six and to his commander, Captain Harold Sells, Frederick Downs asks, "What was I trying to prove? But I answered my own question: The men depend on me. It's my job to keep them alive by giving them good leadership and looking after them. They need me" (191). Tim O'Brien says that when you add things up, "you lost a friend to the war, and you gained a friend" (198). War stories are about "love and memory" and sorrow (91). We are left with names on the Wall.

At the point where the two walls of the Vietnam Veterans Memorial meet, the black granite reflects not only the visitor but also the Washington Monument obelisk. Perhaps it admonishes against foreign entanglements, but it also symbolizes the myth of abstract individual heroism behind the names of the dead, an old archetype that inscribes Vietnam narratives. Likewise, the nearby Lincoln Memorial recalls another period of national divisiveness and reminds us that there is no representational figure of national reconciliation associated with the Wall, only the names of the dead. Frederick Hart's three infantrymen who suggest service and comradeship and Glena Goodacre's three women veterans who represent sacrifice and healing are physically and aesthetically removed to the distant woodline.

As events come to an end, we shape the past, give it a beginning and an end. After wars, stories about the fighting, about the politics, about the society take shape and coalesce into a collective sense of how it was. Each subsequent generation of soldiers relies on this collective sense, these myths of past wars, to prepare themselves for the coming unknown; and, once veterans, they turn to past myths in search of some meaning in the confusion that inevitably was their combat experience. In our collected Vietnam metanarrative, we have replaced the geographical place Viet Nam with that of Nam, an Americanized zone of consciousness that excludes, among others, the experiences of women veterans and the Vietnamese people. It is a state of the American mind where old myths, to include a collective faith in unique American warrior skill and national moral purpose, play out their usefulness. Vietnam veterans trying to find the truth of their war experiences have to contend with these and other sustaining national myths, and we may find upon closer examination that their narratives are as much struggles with old myths as they are attempts at truthful representations of actual experience.

Works Cited

Bradford, William. *Of Plymouth Plantation*. New York: Capricorn Books, 1962

Buck, Paul H. *The Road to Reunion*. Boston: Little, Brown, 1947.

Caputo, Philip. *A Rumor of War*. New York: Ballantine, 1978.

Downs, Frederick. *The Killing Zone: My Life in the Vietnam War*. New York: Norton, 1978.

Goff, Stanley, and Robert Sanders, with Clark Smith. *Brothers: Black Soldiers in the Nam*. New York: Berkley Books, 1985.

Hackworth, David H. *About Face*. New York: Simon and Schuster, 1989.

Hawthorne, Nathaniel. *Life of Franklin Pierce*. Boston: Ticknor, Reed, and Fields, 1852.

Hellmann, John. *American Myth and the Legacy of Vietnam*. New York: Columbia University Press, 1986.

Kovic, Ron. *Born on the Fourth of July*. New York: McGraw-Hill, 1976.

Mason, Robert. *Chickenhawk*. New York: Viking, 1983.

Mather, Increase. *A Detailed Account of the Origin of the War with King Philip*. Ed. Samuel Drake. Boston: 1864.

O'Brien, Tim. *Going After Cacciato*. New York: Delacorte Press, 1975.

____. *If I Die in a Combat Zone*. New York: Delacorte Press, 1969.

____ *The Things They Carried*. Boston: Houghton Mifflin, 1990.

Smith, John. *Travels and Works of Captain John Smith*. Ed. Edward Arber. 2 vols. Edinburgh: John Grant, 1910.

Stallings, Laurence. *Plumes*. New York: Harcourt, Brace, 1924.

Terry, Wallace. *Bloods: An Oral History of the Vietnam War by Black Veterans*. New York: Random House, 1984.

Westmoreland, William C. *A Soldier Reports*. New York: Dell, 1976.

13. Reconciling Vietnam: Tim O'Brien's Narrative Journey

Thomas G. Bowie Jr.

How do you tell a true war story? What makes a story true—the facts that surround it, the memories it evokes, the fidelity with which it records some event? How do you know it is true as you read it or hear it? Why do some stories feel like they are full of truth, while others seem contrived or fabricated?

In the title story in his collection *The Things They Carried*, Tim O'Brien chronicles the "necessities or near-necessities" carried by the typical soldier in Vietnam: "P-38 can openers, pocket knives, heat tabs, wristwatches, dog tags, mosquito repellent, chewing gum, candy, cigarettes, salt tablets, packets of Kool-Aid, lighters, matches, sewing kits, Military Payment Certificates, C rations, and two or three canteens of water. Together, these items weighed between 15 and 20 pounds" (*Things*, 4). Such a list is certainly full of facts— suggesting a truth swirling in the myriad of detail. Then, as this generic catalogue continues, O'Brien slowly personalizes the carriers—bringing the *they* of the "The Things *They* Carried" alive—identifying Henry Dobbins, a "big man," and Rat Kiley, and Norman Bowker, and Ted Lavender, "who was scared" and "carried tranquilizers." Gradually, even these memories give way and our focus shifts again to the *things*. But this time the things these soldiers carry extend beyond the tangible items—like Ted Lavender's six or seven ounces of premium dope—to embrace the fear, the love, even the atmosphere they shared and carried together. As the narrative spirals outward, oscillating between factual detail and imaginative interpretation, O'Brien invites the reader to share a "silent awe for the terrible power of the things they carried" (*Things*, 9). As we feel the strings of memory and imagination pulling us into this awe-full silence, we wonder again, has O'Brien told a true war story? Do the layers and layers of facts make it true somehow? Or do his memories of fellow soldiers impart an air of truth? Perhaps the self-reflexive and silent awe he confesses makes a reader trust his story's truth? Just how should we understand the truth of such a story?

These are some of the questions we bring to any work of war literature—questions that have been concerns of Tim O'Brien's for the past twenty years. O'Brien's narrative journey from his early nonfictional vignettes in *If I Die in a Combat Zone* (1973), to the magical realism of *Going After Cacciato* (1978), to the "factual fictions" of *The Things They Carried* (1990), to his most recent plunge *In the Lake of the Woods* (1994) provides a captivating study of the way the experience of war is reconciled through language, memory, and imagination. As we view the milestones on this journey, studying the narratives that mark the way, we glimpse an ongoing struggle to narrate the "truth" of an experience that haunts both an individual and national journey from war to peace. Through his narratives, Tim O'Brien invites us to consider the complex reality exposed by the stories we tell—the reality we must face as individuals and as a nation if we ever hope to understand and reconcile this experience. O'Brien's own efforts suggest a journey that is as simple as it is complex: a journey to discover the power of stories to mediate past experience, a journey to find a story he can live with.

I don't mean to suggest that O'Brien's journey is necessarily unique. In fact, his struggle to locate an elusive truth through memory and imagination resembles that of many other war authors. From the best known personal narratives of the Great War—especially those of Edmund Blunden, Siegfried Sassoon, and Robert Graves—to those of Vietnam—by writers such as Michael Herr or Philip Caputo—we see a continuous struggle to reconcile war experience through narratives, a continuous struggle to find a story that the writer can live with. And Tim O'Brien is a conscious participant in what he recognizes as an ongoing dialogue with this literary tradition. In interviews he has made conscious comparisons between his work and that of Michael Herr, and he opens *Going After Cacciato* by nodding toward Siegfield Sassoon in his epigraph. In fact, Sassoon's own narrative journey—one that spanned over twenty years and six volumes of fictional memoirs and factual autobiography—makes an interesting parallel with the one O'Brien begins in *If I Die in a Combat Zone.*

O'Brien has explained *If I Die* in a number of interviews as "straight autobiography. All of the events in the book really happened; in one sense it is a kind of war memoir and was never intended to be fiction" (Schroeder, 136). Yet at the same time that he wants to claim the factual support of "straight autobiography," he acknowledges that he borrows many of the techniques of fiction—such as dialogue intensity or ordering chronologies and employing events to heighten the drama. What is more, the text opens itself to a critique of its avowed form and intentions when O'Brien states, "I would wish this book could take the form of a plea for everlasting peace, a plea from one who knows, from one who's been there and come back, an old soldier looking back at a dying war" (*If I Die*, 22). But O'Brien quickly pulls back from such a suggestion, affirming that "none of these notions seems right. Men are

killed, dead human beings are heavy and awkward to carry, things smell different in Vietnam, soldiers are afraid and often brave, drill sergeants are boors,
some men think the war is proper and just and others don't and most don't
care. Is that the stuff for a morality lesson, even for a theme?" (22–3). Faced
with the momentary inclination to sermonize, O'Brien retreats, falling back
to the concrete details of memory, the mental pictures of an old soldier looking back at the war. "Do dreams offer lessons?" he asks the reader. "Do nightmares have themes, do we awaken and analyze them and live our lives and
advise others as a result? Can the foot soldier teach anything important about
war, merely for having been there? I think not. He can tell war stories" (23).
And that is precisely what O'Brien then does for the next 200 pages—tell the
war stories he has catalogued in memory.

In this 23 vignettes that constitute *If I Die*, O'Brien again and again turns
away from the task of overtly interpreting his experience, clinging tenaciously
to the truth he hopes to convey by telling realistic stories. Much like his buddies in the foxhole playing with a night vision starlight scope, O'Brien is trying to get the landscape of Vietnam to come into focus in his text. Just like
Bates and Chip and Barney, we too may distrust the lens he has given us to
look through, but it is all we have to penetrate the night. The stories O'Brien
tells are clearly punctuated with the gritty details of life in Nam, with the
factual representation of a strange and foreign war fought in a mysterious land.
But by the time we finish *If I Die* we realize that the collection of stories is
as much about why O'Brien went to Vietnam, about issues of moral courage
and noble conduct, as it is about his time there. As he points out at the beginning of one of the early stories—titled "Under the Mountain,"—"to understand what happens to the GI among the mine fields of My Lai, you must
know something about what happens in America" (31). Relating the rigors
of boot camp and the agony of his decision to serve in the army, O'Brien
slowly prepares us for the larger agonies of meaning that surround his participation in the war. And all he can do to convey these agonies is tell us his
story as he remembers it.

But an important undercurrent runs beneath these stories. Through them
all, a nagging doubt about the adequacy of stories lingers just beneath the
surface. Reviewing the story of Socrates' courageous decision to embrace death,
O'Brien wonders if Plato got all the details straight—was Socrates, after all,
a reluctant hero? "Certainly, [Plato] must have missed something" (44). And
what about all the cultural narratives that surround people like JFK, or T.E.
Lawrence, or Sergeant York? As writers selected and arranged the details of
such stories, were they accurate and truthful? For O'Brien realizes, shortly
after his arrival in Viet Nam, that language must frequently be modified to
cover experience. And when you begin playing with language, what happens
to the truth of the story? For example, when you call someone an "FNG,"
removing his name for the first several weeks he is in Viet Nam, a wound he

receives or even his death cannot touch you personally. Of course, "fragging" an officer sounds less ominous than murdering him; and O'Brien is troubled by the notion that as long as you "waste slopes and dinks" you never have to think about the purpose or cause of the war (76). As we alter the language used to tell the story—and virtually every story of Vietnam comes complete with its own unique vocabulary, *If I Die* being no exception—we have somehow deferred the truth of the experience in our very efforts to accurately convey it.

Delicately probing the limits of memory, exposing the shortfalls in the stories memory presents, this gap in the stories between the true meaning and its expression haunts O'Brien at the end of *If I Die*. He has done his best to faithfully hold the camera's eye on the war, to faithfully record his individual perspective of what the war meant. But at the end of his narrative—which coincides with the end of his tour in Vietnam—the camera turns inward once again: "the sky you fly in is gray and dead ... you can't see a sign of life. And over Minnesota you fly into an empty, unknowing, uncaring, purified, permanent stillness" (199). Face to face with this overpowering stillness, O'Brien is left with the title question of his final story—"Don't I Know You?" Haunted by what a soldier becomes in war—haunted more specifically by what he has become—O'Brien is also left wondering whether the stories he has told have evoked the truth of his experience. Does he know them? Measuring the adequacy of his rendering, his final tally staggers with ambivalence:

> You add things up. You lost a friend to the war, and you gained a friend. You compromised one principle and fulfilled another. You learned, as old men tell it in front of the courthouse, that war is not all bad; it may not make a man of you, but it teaches manhood is not something to scoff; some stories of valor are true; dead bodies are heavy, and it's better not to touch them; fear is paralysis, but it is better to be afraid than to move out to die, all limbs functioning and heart thumping and charging and having your chest torn open for all the work; you have to pick the times not to be afraid, but when you are afraid you must hide it to save respect and reputation [198].

In this precarious balance has he found truth? Has he told true war stories? The issues of fear, courage, and reputation have been at stake from the beginning of this text, and although factual stories may illuminate these abstractions, we are finally left holding some rather inadequate photos, the photos recorded in memory and faithfully presented in *If I Die*, but somehow inadequate nonetheless.

Something about these photos, just like the careful balancing of the losses and gains of O'Brien's Vietnam experience, ultimately seems less truthful than it should be—less truthful than it must be. So five years later, O'Brien is back telling stories of Vietnam, this time in his acclaimed novel *Going After Cacciato*. Looking back in an interview, he feels that *If I Die* really paved the way for *Cacciato* in important ways: "Yes, I'm glad I got it out of my system. Otherwise I would have ended up writing ... autobiography cast as fiction. The power of *If I Die* is the same sort that one gets from a book like Ron Kovic's. It's just there as a document. It's not art. I didn't know what literature was. *If I Die* is just a straightforward telling: 'here's what happened to me'" (Schroeder, 148). Although this may overstate the case somewhat, the fact remains that, when it comes to assessing the truthfulness of the tale, something about straightforward telling strikes an incomplete chord.

The complexity of *Cacciato*, using a technique often called magic realism to alternate freely between the hours Paul Berlin spends on the watch tower, the memories he has of his experience in the war, and the imagined journey to Paris in pursuit of Cacciato, draws more heavily upon the power of imagination than it does on memory. If the stories in *If I Die* are resolutely committed to faithfully recording memory, *Cacciato* is just as committed to tapping the power of imagination. As O'Brien explains, "I've imagined the events of *Cacciato* just as Berlin imagines them. He doesn't draw any single moral out of the story, and I don't expect the reader to draw any single moral out of it either; but rather, by going through the process of having imagined something, one gathers a sense of the *stuff* that's being imagined, a sense of what a war is and what escape from war is. And that sense can't be pinned down to a message or a moral. It's a story ... "(Schroeder, 140). As O'Brien suggests, the power of imagination generates this sense of the *stuff*—we might say a sense of the *truth*—of what is being imagined. It is a truth of the imagination, a truth of the story.

Let us take the chase that dominates the novel as an example: the sense of pursuing something is powerfully realized throughout the text, driving it, and us, onward. But the object of that chase invites us to consider the truth suggested by imagination. Surely, the characters are pursuing Cacciato on his way toward Paris, but they are also in search of something more—some sense of truth and meaning for their Viet Nam experiences. If O'Brien foregrounds the question of why go to Viet Nam in *If I Die*, *Cacciato* opens the door to the question of "why stay?" What holds a soldier—or a country—in a war like Vietnam? Once again, issues of moral courage and noble conduct anchor this exploration of O'Brien's themes, but the answers, like the style and form, that he poses through *Cacciato* are far less definite, less direct, perhaps less dogmatic than his earlier work. In some sense, though, they are also truer.

About a third of the way through the novel, the platoon pursuing Cacciato falls into a great hole in the earth, and several pages later finds itself in a chapter titled "Tunneling Toward Paris." A North Vietnamese lieutenant—who is holding the squad captive—offers Paul Berlin a look at the outside world through his periscope. Typically, the view through the looking glass offers more questions than answers. "So you see,' said Li Van Hgoc as he brought down the periscope and locked it with a silver key, 'things may be viewed from many angles. From down below, or from inside out, you often discover entirely new understandings'" (*Cacciato*, 82). And that is precisely the point of O'Brien's filtering of his experiences through the lens of imagination in *Cacciato*. Whereas in *If I Die* he was constrained by realistic presentation of memory, in *Cacciato* the power of imagination floods the text, often washing away the anchor or memory. Through the elaborate trip to Paris, through all the imaginative variations on his central themes, through the careful juxtaposition of searing bits of memory with the power to escape them imaginatively, O'Brien forces us to pursue truth in an entirely different register than his memoir provoked.

After all, how can we really take Cacciato's attempt to flee the war seriously? The moon-faced, childlike, often pitiable Cacciato hardly invites consideration as an anti-hero resolutely fleeing the war. At best, he appears as a pathetic victim of circumstance. And yet, by constantly affirming the power of imagination, O'Brien invites us to reconsider our reading of Cacciato's story, to see it, as it were, from a new angle. And this is precisely what Paul Berlin does throughout the novel. The opening lines set the stage:

> It was a bad time. Billy Roy Watkins was dead, and so was Frenchie Tucker. Billy Boy had died of fright, scared to death on the field of battle, and Frenchie Tucker had been shot through the nose. Bernie Lynn and Lieutenant Sidney Martin had died in tunnels. Pederson was dead and Rudy Chassler was dead. Buff was dead. Ready Mix was dead. They were all among the dead. The rain fed fungus that grew in the men's boots and socks, and their socks rotted, and their feet turned white and soft so that the skin could be scraped off with a fingernail, and Stink Harris woke up screaming one night with a leech on his tongue. When it was not raining, a low mist moved across the paddies, blending the elements into a single gray element, and the war was cold and pasty and rotten. (*Cacciato*, 1)

It was a bad time—indeed a totally rotten time. The flesh is rotting from the bone, the litany of the dead and dying grows daily, and the fitful sleep soldiers steal from the night is broken by the screams prompted by leeches violating them. Little wonder, then, that "[i]n October, near the end of the month, Cacciato left the war" (2). Little wonder, then, that during the long, cold, dark night on the observation tower Paul Berlin imaginatively follows Cacciato on his journey away from the war—a journey to Paris.

In an attempt to reconcile Cacciato's desertion from this deadly conflict—to resolve it by apprehending him and forcing him to rejoin his squad—Paul Berlin confronts the possibility of his own reconciliation with the war, and perhaps his salvation from it. Dreamily drifting to the Hotel Phoenix in Delhi, narrowly escaping death in Tehran, passing through Izmir and Athens, Paul and his squad journey towards Paris exploring the profound slippage between "What happened, and what might have happened" (27). For in this novel, each new and outlandish escapade can only be limited by the failure of imagination. The hard memories of Sidney Martin, the crushing weight of death after death, even the deadly plot to frag the lieutenant in "the world's greatest lake country" all can be overcome by Paul Berlin's imaginative process of "slipping out of himself" (145). Dreaming, slipping, imagining, the squad eventually makes its way to Paris where Paul Berlin must measure the cost—and the truth—of this imaginative journey. Along the way, "he tried to explain to himself that it wasn't cowardice or simple desertion. Not exactly. Partly it was Cacciato's doing. Partly it was the mission, partly inertia, partly adventure, partly a way of tracing the possibilities. But it was even more than this. He couldn't put his finger on it, but he knew it had to do with a whole array of things seen and felt and learned on the way to Paris" (154). This journey has taught Berlin to see things in a new way, to understand the war through the lens of the imagination. His final act must then be to measure the fidelity of this perspective, to assess its power to convey truth as it is cast by imagination.

Unlike his earlier account of the war in *If I Die*, in *Cacciato* facts assume an almost irrelevant position. "The facts were not disputed. Facts did not bother him" (288). Paul Berlin *knows* the facts; rather, it is what imagination does with the facts that troubles him. "Billy Boy had died of fright. Buff was dead. Ready Mix was dead. Rudy Chassler was dead. Pederson was dead. Sidney Martin and Frenchie Tucker and Bernie Lynn had died in tunnels. Those were all facts, and he could face them squarely" (288). The dilemma, quite simply, is that once you know the facts you still have to organize them before they have any meaning. "The order of facts—which facts came first and which came last, the relations among facts—here he had trouble, but it was not the trouble of facing facts. It was the trouble of understanding them, keeping them straight" (288). And this is the crux of the matter: what, in the final analysis, do all these deaths mean? How do you organize them so they are more readily understood? How does understanding them help one to understand Cacciato's departure, Berlin's imaginative attempt to follow him, and ultimately O'Brien's efforts to reconcile memory with imagination?

In one final effort to address these mysteries, O'Brien actually stages a confrontation between memory and imagination in the Majestic Hotel in Paris, in a room darkened like a theater stage, with spotlights playing on Paul Berlin and Sarkin Aung Wan. With great care and eloquence, Sarkin Aung Wan pleads for the power of imagination, urging Paul Berlin to step boldly into his dream, "to join [his] dream and to live it? (284). But Paul Berlin's memories of the past—of "prior acts" such as putting on the uniform, accepting promotion and responsibility, tacitly promising his family to serve faithfully—place him beyond "politics or principle or matters of justice" (285). In so doing, they also place him, quite reluctantly, beyond the power of imagination. Confessing the fear and shame that no doubt help motivate his decision, Berlin also claims that "[p]eace of mind is not a simple matter of pursuing one's own pleasure; rather it is inextricably linked to the attitudes of other human beings, to what they want, to what they expect. The real issue is how to find felicity within limits" (286). It is a small step then to the imaginative limits Paul Berlin tentatively recognizes. "Even in imagination we must obey the logic of what we started. Even in imagination we must be true to our obligations, for, even in imagination, obligation cannot be outrun. Imagination, like reality, has its limits" (286). Yet despite the reasoned eloquence of Paul Berlin's position on imagination, despite his confirmation of the limits of both reality and imagination, Paul awakes from a dreamless sleep and joins the lieutenant as he tries to imagine the real Cacciato's successful retreat from the war (301). Thus even with this exhaustive imaginative journey to Paris, even with the recognition prompted by the National Book Award for Fiction, O'Brien's own narrative journey was still not complete.

After all, how do you tell a true war story? As he suggested in a 1984 interview, "truth doesn't reside on the surface of events. Truth resides in those deeper moments of punctuation, when things explode" (Schroeder, 141). *Cacciato* clearly provided one type of explosion, one mode to plumb those deeper moments through the power of the imagination. "The reader has to figure out what it means, if anything.... That's one of those big distinctions, one of the reasons I wrote *Cacciato*—so I could free myself from making authorial judgments and instead present a story. Let the reader make the judgments" (142). Yet even as O'Brien was making this "big distinction," even as he was transferring the judgment of truth to the reader, he knows that a true war story can never privilege memory or imagination; instead, it must fully embrace both.

Having written a memoir and a novel, having measured the truth-telling power of each, he turned one more time to his Vietnam experience in 1990 with a collection of fiction that seems to defy any firm generic label. When asked about what *The Things They Carried* really is, O'Brien stated: "I've never thought of it as a novel. Nor have I ever thought of it as a book of stories. I've thought of it as a work of fiction, that is neither one nor the other" (Kaplan, 2). This indeterminate state, this sense of generic uncertainty, does much, I think, to help us understand the nature of the truths it conveys. Looking back at the exchange in O'Brien's writing between memory and imagination, we find *If I Die* committed to recording memory, and *Cacciato* exploring the power of imagination. Now, looking closely at one selection from *The Things They Carried*, "How to Tell a True War Story," we discover that the dialogue between memory and imagination that has been implicit in much of O'Brien's early work finally becomes explicit.

"This is true. I had a buddy in Vietnam. His name was Bob Kiley, but everybody called him Rat" (*Things*, 75). So begins O'Brien's reflections on how to tell a true war story—a question that has also been implicit in O'Brien's work for over 20 years. Interestingly, it is important for this story to be read as if it were true. The narrator, named Tim O'Brien, wants us to believe in the truth of this tale. But just like the character Bob Kiley—who's also Rat—the truth may be both factual and fictional. The truth might be the truth of memory—a true story about Bob Kiley and the letter he sends to the sister of his good friend Curt Lemon, who is now dead. Or it might be the truth of imagination, the truth of a story "just beyond telling," a story like the one Mitchell Sanders tells about the six-man patrol on a listening-post operation for a week. It gets spooky up in the mountains, night after night, and they begin to hear "wacked-out music," a sort of "crazyass gook concert." As Sanders goes on with the story, embellishing the facts, drawing liberally on imagination, the narrator Tim knows that Sanders cares about the truth of his story. "He wanted me to feel the truth, to believe by the raw force of feeling" (81).

But O'Brien the author senses an even deeper truth exploding beneath the surface of these two stories, a truth he wants his readers to hear in the dialogue between memory and imagination. Because, as he observes,

> in any war story, but especially a true one, it's difficult to separate what happened from what seemed to happen. What seems to happen becomes its own happening and has to be told that way. The angles of vision are skewed.... When a guy dies, like Curt Lemon, you look away and then look back for a moment and then look away again. The pictures get jumbled; you tend to miss a lot. And then afterward, when you go to tell about it, there is always that surreal seemliness, which makes the story seem untrue, but which in fact represents the hard and exact truth as it seemed [78].

And it is the truth of how it seemed, the vision seen when the angles are skewed, that comes as close to the truth in a war story as we can ever get. As we begin to firmly pin the truth to memory, or to blend it liberally with imagination, it slips away from us. "In a true war story, if there's a moral at all, it's like the thread that makes the cloth. You can't tease it out. You can't extract the meaning without unraveling the deeper meaning" (84). The dialogue between memory and imagination points toward these deeper meanings, in the same way it points toward a resting place, not a final destination in O'Brien's narrative journey.

You cannot arrest the motion in this dialectic by generalizing about the truth of war, because generalizations about imaginative truths are just as inadequate as the specific details of memory. O'Brien explains in his story, "War is hell, but that's not the half of it, because war is also mystery and terror and adventure and courage and discovery and holiness and pity and despair and longing and love. War is nasty; war is fun. War is thrilling; war is drudgery. War makes you a man; war makes you dead. The truths are contradictory" (87). So, faced with such contradictions, how do you tell a true war story? What advice does O'Brien finally offer?

War has the feel—the spiritual texture—of a great ghostly fog, thick and permanent. There is no clarity. Everything swirls. The old rules are no longer binding, the old truths no longer true. Right spills over into wrong. Order blends into chaos, love into hate, ugliness into beauty, law into anarchy, civility into savagery. The vapors suck you in. You can't tell where you are, or why you're there, and the only certainty is overwhelming ambiguity.

In war you lose your sense of the definite, hence your sense of truth itself, and therefore it's safe to say that in a true war story nothing is ever absolutely true [88].

But perhaps we need to clarify this just a bit, before we too are sucked in by the vapors, lest we unjustly accuse O'Brien of epistemological nihilism. The important phrase in the quote above is "nothing is ever *absolutely* true."

Neither the truth of memory nor the truth of imagination tells an absolutely true war story. Rather it is the dialogue between them, the questions each raises in its own right, that provides the key to locating a true war story, a story O'Brien can finally live with. And it is precisely such a dialogue that O'Brien insists upon in his most recent return to Vietnam, his novel *In the Lake of the Woods* (1994). Following the advice his narrator Tim O'Brien offers near the end of "How to Tell a True War Story," that "[y]ou can tell a true war story if you just keep on telling it," O'Brien does just that in his new novel (91). So when O'Brien forces his readers to plunge with him *into* the Lake of the Woods in northern Minnesota, he asks once again "have we been listening?"

As O'Brien continues to tell his story, as he continues the search to find a story he can live with, as the dialogue with memory and imagination continues, *In the Lake of the Woods* foregrounds the need for reconciliation with the past in powerful and troubling ways. His latest story is indeed one about "love and memory," and it's a story full of loss and sorrow as well; perhaps then, by his own definition, it can claim to be true. The central character in this novel, John Wade, is haunted by memories of the past—haunted more specifically by the individual and cultural nightmare we call My Lai. Much like Rat Kiley in *The Things They Carried*, John Wade just "couldn't shut off the pictures" (*Things*, 250). Wade's past lurks around him like a damp, cold fog—like the fog that settles over his cabin on the Lake of the Woods each evening. With his life unraveling at the seams, his political career ended, his wife missing—just vanished one day—and himself suspected of her murder, Wade is desperately searching for a story that will once again give meaning to his life. In the days before his wife, Kathleen, leaves, they sit by the lake as the fog drifts in, inventing "happy stories for each other" (3). But Wade knows these stories aren't real, aren't true: "For both of them it was a wishing game. They envisioned happiness as a physical place on the earth, a secret country, perhaps.... To live there would require practice and many changes, but they were willing to learn" (3). Ironically, it is now more than ever that

John Wade needs to find a true war story to tell—and, even more importantly, a true story to live.

In a very real sense, then, O'Brien immerses John Wade, and the readers of Wade's story *in* the Lake of the Woods. Although our joint status is implicit from the opening word of the title, our mutual suffocation—sinking, grasping for air, light, and hope—gradually stifles us throughout the novel. Intricately structured, beyond even the elaborate narrative oscillations of *Cacciato*, O'Brien's *Lake* insists that his readers participate in the dialogue between memory and imagination—he insists, in short, that we listen—even if we drown in the process. For throughout the novel we join John Wade in his struggle to first listen carefully, and then to interpret his story, a story that may well belong not only to him, but to O'Brien and us as well.

Much of the magic of this narrative springs from the intricate structure O'Brien establishes in the novel. In his review for the *New York Times*, Verlyn Klinkenborg identifies three levels of narrative in the book, three levels of stories: the "conventional, remote third-person account of plain facts, the events that can be reconstructed without conjecture"; the "Evidence" chapters that collect everything from personal interviews to quotations from magic books and literary texts; and finally the "Hypothesis" chapters where various possible interpretations of the story are played out (33). Although Klinkenborg is surely right to suggest that the interaction between these narrative lines is central to the emblematic construction of Wade's character, he overlooks a fourth narrative level that in many ways is more important than the first three. With this complex and diffuse narrative structure, O'Brien forces the reader to piece together what happened to Kathleen, and why. In so doing, we must also come to know John Wade more fully, focusing on a myriad of details from memory—both his and others—such as his life-long quest for love from his father, his father's early death, John's interest in performing magic, his role as the "Sorcerer" in Viet Nam, and finally upon his complicity in the events at Thuan Yen on March 16, 1968, events better known as the massacre at My Lai. Deftly stitching these details together with Wade's political career after the war and his marriage to Kathleen, O'Brien dramatizes the process of reconciliation in this novel through the narrative mediation of memory and imagination—a reconciliation that has been implicit throughout the previous twenty years of his own personal narrative journey in search of true war stories.

Interestingly, the fourth narrative level that Klinkenborg neglects is the level where O'Brien's narrator, the voice who has been tracking the disappearance of Kathleen for four long years—assembling the evidence, suggesting the hypotheses, guiding our collective interpretations—intervenes through a dozen footnotes to be sure we as readers have been listening. From his first intrusion, our guiding investigator insists on certain parameters for our dialogue: "I'm a theory man too. Biographer, historian, medium—call me what you want—but even after four years of hard labor I'm left with little more than supposition and possibility" (note 21, page 30). In the same note he goes on to admit that because "there are certain mysteries that weave through life itself" the best we can do at times is to present an "imaginative reconstruction of events" (30). This is not to say that he is willfully distorting the evidence, but to suggest rather that "evidence is not truth. It is only evident" (30). Significantly, these narrational interventions draw our attention not only to the lower case murder mystery surrounding Kathleen Wade, but also to the Murder Mystery we must try to understand as a nation looking back on the events in Viet Nam.

One example of this complex issue in the novel centers around John Wade's struggle to come to terms with the losses in his life. The question of how one copes with loss—whether the loss of love and wife, or the loss of the cloak of protective secrecy that had sheltered him for over twenty years, or the individual and national loss of innocence and belief so characteristic of Vietnam—thus becomes one of the touchstones in the novel. Faced with the overwhelming ambiguity surrounding Kathleen's disappearance, John Wade struggles to find some center to cling to, some truth that will give the loss meaning, some story with a narrative line capable of containing it. Therefore, through all of the games and magic, all of the deceptions, even through John's life of politics built on a life of lies, John Wade still clings to the redemptive power of love. "After all the lies, a couple of minor truths had now appeared, or whatever the certainty was that held his heart when he thought, *Kath, my Kath*" (252). Contemplating what it truly means to have lost her, Wade concludes: "Love, he thought. Which was one truth. You couldn't lose it even if you tried" (252). Much like the truth of a true war story, you can't lose the truth of love because love is always the merging of memory and imagination, always the combination of real people and situations with the ineffable power of romance. And his own disappearance at the end of the novel affirms this position, whether he left to rejoin Kath in some foreign land, or to die in the howling wilderness in atonement for her death, or merely to slip unconsciously into the final embrace of love and life, that of death.

The beauty of the inconclusive, frustratingly ambiguous ending of the novel is that we'll never know which. This much the narrator makes clear in his final note to readers: he wants to stop in the middle of the final "wishing game" of the novel, where happiness abounds, "[b]ut truth won't allow it. Because there *is* no end, happy or otherwise. Nothing is fixed, nothing is solved. The facts, such as they are, finally spin off into the void of things missing, the inconclusiveness of conclusion. Mystery finally claims us" (note 136, p. 304). We are left to contemplate, then, the final nature of such a truth. When the facts of memory dissolve, when the mystery finally claims us, what then is finally true about the story told? The narrator anticipates this question as well in his penultimate note, the longest note in the novel. He begins by reflecting on the mind's ability to erase horror, focusing specifically on the "masterly forgetting trick" John Wade achieved for over two decades. But then the reflection abruptly changes direction, recalling how the narrator himself has only a "handful of splotchy images" that remain from "that ugly war." After briefly recalling the images, *the things* he still carries, he then recalls how "[w]e called in gunships and air strikes. We brutalized. We wasted. We pistol-whipped. We trashed wells. We kicked and punched. We burned all that would burn. Yes, and these too were atrocities—the dirty secrets that live forever inside all of us" (301). And because these secrets live inside *all* of us, as individuals and as a nation, as combatants and non-combatants, we must continue to tell the stories that somehow seek to give them meaning. For as the narrator suggests at the end of this note, John Wade's story has for him—and perhaps for all of us—"a vivid, living clarity that seems far more authentic than my own faraway experience. Maybe that's what this book is for. To remind me. To give me back my vanished life" (301).

Perhaps that is what this complex dialogue between memory and imagination has been about from the very start—the start of the novel and the start of O'Brien's narrative journey. To be true in O'Brien's profound sense, these stories must be continuously retold. For as he says in *The Things They Carried*, "this too is true: stories can save us" (255). When we engage in the powerful dialogue between memory and imagination, when we listen to the voices struggling to reconcile the evidence with the hypotheses, when we embrace the living clarity of fiction in order to understand the swirling muddle of fact, then perhaps we recover a vanishing part of our lives. Reconciling the memories of his own past with the considerable power of his imagination, O'Brien skims "across the surface of his own history" for over twenty years. Much like the ice skating nine-year-old character Timmy in the final story of *Things*, O'Brien loops and spins through the stories he tells, resolutely "trying to save Timmy's life with a story" (273). For in a very real sense, reconciliation is salvation. Just as recognizing the ongoing struggle to reconcile memory with imagination provides the key to understanding Tim O'Brien's personal narrative journey, perhaps honoring it can also help us unlock the mysteries surrounding the national experience we call Vietnam. When we do so, we just might finally hear some true war stories.

Works Cited

Kaplan, Steve. "Playing with Facts and Fictions: An Interview with Tim O'Brien." 9 Feb. 1991. Unpublished text of full interview. An edited version was published subsequently in the *Missouri Review*.

Klinkenborg, Verlyn. Review of *In the Lake of the Woods*, by Tim O'Brien. *New York Times Book Review*, 9 Oct. 1994: 1, 33.

O'Brien, Tim. *Going After Cacciato*. New York: Dell, 1978.

____. *If I Die in a Combat Zone, Box Me Up and Ship Me Home*. New York: Dell, 1973.
____. *In the Lake of the Woods*. Boston: Houghton Mifflin, 1994.
____. *The Things They Carried*. New York: Penguin, 1990.
Schroeder, Eric. "Two Interviews: Talks with Tim O'Brien and Robert Stone." *Modern Fiction Studies* 30:1 (Spring 1984): 135–151.

14. Coming Home: Difference and Reconciliation in Narratives of Return to "the World"

JAMES CAMPBELL

"Vietnam Vietnam Vietnam, we've all been there" is the famous last sentence of Michael Herr's *Dispatches* (260). What I'd like to do here is look at this assertion that we've all been there and ask, in what sense? And what effect does this claim have on the question of reconciliation of veterans and the civilian society into which so many have found it so difficult to fit? More specifically, I want to question the terms of sexual difference through which narratives of return to 'the world' have been constructed. Besides *Dispatches*, I also want to address two novels of reconciliation (or lack thereof) between veteran and civilian, Bobbie Ann Mason's *In Country* and Larry Heinemann's *Paco's Story*, along with the film *Coming Home*.

Placing *Dispatches* in the context of American civilian-to-combatant relations presents us with an unusual encounter: instead of the typical Vietnam combat veteran struggling to readjust himself to civilian America, we have the civilian noncombatant who lives, walks, and does nearly everything but fight along with the grunts (or so Herr would have us believe). A careful reading of *Dispatches* reveals numerous moments when the civilian-combatant encounter borders closely on confrontation: Herr's ruminations on the parasitic role of the war correspondent spring immediately to mind (e.g. 228–29). Yet all of these encounters between reporter and soldier, whether napalm-induced male bonding or barely contained hostility, take place on the soldiers' turf: they are in country. Herr's text gives us an important introduction to the study of narratives of return because it presents us with a struggle to reconcile the civilian with the combatant even while the war is still on.

It may well be that this rather strange situation gives rise to the rather strange reconciliation that Herr offers. If the civilian is, like Herr, in the combat, then perhaps it becomes easier to place the combatant into civilian territory. Or at least it becomes easier as a metaphor, a mental exercise. The process becomes apparent with the very first encounter with a veteran that Herr describes. Speaking to a spaced-out, borderline psychopathic LURP, Herr presents him thus: "His face was all painted for the night walking now like a bad hallucination, not like the painted faces I'd seen in San Francisco only a week before, the other extreme of the same theater" (6). Significantly, Herr glances at difference by mentioning the dissimilarity: the LURP's face paint is unlike that of the Haight-Ashbury acid-heads, at least superficially. Yet, on an essential level, this long-haired, earringed, silk bandanna clad LURP fights the same war as his rock 'n' roll counterparts on the other side of the Pacific— say, the similarly long-haired, jewel-clad, headbanded, technologically equipped Jimi Hendrix. Like Hendrix, the LURP is simultaneously an expression and a victim of the Sixties. Or, as Herr puts it at the end of the book when confronting his own difficult return to the world: "Out on the street I couldn't tell the Vietnam veterans from the rock and roll veterans. The Sixties had made so many casualties, its war and its music had run power off the same circuit for so long they didn't even have to fuse." (258) For Herr, the Vietnam War is a symptom of the Sixties. It's an essential generational experience, like trying drugs and listening to the White Album backwards. And, like those examples, it doesn't really matter whether you actually, physically participated (inhaled?) or not. The Sixties generation had a proximity to drugs (and sex and rock 'n' roll and gonzo journalism) which helped to define it culturally. For Herr, Vietnam is a part of that culture, it's a part of that generation, whether or not any given member of that generation actually fought in it. Hendrix died at Khe Sanh.

Herein, I believe, lies Herr's solution to the reconciliation problem. If the horrors of Vietnam are simply the exported version of an essential Sixties culture, as Herr seems to imply, there is an awful lot of common ground between veteran and civilian. The veteran can be welcomed back just like anybody else who has had a bad trip. We who were not there can come to terms with 'the Vietnam experience' because it remains essentially the same as our own experience of the civilian 1960s.

This, of course, begs the question that we have a Sixties experience, besides, perhaps, being born and growing up with a war on the six o'clock news. Bobbie Ann Mason's *In Country* addresses this intergenerational problem through the character of Sam Hughes, a seventeen-year-old girl whose father was killed in Viet Nam before her birth. Her name, almost the only legacy she consciously retains from her father, allows her to confront the specter of Vietnam in a unique and unmistakably iconic manner when she finds "Sam Hughes" inscribed on the Wall of the Vietnam Veterans Memorial. The final scene of the novel, in which Sam, her paternal grandmother, and her veteran uncle confront the Wall, presents us with another version of reconciliation via an identification with veterans. "She touches her own name. How odd it feels, as though all the names in America have been used to decorate this wall" (243). The implication is clear and, in a sense that I do not wish to elide, admirable. All of America, including that part of it barely even born during the war, lived through the war and continues to live with its traces. In a certain sense, we all have a stake in the Wall, and we must all confront it and find our own name on it. Or, as Sam's grandmother puts it as she gazes up at the Memorial: "All I can see here is my reflection" (244).

Yet, in a certain sense that I also do not wish to elide, this resonant final scene erases difference and thus does further violence to veterans. Granted, I have taken this final scene out of the context of the novel as a whole, yet its self-consciously emblematic deployment does little to discourage this. It remains important to remember Sam's earlier experiences, when her Vietnam obsession and identification with the veterans led her to construct a sort of civilian's version of the veteran's flashback. After spending the night at Cawood's Pond confronting imaginary "VC rapist-terrorists," Sam must face the fact that a swamp in rural Kentucky is not the Viet Nam jungle, and that she cannot really experience the trauma of her uncle and his friends: "It hit her suddenly that this nature preserve in a protected corner of Kentucky wasn't like Vietnam at all" (214). Mason places her heroine between the urge to bear the cross of the veterans and the realization that, as Sam herself puts it, "she will never really know what happened to all these men in the war" (240). Yet the fact that Mason ends the novel with Sam's discovery of her own name on the Wall tends to privilege the identification half of the dilemma. Even though Sam realizes that her experience is qualitatively different from that of her uncle Emmett and the other veterans, she is nonetheless comfortable with having her name on the Wall. Mason leaves us with a sense of the appropriateness of the double meaning of Sam Hughes, signifying both a dead American soldier from Texas and a living American teenager from Kentucky (or, alternately, a fictive character emblematic of civilians who have grown up in the shadow of the war).[1] Mason's "we" is less a generational construct than Herr's. In fact, it's a broader "we," inclusive of not only the standard issue Sixties generation, but of that generation's parents and children as well. Nonetheless, Vietnam is still the place we've all been.

It is this aspect of Mason's text that I find most difficult. Pushed a bit further than I've yet done, her compelling final scene can disturb as well as uplift. Does Samantha Hughes' finding her name on the Wall take anything away from the Sam Alan Hughes whose name had been there before her discovery of it? Does Samantha erase any of the particularity of Sam Alan Hughes's experience, or appropriate it by identifying herself with his name, and the death it signifies? The metaphor is certainly a powerful one, but for all its power, can we not say that it appropriates an identity for civilians that is not theirs? I mean this in at least two senses: first, that Samantha and Sam Alan Hughes are two different people (only one of whom has access to a voice in the novel and only one of whom was killed in Vietnam); second, that the association of these two people under one name obscures the reason why the inscription "Sam A Hughes" appears on the Vietnam Veterans Memorial. In the sense that I assume Mason intends, Samantha Hughes is a veteran of Vietnam—if by "Vietnam" we mean neither a war nor a nation but a particular historical moment in American culture. But the Vietnam that killed Sam Alan Hughes is not merely a phase of domestic American culture, but a physical, political, and military chiasmus in Southeast Asia. Like "Sam Hughes," "Vietnam" carries several significations. And Samantha Hughes is not a veteran of this second Vietnam. If we are all Vietnam veterans, if "we've all been there," there is also a very important sense in which the name on the wall is not our own. We are not all (dead) Vietnam veterans. And, hopefully, the Vietnam Veterans Memorial is not only a memorial of America to itself for bearing the burden of Vietnam (sense #1), but also a memorial of those very particular men and women who died in Viet Nam (sense #2).[2]

Finally, I want to investigate another way in which Mason explores reconciliation, one which I will call the *Coming Home* metaphor from the 1978 Jane Fonda movie. The metaphor constructs the reconciliation of the (male) Vietnam veteran with American culture as a sexual relationship. Furthermore, there is always some physical barrier to this relationship. In the *Coming Home* film itself, of course, the unintegrated Vietnam vet is paraplegic. In Mason's *In Country*, the problem is less overt. The metaphor is most obviously played out between Sam and Tom, the Vietnam veteran who has been psychologically damaged by the war, resulting in his impotence. Sam suspects that Emmett and his sometime girlfriend Anita may be playing it out too. Sam and Tom are unable to consummate their admittedly tenuous relationship, despite mutual desire, because "Vietnam" intervenes. The difficulty, perhaps even the impossibility, of the sex symbolizes the difficulty both veteran and civilian experience in attempting to achieve reconciliation, and the embarrassment this causes them both. The Tom and Sam relationship does not pretend that reconciliation is easy or inevitable.

Likewise, Larry Heinemann's *Paco's Story* also presents the reconciliation (or lack thereof) of a Vietnam veteran via sexuality.[3] In fact, it is relatively easy to read Paco's relations with women as an allegory of American civilian reception of the Vietnam veteran. Initially, Paco's reception into the quasi-anonymous town of Boone remains relatively ungendered. He is met with distrust and suspicion as a gimp and a drug addict looking to disturb life in peaceful but narrow-minded America. His encounters with townspeople are bitter and short until he happens into the Texas Lunch, where he finds two people. In the first, Ernest Monroe, a World War II Marine and veteran of Guadalcanal and Iwo Jima, Paco finds both a comrade, someone who understands the lifelong burden of combat experience, and, perhaps more importantly for the purposes of our allegorical excursion, imparts a certain legitimacy to Paco's war experience by putting it into the tradition of the more "normal," "heroic," and "acceptable" experiences of World War II. In the second character present at the diner, we find evidence of Paco's sexual attractiveness, or, more properly, the attractiveness of his scars. Betsy, the young woman in question, fantasizes about Paco's scars: "the swirled-around scars up and down his back, and how they disappear over his shoulder and up into his hairline; how she would lay her head on his shoulder and stoke the scars of his belly .... She sees herself drawing on his scars as if they were Braille, as if each scar had its own story" (100–01). It is not coincidental that this revelation of Paco's attraction to a woman occurs at the moment of his legitimation as a veteran, due to his link with Ernest Monroe. Furthermore, in the spirit of the *Coming Home* metaphor, I would allegorize this moment to correspond to the general turn-around in American culture, sometime in the early 1980s, when it suddenly became cool to be a Vietnam veteran. We went from the murdering, drug fiend, Hawaii Five-O stereotype villain and *Taxi Driver's* psychopathic Travis Bickle to the heroic and socially vindicated Rambo and Magnum, P.I.—the first the apparent sociopath turned ultra-macho war hero, the second the perfectly integrated vet who turns violence into social good. Vietnam veterans became sexy. Their scars began to be seen as legitimate and alluring.

Heinemann's answer to this change in attitude occurs, like Mason's, in an emblematic final scene. One of Paco's neighbors in the run-down hotel in which he lives is a young college student named Cathy. Cathy, like Betsy, finds Paco's scars sexually fascinating ("Cathy would ponder the tight, dark bulge in his crotch and the endless mosaic, the wonder, of all those scars" [199]) but, again like Betsy, the relationship goes no further than fantasy. In fact, as Paco discovers when he sneaks into Cathy's room and reads her diary, weeks of living in close proximity to Paco and his scars, both physical and psychological, diminishes their sexual appeal. After seeing Paco come home drunk and take large amounts of prescription pills, as well as hearing his weeping when he has nightmares, Cathy decides that, instead of being cute or sexy, Paco is really "a dingy, dreary, smelly, shabby, *shabby* little man" (205). Finally, in a sequence related in her diary, Cathy dreams of having sex with Paco, then being pinned by him as he strips off his scars and lays them on her: "And when each scar touches me, I feel the suffocating burn, hear the scream" (209).

Given an allegorical reading, the implications are clear enough: American civilian culture, in the character of the sexually intrigued woman, finds the Vietnam veteran appealing once he has attained some amount of traditional legitimacy. Then his physical and psychological scars make him human, as when Rambo cries over his frustration at his inability to integrate himself into society; the scars make him sexy, as when the handsome and suave Thomas Magnum has occasional low-level flashbacks to his days as an elite soldier in Nam. But, on closer examination, this attraction proves ephemeral.

American civilian culture enjoys being titillated by this new image of the veteran, but when it comes to actually bearing those scars, to wearing them instead of merely seeing and thinking about touching them, we "get the creeps," to use Cathy's term. Integration is a bit too difficult for this rather facile paradigm shift to accomplish. The Vietnam vet is different from his military forebears, and he is different from noncombatant civilians. We may flirt with other possibilities, that we've all been to Vietnam, or that our cultural experience allows us to understand the veteran. However, if we allow ourselves this erasure of difference, of claiming that our generational experience of sex, drugs and rock 'n' roll gives us an understanding of what it was really like in Vietnam, or that our cultural struggles with Vietnam make us all casualties of that war, then we will never allow reconciliation with the veteran. Without this sense of difference, we will remain with our easy fantasies of attraction to the scars of Vietnam vets, but never even getting so far as a one night stand.

It would be relatively easy to end with this paean to difference, with the otherness, as well as the alienation, of Heinemann's hero safely intact. But there's something troubling here. Granted, Heinemann, like Mason, refuses any easy answers: he does not say that reconciliation is easy, for the Vietnam veterans' experience is one that is truly different from the civilian experience, and we must respect that difference if we are to offer any real hope for reconciliation. But perhaps the way that the question is raised is also important. My problem is not so much with the *Coming Home* metaphor as such, but rather with what we have in the sexual relationships in *Paco's Story* when we stop seeing them as metaphors. In *In Country*, when we cease to see Sam Alan Hughes as symbol and begin to see him as an individual Vietnam casualty, we realize that the symbolic meaning of Samantha Hughes' finding her own name on the Wall must be, at least, qualified. Likewise, if we strip away the allegorical context that I have constructed around sexual relations in *Paco's Story*, the very unsympathetic treatment of the character of Cathy becomes simultaneously unavoidable and less excusable. Cathy as "prick tease" (186) is somehow easier to accept when she represents the fickle taste of the American public in their embracing of a Hollywood version of the veteran and their subsequent balking when faced with someone who doesn't fit the image of this jungle-fatigued sex symbol. As a story of one man, even if that man is a wounded Vietnam veteran, and his relationship with the people of Boone, especially one particular woman, it's more problematic. Were I to say that *Paco's Story* presents an unsympathetic view of women, this would be nothing new; Susan Jeffords in "Tattoos, Scars, Diaries, and Writing Masculinity" has developed a very sophisticated reading of the text that foregrounds its abstraction and elision of sexual difference in portraying Paco's victimhood. Likewise, Lorrie Smith in "Back Against the Wall" cites *Paco's Story* in her construction of narratives that fail to adequately question patriarchy, and Donna Connolly states in her 1991 dissertation that "the feminine in this novel is a strong yet negative presence" (141).[4] The book's graphically realized rape scene and its relation to the final dream sequence practically guarantee this reputation, deserved or not. And, once denuded of its allegorical significance, the novel's misogyny is hard to miss: all the women function exclusively as sexual objects for Paco, whose ubiquitous phallic cane is as much his symbol as his scars.

Then again, perhaps the problem is, after all, with the *Coming Home* metaphor. The metaphor determines that woman represents the civilian culture, thus placing her in an antagonistic role as representation of that from which the Vietnam veteran is excluded. The veteran desires to reintegrate himself with society or, in the terms of the metaphor, to develop a sexual relationship with the woman, yet the woman herself is also the object of his anger at his alienation; she is both what enables and prevents his reconciliation. Hence the difficulties in the relationships, from *Coming Home* itself on. The woman's position in the metaphor is, for herself, untenable. She is stuck within this double-bind of being at once object of desire and object of frustration. All too often, in these texts and in others, the women themselves are given little to say about their own desire. Even in *In Country*, when the protagonist is a woman (though, significantly, an immature one), her final moment of epiphany at the Wall is less a product of her own desire than of her uncle Emmett's, who provides the impetus, if not the material means, for the journey to Washington.[5]

And just how literal do we wish to make the *Coming Home* metaphor? Is there perhaps a pun implied in the title of the film? Recalling its two scenes of sexual intimacy, we know that Sally's sexual life with her career Marine husband Bob is unfulfilling (she stares at the ceiling while he groans), while it is Luke who, despite his wounds, gives Sally her first orgasm. Luke's return to civilian life, his coming home, is thus linked with Sally's sexual (and thus to some extent political—this is the Sixties, after all) *coming* home. The metaphor is very literal indeed; coming home is coming to sexual climax. Likewise with Mason's Sam and Tom: his inability to come and thus make her come unmistakably marks his continued lack of reintegration with non-combatant America. The possibility of an end to this bind, the technological "prick pump" (129), is an expensive dream, dangled out of reach by an insensitive United States government. Like all the veterans of *In Country*, Tom has yet to *come* home.

Similarly, although we are given hints of Paco's sexual activity prior to the events described in the text, neither of the two aforementioned possible relationships develops beyond fantasy. Instead, overhearing Cathy and Marty's sex prompts two reactions in Paco. The first is a violently jealous fantasy of tearing Marty away from Cathy and replacing him as her sexual partner, which prompts this response from the ghostly narrators:

And he's just a man like the rest of us, James, who wants to fuck away all that pain and redeem his body. By fucking he wants to ameliorate the stinging ache of those dozens and dozens of swirled-up and curled-round, purple scars, looking like so many sleeping snakes and piles of ruined coins. He wants to discover a livable peace [173–74].

Yet this wish is replaced by his second reaction, the unavoidable memory of the rape of the Viet Cong girl which, we are to understand, has ruined all sexual associations for Paco, making it impossible for him to "fuck away all that pain and redeem his body." Thus Paco finds himself in the same situation as Mason's Tom: unable to complete his return to civilian life, unable to *come* home. Heinemann, however, makes a more overt claim as to the stakes involved, as he implies that Paco's scars will never stop hurting until he *comes* home.

Having thus literalized the *Coming Home* metaphor, its difficulties become more obvious. With its simple assignment of masculine and feminine roles, it leaves us with very few possibilities. We are given women who cannot make their men come home, yet it is too simple to say that the war has emasculated these men. Luke, Tom, and Paco all retain the capacity to attract women— as we have seen, their scars seem to increase their sexual appeal. Yet it all comes down to the phallus. These veterans remain unintegrated inasmuch as they have yet to come home. And the women, which is to say the civilian world, likewise remain unfulfilled. Luke may prompt Sally to come into some form of politically increased awareness (although Milton Bates rightly questions the politics of the film in *America Rediscovered* [44-48]), but neither Tom nor Paco seems to have much hope of coming home. Meanwhile, her desire for Tom has left Sam dissatisfied with her civilian boyfriend Lonnie Malone, and Cathy is stuck with Marty-Boy, whose name alone questions his masculinity. Even Sally's husband Bob is emasculated by the unheroic circumstances of his wounding, as well as losing his woman to a "jody-boy," leaving him to kill himself by swimming westward into the ocean—back, perhaps, towards Viet Nam and his warrior manhood.

Such is the result of the *Coming Home* metaphor. Women are attracted to these real men with their sexy physical and psychological scars, leaving their civilian men seeming pale and anemic in comparison. These sexual cripples, Luke, Tom, and Paco, are infinitely preferable for the principal women in the texts to the civilian men. "Civilian men" is almost an oxymoron. Thus the metaphor, despite its sensitive treatment of the veteran's pain, still upholds the great myth that combat proves masculinity, even as it destroys these veterans' sexual lives. The sexual dysfunction at the heart of the metaphor does justice to the particular difficulties that Vietnam veterans have experienced with reintegration, yet the sexual metaphor itself limits what few reintegrative possibilities remain. The fact that the novels of veteran-civilian reconciliation that have generated the most attention remain fully and unquestioningly within this metaphor only foregrounds the further difficulty that veterans of this war have undergone and continue to undergo.[6]

Finally, I would like to point out that the identification of woman with the civilian social sphere, the very identification on which the entire metaphor depends, is not exactly postmodern, or even modernist. It is, in fact, rather Victorian, though it certainly has played itself out throughout the twentieth century. The metaphor itself limits the possibilities of the reconciliation that it is designed to aid. Mason and Heinemann have, I believe, pushed the metaphor as far as it will go. Its tour of duty, like those of the veterans it is trying to serve, should now be over.

Notes

1. My argument here runs counter to Katherine Kinney's in "'Humping the Boonies': Sex, Combat, and the Female in *In Country*," in which she states that

> reconciliation is earned not by denying the differences of age and gender which separate Sam from the Sam Hughes who died in Vietnam, but by Mason's insistent illustration that self and other, male and female are not static, absolute terms but multiple, interactive constructions which can aid as well as hinder imaginative identification [47].

I do not wish so much to deny Kinney's argument as to investigate it. I think that Kinney is right in discovering what Mason is attempting; I also think that a price of this attempt is a certain amount of denied difference that follows from this "imaginative identification." I can only add that my conception/construction of otherness, or alterity, is greatly indebted to Emmanuel Levinas's writing in such texts as *Totality and Infinity* and *Otherwise Than Being or Beyond Essence*, in which the difference of the other is inviolable.

2. W. D. Ehrhart questions the iconic use of the Wall both in and out of Mason's text in his comments on the novel, given at La Salle University in 1991 and published in *Viet Nam Generation*.

3. Heinemann's first novel, *Close Quarters*, likewise portrays the process of coming home largely through the sexual relationship of the masculine protagonist, Philip Dozier, and his girlfriend and eventual wife, Jenny. Other novels more or less within this paradigm include Philip Caputo's *Indian Country*, much of Robert Olen Butler's work, and, to a lesser extent, Stephen Wright's *Meditations in Green*.

4. Similarly, Philip Jason ("Sexism and Racism in Vietnam War Fiction" [129–33]) and Kalí Tal ("The Mind at War" [82–83]) have critiqued the misogyny of Heinemann's *Close Quarters* in terms that, I feel, would largely apply to *Paco's Story* as well. For a more general view of the subject of treatment of women in Vietnam War literature see Nancy Anisfield's "Sexist Subscript in Vietnam Narratives." For the non-literary war see Jacqueline Lawson's "'She's a Pretty Woman ... For a Gook': The Misogyny of the Vietnam War."

5. Both Susan Jeffords and Milton Bates have questioned *In Country*'s feminism, Jeffords contending that "in spite of the novel's apparent focus on women, the mechanism for the generation of collectivity is still ... the masculine bond" (*The Remasculinization of America* 63), while Bates claims that it, along with *Coming Home*, is a "complacent work" that fails to truly challenge notions of masculinity and femininity (*America Rediscovered* 55). On the other hand, Matthew Stewart objects to the ending of Mason's novel precisely because this radical change in Emmett remains insufficiently motivated ("Realism, Verisimilitude, and the Depiction of Vietnam Veterans in *In Country*"). Stewart's praise of the earlier parts of the text, however, are based on his perception of a certain realism and

authenticity that, in his view, the ending betrays. I am less concerned with critiquing the novel's validity as a mimetic exercise in determining what a real veteran would actually do than in attempting to understand the implications of those actions that her characters do take.

6. I mean "attention" not merely from academic audiences, but within American pop culture as well. *In Country* was made into a film, with adventure movie hero Bruce Willis as Emmett, while *Paco's Story* won the National Book Award and, rumor has it, will itself soon be filmed.

Works Cited

Anisfield, Nancy. "Sexist Subscript in Vietnam Narratives." *Vietnam Generation* 1.3–4 (1989): 109–14.

Bates, Milton J. "Men, Women, and Vietnam." *America Rediscovered: Critical Essays on Literature and Film of the Vietnam War.* Ed. Owen W. Gilman, Jr. and Lorrie Smith. New York: Garland, 1990. 27–63.

Connolly, Donna M. "The Face of the (Other) Enemy: Aspects of the Feminine in Vietnam War Novels." Dissertation, University of Notre Dame, 1991.

Ehrhart, W. D. "Who's Responsible." *Viet Nam Generation* 4.1–2 (1992): 95–100.

Heinemann, Larry. *Paco's Story.* New York: Penguin, 1989.

Herr, Michael. *Dispatches.* New York: Vintage-Random House, 1991.

Jason, Philip K. "Sexism and Racism in Vietnam War Fiction." *Mosaic* 23.3 (Summer 1990): 125–37.

Jeffords, Susan. *The Remasculinization of America: Gender and the Vietnam War.* Bloomington: Indiana University Press, 1989.

——. "Tattoos, Scars, Diaries, and Writing Masculinity." In Rowe, John Carlos, and Rick Berg, eds., *The Vietnam War and American Culture.* New York: Columbia University Press, 1991. 208–23.

Kinney, Katherine. "'Humping the Boonies': Sex, Combat, and the Female in *In Country.*" In Jason, Philip K., ed., *Fourteen Landing Zones: Approaches to Vietnam War Literature.* Iowa City: University of Iowa Press, 1991. 38–48.

Lawson, Jacqueline. "'She's a Pretty Woman … For a Gook': The Misogyny of the Vietnam War." In Jason, Philip K., ed., *Fourteen Landing Zones: Approaches to Vietnam War Literature.* Iowa City: University of Iowa Press, 1991. 15–37.

Mason, Bobbie Ann. *In Country: A Novel.* New York: Perennial–Harper and Row, 1986.

Smith, Lorrie. "Back Against the Wall: Anti-Feminist Backlash in Vietnam War Literature." *Vietnam Generation* 1.3–4 (1989): 115–26.

Stewart, Matthew C. "Realism, Verisimilitude, and the Depiction of Vietnam Veterans in *In Country.*" In Jason, Philip K., ed., *Fourteen Landing Zones: Approaches to Vietnam War Literature.* Iowa City: University of Iowa Press, 1991. 166–79.

Tal, Kalí. "The Mind at War: Images of Women in Vietnam Novels by Combat Veterans." *Contemporary Literature* 31.1 (1990): 76–96.

15. New Battles: Cultural Signification in Contemporary American Narrative

Maria S. Bonn

Vietnam has always been disputed territory. The political and physical battles waged over that terrain now become refigured as battles over metaphor and experience, signification and cultural presence. A few years ago I attended a conference on the war and its cultural effects which ended with a call for reconciliation. The final speaker urged that now we should *all* sit down and talk about the war—those who fought it and those who fought against it. Then in my mid-twenties, my deepest experience of Vietnam came from sleepy childhood Sunday evenings watching the news, half-understood headlines, and long months of dissertation work, charting out a literary cartography of this war. I was no soldier, either for war or peace. Where then did this leave me? Shut out of the conversation?

The presence of this essay testifies that I am obviously not shut out of the conversation. But as I have defined my own relationship to my work and pondered the tensions and forces that operate within the literature of the war, I have often found myself confronting the problematic of authenticity and experiential credentials. All Vietnam scholars, all readers, all Americans participate in the synergistic cultural production of Vietnam; yet at the same time there exists within this production a privileging of verisimilitude, of personal experience, of "Having Been There, Man." This privileging is certainly not unique to this literature; it is symptomatic of all marginalized discourses that reclaim that margin as a site for counter-hegemonic articulation. Many of us are engaged these days in interrogating the literary politics of experience—this interrogation is important to apply in the context of contemporary American representation of Vietnam.

There is a set of ethical and aesthetic questions which we need to employ in this interrogation: To what political, social and literary uses do we wish to put our narratives of this war? Do we want them to stand as memorial to a specific set of events both triumphant and atrocious? Or do we wish them to help us recognize that whatever happened in Viet Nam is embedded in a larger cultural context of violence and fragmentation for which the war can be a powerful signifier? Do we want to say this is unique or common evil? And as we talk with veterans do we wish to privilege the special quality of their experience or claim that experience as a mirror of our own? The movement from viewing the war as a specific historical event to a general cultural metaphor is one which is fraught with ethical perils but may also have larger political benefits. We need to balance these carefully against each other as we consider the construction of the literary signification of the war. So far, I would argue, we have valorized personal and historical specificity, but, I would further argue that we are in a moment of transition toward a shared metaphorical sense of the war and what it means in our culture.

The primacy of first-hand experience in Vietnam War representation both generates and is generated by the canon, such as it is, of Vietnam War literature, which has primarily consisted of literature written by war veterans and war correspondents. The texts which constitute this canon have had to struggle for recognition as a valid body of literature in their own right and as significant movement within the larger trajectory of American literature. And this is a struggle that is not yet over (scholars studying the literature of this war are still frequently asked, "*Is* there much Vietnam War literature?"). The difficulty of attaining academic and popular recognition and legitimacy has paralleled the difficulty of veterans themselves in attaining recognition and legitimacy. The veteran-authors' battles to be published, to reach a wide audience, and to be acknowledged as engaged in the task of important literary and cultural production are both reflection and direct consequence of American attitudes towards Vietnam veterans on the whole.

But that said, those attitudes have changed in the past ten years. The Vietnam experience has been popularized, revised, appropriated, and mainstreamed within the larger cultural framework for all kinds of political, social and financial profit. A lot has been and will be said about the uses and abuses of Vietnam as cultural signification. It is easy to point to the varieties of opportunism that have reconstructed the war in the American imagination; but we also need to turn our critical scrutiny upon a whole collection of contemporary texts in which Vietnam is a less overt but nevertheless influential presence. The generation that is now taking up the task of literary production is a generation that came of age with Vietnam as a primary, if sometimes mysterious, cultural presence. For some it was formative political event, for others the background noise to growing up. But it was always a central structural element of our milieu—one of our key reference points in the construction of late twentieth century American existence.

If we track the presence of Vietnam in contemporary American literature (and once one is attentive to that presence, one can find the war in a great many current narratives), we find it manifested in a few different ways. I would like to investigate these trends and to give a few examples of where we can see them at work.

The first of these is an extension of the veteran literature. We have the veteran in the world—1990's style; this is a literature of reaching middle age, of legacy and of reconciliation, of men and women twenty-five years away from Vietnam, struggling to come to terms with lives irrevocably touched and shaped by war-time experience. These texts continue to be written by veteran-authors—one thinks of Tim O'Brien's *The Things They Carried* or Philip Caputo's *Indian Country*, but while all of this literature engages in the same thematics as those of narratives by actual veterans, they are not necessarily just by veterans anymore. Because the experience of the American soldier in Vietnam *has* been illuminated in the past ten years, it is now accessible to authors who lack firsthand experience of Vietnam. So now we have writers such as Susan Fromberg Schaeffer in *Buffalo Afternoon*, Sydney Blair in *Buffalo*, Larry Brown in *Dirty Work* and, god help us, Danielle Steele in *Nam* exploring the terrain of the Vietnam War and its effects upon a generation of Americans.

There has also been a parallel development of a literature of voices from the home front. These texts are often by women and speak of the absence and presence of brothers, fathers, husbands and friends whose lives have been altered by the war. Texts like Maxine Hong Kingston's *China Men*, Toni Morrison's *Tar Baby*, Jayne Anne Phillips' *Machine Dreams*, Louise Erdrich's *Love Medicine* and Bharati Mukherjee's short stories record the pain of having someone "out there," describe alienation and loss, and show us how American soldiers in Viet Nam were and are located within a whole network of past and present social relations, all of which are altered by the war.

Texts such as these have broadened our understanding of the impact of the Vietnam war on American lives, but there is, I believe, an even more interesting and pervasive manifestation of Vietnam in contemporary American fiction. The war, both in its physical, military unfolding on the soil of Viet Nam and in its social and political unfolding in the United States, was a radically decentered and ambiguous event that can be recognized and constructed as a quintessential postmodern moment. Thus cultural production and reproduction of the war has begun to make use of Vietnam as cultural code, as experience in national consciousness, as a kind of shorthand for the fragmentation and brutality of our historical moment.

An example might illuminate this manifestation in greater detail: A few years ago, at the height of the media interest in war veterans, one of the television news shows followed a group of veterans with post–traumatic stress disorder on a therapeutic trip back to Viet Nam. One odd element of this rather voyeuristic episode was that one of the veterans had never actually been in Viet Nam; he served out his tour of duty in California, supplying the war effort. So, we might ask, can you have the Viet Nam version of PTSD without ever having been there? Or, as Michael Herr famously claims at the end of *Dispatches*, have we all been there? And, if we've all been there, are we all somehow suffering from PTSD? Or is PTSD perhaps a natural expression of the postmodern condition, of a world in which we live without connection? In our current cultural narrative and in texts which articulate that narrative there pervades a sense of Vietnam as more than a self-contained military and political event. The war has become a set of signs about the way we live now.

Leslie Marmon Silko in her long and complicated novel *Almanac of the Dead* points to this metonymic use of the war. One of the many plots revolves around the "Army of the Homeless," a group of organized homeless men led by an ex–Green Beret. All of the men in the Army claim to be veterans of the Vietnam War, but as Roy, the leader, points out, all one has to do is look at many of the young faces and do the math to realize they would have been children in the Sixties. But Roy recognizes that the claim of these young men is a means to make concrete the abstract, confusing nature of their existence. Roy thinks:

> What difference did it make years later whether a man had actually served in Vietnam and was now wandering the streets, or only repeated stories he'd heard from older guys who had been in combat? Roy was not going to pass judgment on what were lies and what were truths. The U.S. had used false figures; the enemy body count had been inflated .... In America a man needed some kind of story to explain himself, to explain why he was here and how he had got here. The only good they would recognize from that war were the stories [396].

That notion that Vietnam provides a story, a fable for our times, is central to one of the most interesting recent narratives that makes use of the war: Fredrick Busch's 1991 *Closing Arguments*. *Closing Arguments* is the story of Mark Brennan, a small-town lawyer who is involved in a sexually incendiary murder case (he is the lawyer and eventually the lover of an accused woman who has killed her previous partner during violent sex), and, at the same time, is apparently trying to resolve his wartime experience and his troubled marriage. Fredrick Busch is not himself a veteran, but he has obviously acquainted himself with the Vietnam genre and his novel has the air of an authentic Vietnam narrative. It uses a flashback structure, which is common in the veteran literature as a means of conveying fragmentation and the process of recovery. It demonstrates a mastery of the language of the Vietnam narrative— both of official military language and the subversive discourse of the grunt. In many ways it seems as if it conforms to the pattern of my first category, and one part of its thematics revolves around reconciliation and recovery as Schell, Mark's wife and a former antiwar activist, works to get a war memorial built in their little town. The memorial will then heal rifts—in the marriage, in the Vietnam generation, in one small part of a conflicted nation.

So the novel initially seems like a further articulation of the narrative we all have access to now; one we've grown to understand. But there is a twist in this book, and what we gradually come to understand through Mark's narration is that in fact he never was in Viet Nam at all, but is a victim of protracted and brutal child abuse. His life is indeed marked by violence, but not the violence of warfare. This is a narrative of trauma, but, ironically, Vietnam, that event which has been figured in our collective consciousness as unknowable and unspeakable, has become the means of articulating *another* experience beyond words, a way of controlling and conveying the legacy of abuse. Mark's narration, which turns out to be a long confession of a life full of lies, begins with the claim "the best defense is a good story" (1), and the war becomes the setting for the story he has used to explain his life and to defend himself against the dangers of memory.

This thematic is further compounded by the history of Estelle, the accused murderer. Mark comes to realize that she too has a past history of sexual and physical abuse by her parents, and he decides to base her defense on claiming that she suffers from PTSD and that the violence that precipitated the murder was brought on by a flashback induced by rough sex. In the midst of this he is not at all unaware of the further complications of the dynamic; he is the town's supposed war hero and a returned POW, arguing PTSD as extenuating circumstances for a murder. A complicated thematic and narrative brew, but the point I wish to make here is that the war, so often viewed as the heart of darkness (to use a popular Vietnam analog) now provides an iconography for rape and brutality—the unarticulated horror finds a language in this war.

The drive of the novel is toward an acknowledgment that war stays with us, that battles are fought on the civilian landscape, that there's really nothing remarkable in Mark's calling his broken foot (broken by his father in a fit of rage) a war wound; everywhere people are battle-scarred. Mark and Estelle make explicit this position when Estelle takes the witness stand during the trial. Mark questions Estelle about PTSD as a potential cause of violence: "Because of the flashback? Because war stays with you? Because even when you think it's over it isn't, am I right? That very often you can't end a war—or the stress of 'battles' in civilian life." Estelle responds, "Like war. Very much like war" (275). But this contention does not go undisputed. Sydney Birnbaum, the reporter who's doing a story on Mark, Schell and the memorial, discovers that Mark's past is a fiction and, specifically on the basis of his own experience as a soldier in the war, feels compelled to expose Mark. Sydney insists that the war is not just part of some common contemporary malaise, but a uniquely important experience in and of itself, and he privileges the authenticity of the veteran. He tells Mark he must expose him and explains, "You see ... I was there ... That's the whole thing ... I was there" (257).

Which leads us back to the central dilemma in this construction of Vietnam as metaphorical presence. If we embrace the war as a kind of catch-all metonymy for contemporary existence, do we then cheapen the very real and often painful experience of people whose lives were directly and immediately altered by the war? Or by investigating the shared nature of fractured, postmodern life do we in some way participate in a community of understanding with those same people? The obvious analogy to consider here is the discourse of the Holocaust and our debates over whether that event should be remembered and discussed as the greatest aberration in human history or as the most striking manifestation of the very nature of human history. Unique or common evil? In writing and reading narratives of the Vietnam War we will continue to struggle over the merits of respecting the authenticity of individual, lived experience versus the political and educational benefits of participating in a discourse which we can all have access to. As we move farther away from the war there continues to be produced a variety of texts that keep us engaged with these issues and with the question of whether Vietnam will continue to be disputed territory or will become common ground.

Works Cited

Busch, Fredrick. *Closing Arguments*. New York: Fawcett Columbine, 1991.
Silko, Leslie Marmon. *The Almanac of the Dead*. New York: Simon and Schuster, 1991.

Making Friends

Twenty years since my life was changed
Twenty years making a friend of death
Knowing it
Respecting it
Wishing for it at times
Fighting with it as friends sometimes do.

But the nightmares of war have faded as I've healed
My dreams are now of peace
Peace of mind
Peace of heart
Hoping for Peace on earth
It's time I made a friend of Life.

—LYNDA VAN DEVANTER, 1990

V.
VIETNAM VETERAN
WRITERS
SYMPOSIUM

16. Roundtable Discussion with John Balaban, Robert Olen Butler, W.D. Ehrhart, Larry Heinemann, and Marc Leepson—Moderator

Introduction

Writers, poets and artists of all kinds have focused on wars and warriors since the first humans began drawing on their cave walls. Veterans of modern wars have used their battlefield experiences as fodder for imaginative works that have become classics. Veterans of Vietnam have produced a substantial body of literary work, including novels, short stories, literary non-fiction, plays, and poetry. Four of the best known and most accomplished Vietnam veteran writers, John Balaban, Robert Olen Butler, W.D. Ehrhart and Larry Heinemann, took part in a roundtable discussion at the Notre Dame conference. They discussed their creative work in a 90-minute discussion moderated by Marc Leepson, the arts editor and columnist for *The Veteran*, the national newspaper published by Vietnam Veterans of America. Some excerpts follow.

The Discussion

Leepson: I found a terrific quote from a review by Verlyn Klinkenborg of a book called *A Moment of War*, a memoir of the Spanish Civil War:

It says: "For some artists and writers, I think of Goya or Michael Herr, war is a kind of fugue state from which they return with a lingering vision in which you feel an expressive haste, a hysteria under flushed skin. These are the kinds of artists and writers for whom war retains a kind of esthetic sublimity—immoral, to be sure, and always undercut by the blatant ironies of combat, but with the mix of fear and beauty that Wordsworth could find in a mountain landscape, unmolested by shellfire, or that Byron could find in

217

incest. The emotion with which such works are charged is a commentary on war and a gauge of authenticity.

"But there is another school of artists and writers for whom war obviates all commentary, for whom war, austerely depicted, is itself a commentary on human civilization."

My question is: Which one of these comes closest to why you began writing about the war in a creative way?

Balaban: I have another quote, which is similar. It's something I discovered after I returned and it's a quote from Dante: "The proper subjects of poetry are love, virtue and war." That's from *De vulgari eloquentia*, a Latin essay he wrote. "The proper subjects of poetry are love, virtue and war."

What that means for me is that these things are displayed extravagantly during warfare. People do extraordinary things for and against each other. They betray themselves. They give their lives for strangers. Love and virtue are supremely tested during warfare.

I guess the reason that I continue to write about Vietnam is that I'm still learning from experiences—in fact, in some cases [I deal with the] same events in nonfiction, in fiction and in poetry. All, I think, because there's an instruction there in love and virtue that is still instructive to me, that at least I'm still learning.

Butler: It seems to me that artists are not intellectuals. We are sensualists. And art is intensely sensual. That's why it exists as a mode of discourse separate from any other.

In war and the conditions around war, especially in a war where the front lines were often nonexistent, one finds one's sensual self pitched very keenly. The world becomes extremely vivid. And, indeed, for that year you find that all the cosmic issues confront you every morning when you wake up and linger in your dreams at night. And those issues are intensely imbedded in the sensual experience around you.

The combination of the cosmic and the sensual is as good a definition of art as I could think of. So for the nascent artist the world in which these things are heightened to that extent must then produce and generate your art. I am thankful, and I think my fellow panelists would be thankful, that we had art to turn to.

This is not really a digression; it's an extra thought on this. I think a lot of post–traumatic stress syndrome, much of it, has to do with not being able to shake off the horrors. But maybe not as much of it as we tend to think.

I have a hunch—and I know people who have this feeling—that it wasn't the horror of the past that is keeping them stressed, it's the blandness of the present. After a year of that kind of heightened sensitivity to the world and the cosmos, to return to a world of pop culture and superficial values, the discrepancy—the sense of having lost something—that if horrifying at times, if difficult at times, if politically bizarre and evil at times, at least one was aware intensely always of your presence in the universe.

Heinemann: I started writing because I simply couldn't shut up about what I had seen and what I had done and what I had become.

My youngest brother was a two-tour Marine and he came home for the second time and he and I did not exchange a word for ten years. He basically went to his room and has been eating his liver out for about 25 years.

But I was not one of those people. I came back and discovered very quickly that there was something about what was going on overseas, that with all the information that was coming back, there were still tremendous distortions and tremendous—well, I don't want to call it misunderstanding because it was more serious than that.

Like a lot of other veterans, I went back to school on the G.I. Bill, for what that was worth, and encountered people who were against the war and serious about their antiwar activities and serious about their opposition to the war and some of them went to prison.

It was not ever a calm undertaking.

I started writing when the information and my own energy was very raw. Raw in a lot of ways. I was not a very good student, not a very good writer. The first couple of years I was writing, I was reading bonehead English books and dictionaries.

One of the things I learned from *Moby-Dick* is that if you take a story like this and sort of nail it with what the work was, the story can proceed from that and grow out of that. The other thing I very quickly discovered was that the writing had nothing to do with what everyone told me was going to be a cathartic experience. I've written two novels the best I know how to write and neither book was a catharsis in any way, shape or form.

I can't tell you the number of times that *Close Quarters* was abandoned, simply abandoned. The same with *Paco's Story*. "I can't think about this any more."

It's also a considerable irony—this may be off the subject, but I may as well say it while I'm thinking about it—a considerable irony that I discovered what apparently is my life work as a writer because of what happened in the war and what I did.

Ehrhart: I've often talked about my writing as being a writing of witness: essentially all this really rotten stuff happened to me in Viet Nam and it took me by surprise because I thought I was going there to do good and I thought that my country was doing good.

I'm really simplifying here, but when you're eighteen years old and they give you a gun and they send you through all this training and they send you out there and you discover that things are not the way they told you they were, it's a long way to the bottom of the shaft.

And I came back really, really fucked up. I was really angry. I was confused, lost and did not know how this had happened to me or to my country. Mostly I wanted to know what happened to me. I ignored this for about a year and a half, but eventually realized I was ignoring it and I began to explore what had actually happened to me and why.

Part of the way that I used to explore that was writing. I had done some writing before I ever went into the military as a lot of high school kids do.

So I can say it was this terrible need to discover what was in me, to articulate what had happened to me. As all of you know, we learn what we think by writing.

So I used the writing—I think Bob was right—I'm very grateful I had the writing. I would have been a statistic if I didn't have that. I damn near was anyway.

I wanted to be able to communicate this to people around me. I used to shove my poems at people. I went to this college where I was the only veteran. It was a very politically aware place. So I was very conspicuous. Nobody had a clue what I was trying to deal with. I didn't have a clue what I was trying to deal with. Neither did they. How could they possibly?

But I would show them these poems. And, again, what's going on here is that I'm trying to explain things consciously that I did quite unconsciously. When I picked up the pen, this stuff began to happen. And I don't quite know why.

But if I say that I'm the guy who was just trying to bear witness, and I have been quoted in print as saying "I don't give a goddamn about art. My writing is a tool of education." And jumping up and down as some of you have seen on multiple occasions.

I think that's true. But at the same time people—and some of them are in this room—have called me out on that statement, and said, "But you are producing art." And, in fact, there has been a part of me that has had some artistic pretensions.

I have always written poems—not so much the prose, but the poems—that have dealt with things other than the Vietnam war—entirely divorced from the war: geese in the autumn, broken-hearted love poems and all that stuff.

So, finally, I answer you by saying, I don't know what a fugue state is and I don't know what side of that business I come down on. I'm not sure what fueled me. It just happened. And in some ways this makes me uncomfortable, trying to explain this stuff.

You actually saw what I do on Thursday afternoon [a poetry reading]. That's what I do. This isn't what I do. Sitting here talking about it is not what I do. What I do is what you heard. I'm much more comfortable doing a reading than trying to explain because, ultimately, I'm not sure but what I'm doing is sitting here now trying to give you conscious explanations of things I haven't really got a clue why they happen, why this thing happens.

Leepson: You gave a pretty good answer, nevertheless.

You just brought up an issue that's been a recurring theme here at the conference, the issue of the war seeping into your non-war work, whether poetry, novels or literary nonfiction. I'd like you all to address that issue of how the war doesn't go away and how it remains in your work.

Butler: The novel I read from [*They Whisper*], my new novel which is coming out at the end of January [1994], is a book about something quite different. It's a serious literary novel about human sexuality.

But all of the issues that as artists we find most insistent in our unconscious surely have been shaped by our most insistent and vivid experiences in life. That is inescapable for any real artist. So Vietnam will always be there, just as all of my other experience comes into Vietnam.

I'm often—particularly with *A Good Scent from a Strange Mountain*, which is fifteen stories in the voices of Vietnamese—I'm constantly having to let people know, because their assumptions go elsewhere, that of those fifteen first person speakers, those fifteen quite different characters, not one of them has a real life counterpart, not one.

I love to quote—paraphrase actually, because I can never remember the quote—Graham Greene when he said that good novelists have bad memories. He says what you remember comes out as journalism. What you forget goes into the compost of the imagination.

So there have been a lot of other things in my life. I have been married three times. Sole custody of my son at age twelve. I grew up in a steel mill town in the Midwest. Worked the mills. I've done a lot of things. I did a lot of things in my life, a lot of relationships of all kinds.

Just as all of that non–Vietnamese stuff I know in my heart was in that compost heap and helped to shape the fifteen characters in *Good Scent*, so too has my experience in Viet Nam come out of that compost heap and shaped a book like *Countrymen of Bones*, for instance, which is set in the Alamogordo Desert in 1945 with the birth of the atom bomb. Needless to say, there's not a word about Vietnam in there.

Yet my vision of the world, my vision of humanity, is profoundly shaped by my having been to Viet Nam and been intimately close to and loved those people and their culture. So it flows both ways. We are, as artists, the indistinguishable sensual sum of all of our experiences. Vietnam informs everything and everything else informs Vietnam.

Heinemann: Bob says it pretty accurately.

It would be foolish for any writer, any artist, to ignore those things that come to him that are the most powerful and the most present. To deny those things that are the most powerful in your work or the foundation of an imagination or mind-set, perception, whatever, is kind of foolish.

I'm jealous of people like William Faulkner who had a whole history and a whole people and a whole community going on in his imagination all of his life. Somebody like Garrison Keillor has this—good, bad or indifferent; how well or how ill he does it—nevertheless has this advantage of this remarkable place and these people to grow upon.

It would be foolish of any artist, any writer, any poet, et cetera to deny these things. I got to a point—this was a couple of years ago when I first started working on this book on PTSD which is still in a box in the corner of my room—[where] I was earnest about getting the war out of my house once and for all. And then, like a lot of other people is [this] room, I traveled back to Viet Nam and talked a great deal about different experiences that people have had going back.

It suddenly occurred to me when that happened that that story has changed. That good, bad or indifferent, not only as I a Chicago writer, but I am also a Vietnam writer. I used to [say] "I don't want to do that anymore." But now the story has changed. It's not about the war. It's about this other more remarkable, really much deeper relationship with all of that.

Sometimes I have to remind myself out loud that that was one year out of my life. I'm farther away from it now than I was old when I was there.

I welcome that kind of connection with material. There are artists and writers who would pay for something like this. I've come to understand that kind of relationship with—we'll call it material. The relationship with the material is gold as far as I'm concerned. For my job as a writer this is golden because I can draw on this all my working life and not everybody gets to do that.

Ehrhart: Americans tend to use the word "Vietnam" meaning this thing that happened to a bunch of nineteen-year-old kids twenty-five years ago. And, in fact, Viet Nam is this place that exists in the world today.

My experiences in Viet Nam continue to inform my writing in the way that Bob mentions specifically because—for good or ill—it shapes what I see when I open my peepers and look out on the world. It shapes the way I understand the world that I live in and my relationship with it.

People call me a Vietnam writer when they talk about me. That bothers me because I'm not a Vietnam writer. I'm a writer who went to Viet Nam. They tend to talk about my political poems. I really am a Vietnam writer—even the innocuous love poem to my daughter is a Vietnam poem. Everything that I write is a Vietnam poem because that's what shaped me.

There's a second way in which I keep circling back to the war and my experiences in it. I guess that's that sort of messianic part of me that wants to bear witness. Just the other month when those horrible pictures of those American bodies being dragged through the streets of Mogadishu [were broadcast] I looked on the television screen, and [thought], What did those kids die for?

We're not catching on. It's impossible not to hearken back to what I saw and did and learned in Viet Nam when I see that stuff going on now. I'm forced constantly to go back, not only to Viet Nam as a place, but to my experience and what I learned and what we as a nation learned and didn't learn.

I keep getting my face rubbed in the war every time I turn on the television or open up a newspaper. When we wise up, I'll finally let that whole business go. We all know how soon that's going to happen. So I guess I'm stuck with it for the rest of my life.

The older I get, the more I'm beginning to come to terms with that. I'm beginning to understand, not in an intellectual way, but in my gut, that it's okay for me not to let it go.

Balaban: I had a very careful stash of cigars that I brought with me from Miami. I was saving the butts outside the door. The janitor took them away. In a state of panic I went through the trash cans with him. We were diving down in the trash [and] as we were throwing the trash back in ... there was a six-foot fluorescent lamp which blew up or shattered and I had all this glass that I was picking out of hair.

As it banged over my head, my instincts took me immediately to Viet Nam. I remember walking with Donald Duncan, the great reporter who was once the most decorated soldier in Vietnam, a Green Beret. He turned against the war. We were walking in Cholon and something dropped, a piano, out of a building or something. I jumped and looked for Duncan and I couldn't find him because he was on the ground. He had just fallen flat because the tonality of the drop was reminiscent for him.

This is a roundabout way of telling you about the cigars again. A very nice woman whom I've met at the conference, Wendy Green, took me down to the mall where there was a good cigar store. On the way we were talking about the world and we passed a corner where a child was killed and I remarked about the way children are being snatched off streets.

"What can that be about?" I said. "I can't understand it. Why didn't it happen before in this country?"

And she said, "Vietnam?"

Then she took it back. She said, "Oh god, so much is being blamed on Vietnam."

And I said, "Well, I guess you could run a line of argument that way." You could talk about the dissolution of values.

In other words, there's another way of arguing it. Why would Americans be interested in writers whose instincts or reflexes are set in Viet Nam? Who, as my friend John Steinbeck said, grew up in Viet Nam in a very real way.

I'll never be this person I was before I went there. Not just because I'm twice as old. But all my values and beliefs and trusts in other people changed irrevocably as everyone's was. I became a Buddhist in Vietnam. My whole religious system changed.

But why would this country care about us and why would it be important to hear about Vietnam in fiction and poetry and plays and in any creative media? The answer is that Vietnam was part of a series of disasters, but it was really a first-rate disaster.

Vietnam was huge persuasive power throughout American society. I suppose we as writers in some way address it even when we're not addressing it openly and directly. So that's why it remains important. So inevitably, it's an important thing. Whether we continue writing or not is irrelevant, but the need for that writing seems to be essential.

Leepson: I want to get your thoughts about something all of you have written about in one degree or another through fiction or poetry, this image of the veteran.

Does that concern you in your writing, the implications of these [stereotyped] characters that tend to pop up one way or another in the literature?

Heinemann: It's a kind of complicated question. I'll try not to complicate the answer.

I wanted to write a war story. So I thought to myself that probably the easiest way to do that was to read some war stories because you have to basically find out what the form is and what the structure of the war novel is. So I started reading every war story I could get my hands on.

I read the *Iliad* and then I skipped a couple thousand years and read *War and Peace* and on and on and on and on. I read the work that came out of World War I, that work that came out of the Civil War, World War II.

Parenthetically, I came to admire and really learned a great deal from James Jones. He died before I could meet him, which I think, for me anyway, is a pity because I really would have liked to tell him a number of things.

One of the things I discovered was that there is this, of course, universal experience of men as soldiers: the problem of rediscovering who you are as a man after you've been a soldier for a time and to rediscover those things that made you a soldier.

There is a commonness about that, too. I believe that the difference with the literature that came out of Vietnam and the literature that emerged from other wars is that all war is evil, but some wars are evil with the saving grace of getting rid of Nazis or Japanese fascists or putting a stop to this or that or the other. There's an actual arguable reason.

With Vietnam there wasn't. No one has ever come to me and said to my face and given me a reasonable explanation for the goddamn thing.

All soldiers have this sort of universal process and they emerge from this universal process as someone not simply different or crazy, just changed. Everybody in the room knows it. You become a person that you don't recognize when you come back. But after Vietnam there was no—how to say this?—there was no saving grace [or] decent excuse. This was an absolute bullshit evil and there was no explaining it away and there were no excuses. As individuals, just the way the war and the postwar experience was structured, everybody was sort of left to hang by themselves.

And another reason. There was such an odd, confused ambivalence about who we were among the culture at large. After Vietnam there was a great deal of energy of considerable velocity that was directed inward. I'm no pro, but I do know enough about what it is to be a human being to know that when you take something like that and point it inward, you shouldn't. It's one of the things that does make the war unique.

Question from the Floor: I wonder if you'd be willing to comment on a very famous scene by Nietzsche in *Thus Spake Zarathustra,* which seems to me to relate to a number of things that you've said.

Zarathustra is sitting and he says, "The broken tablets of the law lie around my feet and here in my lap are the unwritten tablets of the new law." It's often struck me that [some] veterans are in exactly this position. All of what is right has been shattered and demolished and they are in this painful and enormous awe inspiring task.

Butler: It sounds like a wonderful answer to some other question. So your exegesis on that seems perfectly adequate to me.

Ehrhart: Certainly it's perfectly true for—and this goes back to what I was saying earlier—what happened to me. I rather crudely described the condition I was in when I came back. I ought to be more articulate about that. And, in fact, that's what you're talking about.

The entire value system that I had been inculcated with in the first eighteen years of my life was destroyed in Viet Nam and I came back and had to build something new. I had to build a new house of values. I write to write new laws for myself. I think that was true for a great many others, maybe most of us.

It certainly was true for me. I didn't know what right and wrong meant anymore. I thought my country was right. All sorts of things that I thought were wrong turned out not to be and I had to go figure out what was right.

Question from the Floor: I have a question for you as professional writers.

This is a Vietnam conference and you're gathered here as essentially genre writers: Vietnam war writers. Whether you like it or not, sitting on that panel places you there. I'm interested in how you see yourselves as part of a community of writers who write about the war. Do you have a heritage that you grow upon? Who were your mentors? Where do you place yourselves as professionals in this field?

Butler: I'm going to give an answer that I've given in public before, but it's directly applicable to this because it's a perfectly legitimate question.

We are artists here. The artist approaches the things that he or she creates from encountering the chaos out there, and yet having some inchoate conviction that it makes sense, that there's order out there. We are moved to express that vision of order by telling stories or writing poems.

And insofar as that's the case, to call us Vietnam novelists or Vietnam poets is like calling Monet a lily pad painter. It's just the surface material that we use to find the deeply universal shapes, the colors, the forms that are the real subject of what we say.

Question from the Floor: Douglas Pike in his presentation articulated clearly a sentiment that seems to be fairly widespread. He mentioned that he found the people in Viet Nam much less preoccupied with the war than Americans. He suggested pretty strongly that American preoccupation with the war in a lot of ways is not a very healthy thing—that, in fact, we needed to get beyond it, to get it behind us, to think about other things. I'd like your answers on that.

Ehrhart: I lump that into the same category as healing. I've been hearing the terms healing and reconciliation for, I don't know, fifteen years. And what I find—what people generally seem to mean by that is: by healing they mean, stop disturbing us by talking about this, stop giving us nightmares. We thought that the nightmares had stopped when the war ended.

By reconciliation, do they mean that I am supposed to embrace Henry Kissinger or Robert McNamara? I'm not interested in reconciling with those people. People who say that, what they mean is: Stop troubling us with this.

I'm not going to stop talking about this until we've learned something from it. That means I'm going to be talking about it until they shovel the dirt in my mouth because we're not catching on.

Leepson: As far as a literary response to the war, we didn't have one in the beginning. We weren't allowed to. Nobody wanted to hear about it. That was as harmful to reconciliation or healing as was the nation's total amnesia about the war in the beginning, when nobody wanted to talk to us.

When I came home from Viet Nam I didn't get called a baby killer or spat upon. I didn't have to. I knew that this wasn't what people wanted to hear. So I did what most vets did and shut up about it. It wasn't until—who know when; a convenient date is the return of the hostages from Iran in 1982—that the nation sort of forgave us and the writing started coming.

So, I would just say: What are we supposed to do, go back to this time—just push it under the rug, we don't want to hear about it, let's move on to something else?

I want to see Vietnam books and poetry and films and plays and operas continue—not to the exclusion of everything else, but the more that's written, especially through art, the better it will be for everyone.

Question from the Floor: We've talked a lot about how serious that experience was and the writing experience. Where is the laughter? Where does that come in among all this?

Butler: You pointed to me, I guess, because a couple of the stories in *A Good Scent from a Strange Mountain* certainly are funny.

We do not know the effect [of what we write]. We do not know the emotion. We do not even necessarily know the political implications of what we write. We don't know if you're going to laugh or if you're going to cry or if you're going to do both or if you're going to do neither.

We don't know if the Vietnamese or the Americans are going to come off as good or bad or indifferent or whatever. We pursue through story the vision of the world that we deeply feel but we don't even yet understand until the object is created.

Balaban: It works the same for poetry.

Robert Frost had this maxim. He said, "No surprise for the writer, no surprise for the reader." The discovery is there in the poem. And what a wonderful thing, to find in the landscape of Vietnam some laughter, its benediction.

VI.
EPILOGUE

A Farmer from Vinh

"The airplane crashed into my rice paddy on the night of December 21, 1972,"
says the old farmer from Vinh.
"It fell like a star out of the heavens,
and knocked me and my wife right out of our bed!

"The Army soldiers who came running said it was a fighting jet,
and that the driver was still inside.
But after the terrible burning was over,
it looked only like a huge lump of charcoal in my field.

"My wife was afraid of the plane, and wouldn't go near.
But I knew its hurting days were finished,
and since the American had no one to say prayers over him,
I built a small altar on the wreckage.

"Each week, I still burn some joss for that young man
who died all alone so far from his ancestors.
Many times the local cadres have ordered me to stop doing that,
but they are all too young to know about important things."

—LARRY ROTTMANN

17. Salem

FICTION BY ROBERT OLEN BUTLER

I have always been obedient to these true leaders of my country, even for their sake curling myself against a banyan root and holding my head and quaking like a child, letting my manhood go as we all did sooner or later beneath the bellow of fire from the B-52s. I said yes to my leaders and I went into the jungle and gave them even my manhood, but I sit now with a twenty-four year old pack of Salem cigarettes before me and a small photo trimmed unevenly with scissors and I whisper softly no. I whisper and I raise my eyes at once, to see if anyone has heard. No one has. I am alone. I look through my window and there is a deep-rutted road, bright now with sunlight, leading into the jungle and we are at peace in Vietnam, hard stuck with the same blunt plows and surly water buffaloes but it is our own poverty now, one country, and I turn my face from the closing of trees a hundred meters down the path. I know too much of myself from there, and I look at the objects before me on the table.

He was alone and I don't know why, this particular American, and I killed him with a grenade I'd made from a Coca-Cola can. Some powder, a hemp fuse and a blasting cap, some scraps of iron and this soda can that I stole from the trash of the village: I was in a tree and I killed him. I could have shot him but I had made this thing and I saw him in the clearing, coming in slow but noisy, and he was very nervous, he was separated and lost and I had plenty of time and I lobbed the can and it landed softly at his feet and he looked down and stared at it as if it was a gift from his American gods, as if he was thinking to pick up this Coca-Cola and drink and refresh himself.

I had killed many men by that time and would kill many more before I came out of the jungle. This one was no different. There was a sharp pop and he went down and there was, in this case, as there often was, a sound that followed, a sound that we would all make sooner or later in such a circumstance as that. But the sound from this particular American did not last long. He was soon gone and I waited to see if there would be more Americans. But I was right about him. I'd known he was separated from his comrades from just the way he'd picked up one foot and put it ahead of the other, the way he'd moved his face to look around the clearing, saying to himself, Oh no, no one is here either. Not that I imagined these words going through his head when I first saw him—it is only this morning that I've gone that far. At the time, I just looked at him and knew he was lost and after the grenade I'd made with my own hands had killed him, I waited, from the caution that I'd learned, but I knew already that I'd been right about him. And I was. No one appeared.

And then I came down from the tree and moved to this dead body and I could see the wounds but they did not affect me. I'd seen many wounds by then and though I thought often of the betrayal of my manhood beneath the bombs of the B-52s, I could still be in the midst of blood and broken bodies and not lose my nerve. I went to this dead body and there were many jagged places and there was much blood and I dug into each of the pockets of the pants, the shirt, and I hoped for documents, for something to take back to my leaders, and all that I found was a pack of Salem cigarettes.

I do not remember if the irony of this struck me at the time. I was a young man and ardent and at turns full of fury and of shame and these are not the conditions for irony. But we all knew, even at that time, that one of the favorite pleasures of the dear father of Vietnam, Ho Chi Minh, was to smoke a Salem cigarette. A captain on our popular forces had a personal note from father Ho that thanked him for capturing and sending north a case of Salem cigarettes. This was all common knowledge. But I, too, liked American cigarettes, encouraged in this by the example of our leader, and I think that when I took this pack of Salem from the body, I was thinking only of myself.

Like now. I am, it seems, a selfish man. Ho Chi Minh died that same year and we all went through six more years of fighting before our country was united and I owe my obedience to those who have brought us through to our great victory, but they have asked something now that makes me sit and hesitate and wait and think in ways that surprise me, after all this time, after all that I have been through with my country. The word has come down to everyone that we are to find any objects that belong to dead American soldiers and bring them forth so that the American government can name its remaining unnamed dead and then our two countries can become friends. It's like my wife's old beliefs and her mother's. These two women live in my home and they love me and they care for me but they do not change what they deeply believe, in spite of what I've been through for them, and they would understand this in their Buddhist way. It is as if we had all died and now we were being reborn in strange new bodies, destined to atone in this particular new incarnation for the errors of our past. The young V.C. and U.S. soldier reborn as middle-aged friends doing business together, creating soda cans and cigarettes.

Is it this that makes me hesitate to obey? I only have to ask the question to know that it is not. In the clearing, I put the pack of Salem cigarettes in my pocket and then I slipped back into the jungle and I smoked one cigarette later in the afternoon, shaking it out of the pack with my mind elsewhere as I sat beside a stream, a little ways apart from my own comrades. I did not wish to share these cigarettes with them and when I lit one and drew the smoke into my body, there was that familiar letting go from a desire both created and fulfilled by this thing I did, and I looked down the stream away from the others and in a few hundred meters the jungle closed in, black in the twilight, and I blew the smoke out and my nostrils flared from an odd coolness. I had never before smoked this favorite cigarette of Ho Chi Minh and for a moment I thought this soft chill in my head was somehow a sign of him. Such a thought—the vague mysticism of it—came easily to me and I never questioned it, though I think Ho himself would have been disappointed in me because of it. This was not the impulse of a mature communist, and much later, when I learned that there was a thing called menthol in some American cigarettes, I remembered my thoughts by the stream and I felt ashamed.

But at the time, I let this notion linger, that the spirit of Ho was inside me, and I took the pack of cigarettes out of my pocket and now I looked at it more carefully: the blue-tinted green bands of color at the top and bottom, the American words, long and meaningless to my eyes except for the large *Salem* in a central band of white—this name I'd known to recognize. And there was a clear cellophane wrapper around the pack, which I ruffled a little with my thumb and almost stripped off, but I stopped myself. This was protection from the dampness. Then I turned the pack over and there was a leaping inside me as if a twig had just snapped in the jungle nearby. A face smiled up at me from my hand, a woman's face, and I stopped my breath so that she would not hear me. I suppose that this reflex ran on even into my hands where I was ready to draw my weapon and kill her.

And she is before me now. The pack of Salem is in the center of the oak table that I made with my own hands, breaking down a French cabinet from an old provincial office building to make a surface of my own. The cigarette pack lies in the center of this table and the photo looks up from behind the cellophane, just where he put it, the man from the clearing. I have never taken the photo out of its place and I have never smoked another cigarette from the pack and these are things that I knew right away to do, even before my hands calmed and the beating of my heart slowed again beside the stream, and I did not ask myself why, I just knew to look once more at the woman— she had an almond-shaped face and colorless hair and a vast smile with many teeth—and then to put the cigarette pack into my deepest pocket with the amber Buddha pendant my wife had slipped into my hand when I went away from her.

I expect her soon, my wife. I look through my window and down the path and she and her mother will come walking from out of the closing of the trees and she will be bearing water and her sudden appearance there along this jungle path will make my hands go soft and I am wrong to say that the hair of this woman in the picture has no color, there are times of the day when the sunlight falls with this color on our village and her hair has no color only against the jungle shadow of my wife's hair.

I wish I had the reflexes of the days when I was a freedom fighter. Instantly I could decide to kill or to run or to curl down and quake or to rob a dead man's pockets or I could even make such a strange and complicated decision as to put this pack of cigarettes into my pocket with the secret resolve—secret even from myself—to preserve it for decades. Now I sit and sit and I can decide nothing. Something tells me that my leaders will betray all that they have ever believed in and fought for, that they will make us into Japanese. But even shaping that thought, I do not have a reflex, my hands do not go hard, they just lie without moving on the tabletop before the smile of an American woman, and perhaps what began beneath the bombs of the B-52s is now complete. Perhaps I am no longer a man.

Still, I will not act in haste about this. That is the way of a twenty year old boy. I am no longer a boy, either. And even the boy knew to put this thing away and not to touch it. Why? I bend near and I wait and I watch as if I am hidden in a tree and watching the face of the jungle across a clearing. The photo has three sharp, even edges, top and bottom and down the left side, but the right side is very slightly crooked, angling in as it comes down through a pale blue sky and a dark field and past the woman's shoulder and then it seems as if this angle will touch her at the elbow, cut into her, and the edge veers off, conscious of this, leaving the arm intact. I speak of the edge as if it created itself. It is of course the man who made the cut, who was careful not to lose even the thinnest slice of the image of this woman he clearly loved. He trimmed the photo to fit in the cellophane around a pack of cigarettes and I understand things with a rush: he placed her there so that every time his unit stopped and sat sweating and afraid by a jungle stream and he took out his cigarettes to smoke, she would be there to smile at him.

Is this not a surprising thing? A sentimental gesture like that from an American soldier who has come across an ocean to do the imperialist work of his country? Perhaps that is why I kept the pack of cigarettes. I am baffled by such an act from this man. Even my wife has such ways. We still have an ancestor shrine in our house. A little altar table with an incense holder and an alcohol pot and a teakwood tabernacle that has been in her family for many years and there is a table of names there, written on rice paper, with the names of four generations, and she believes that the souls of the dead need the prayers of the living or they will never rest and I tell her that this is not clear thinking in a world that has thrown off the tyrannies of the past, but she turns her face away and I know that I hurt her. This altar and the prayers for the dead do not even fit her Buddhism, they are from the Confu-cianism of the Chinese who oppressed us for centuries. But she does not hear me. It is something that lives apart from any religion or any politics. It is something that comes from our weakness, our fearful hopes for a life beyond the one that we can see and touch, and it is this that allows governments to oppress the poor and create the very evils I helped fight against.

But as I look more closely at these objects and think more clearly, I realize I should not have been surprised at the sentimentality of this American soldier. I am confused in my thinking. His wife was alive. This was the picture of a living person, not a dead ancestor. And whatever excess of sentiment there was in his wanting to see his wife in the jungle each time he stopped to smoke a cigarette, his government had bred such a thing in him— it was their power over him—and I look beyond this smiling woman and there is a sward of blue green nearby but then the land goes dark and I bend nearer, straining to see, and the darkness becomes earth turned for planting, plowed into even furrows, and I know his family is a family of farmers, his wife smiles at him and her hair is the color of the sunlight that falls on farmers in the early haze of morning and he must have taken as much pleasure from that color as I take from the long drape of night-shadow that my wife combs down for me and the earth must smell strong and sweet, turned like that to grow whatever it is that Americans eat, wheat I think instead of rice, corn perhaps. I am short of breath now and I place my hand on this cigarette pack, covering the woman's face, and I think the right thing to do is to give these objects over to my government. I have no need for them. And thinking this, I know that I am trying to lie to myself, and I withdraw my hand but I do not look at the face of the wife of the man I killed. I sit back instead and look out my window and I wait.

Perhaps I am waiting for my wife: her approach down the jungle path will make it necessary to put these things away and not consider them again and then I will have no choice but to take them into the authorities in Da Nang when I go, as I do four times a year to report on the continued education of my village. If my wife were to appear right now, even as a pale blue cloud-shadow passes over the path and a dragonfly hovers in the window, if she were to appear in this moment, it would be done, for I have never spoken to my wife about what happened in those years in the jungle and she is a good wife and has never asked me and I would not tempt her by letting her see these objects. But she does not appear. Not in the moment of the blue shadow and the dragonfly and not in the moment afterward as the sunlight returns and the dragonfly rises and hesitates and then dashes away. And I know I am not waiting for my wife, after all. It is something else.

I look again at the face of this woman. The body of her husband was never found. I left him in the clearing and he was far from his comrades and he was far from my thoughts, even after I put his cigarettes in a place to keep them safe. Perhaps she has his name written on a shrine in her home and she lights incense to him and she prays for his spirit. She is the wife of a farmer. Perhaps there is some belief that she has that is like the belief of my own wife. But she does not know if her husband is dead or he is not dead. It is difficult to pray in such a circumstance.

And am I myself sentimental now, like the American soldier? I am not. I have earned the right to these thoughts. For instance, there is already something I know of that is inside the cigarette pack. I understood it in a certain way even by the stream. I think on it now and I understand even more. When I shook the cigarette into my hand from the pack, the first one out was small, half-smoked, ragged at the end where he had brushed the burnt ash away to save the half cigarette, and I sensed then and I realize clearly now, that this man was a poor man, like me. He could not finish his cigarette, but he did not throw it away. He saved it. There were many half-smoked cigarettes scattered in the jungles of Vietnam by Americans—it was one of the signs of them. American soldiers always had as many cigarettes as they wanted. But this man had the habit of wasting nothing. And I can understand this about him and I can sit and think on it and I can hesitate to give these signs of him away to my government without thinking myself sentimental. After all, this was a man I killed. No thought I have about him, no attachment, however odd, is sentimental if I have killed him. It is earned.

Objects can be very important. We have our flag, red for the revolution, a yellow star for the wholeness of our nation. We have the face of the father of our country, Ho Chi Minh, his kindly beard, his steady eyes. And he himself smoked these cigarettes. I turn the pack of Salem over and there is something to understand here. The two bands of color, top and bottom, are color like I sometimes have seen on the South China Sea when the air is still and the water is calm. And the sea is parted here and held within is a band of pure white and this word *Salem*, and now at last I can see clearly—how thin the line is between ignorance and wisdom—I understand all at once that there is a secret space in the word, not *Salem* but *sa* and *lem*, Vietnamese words, the one meaning to fall and the other to blur, and this is the moment that comes to all of us and this is the moment that I brought to the man who that very morning looked into the face of his wife and smoked and then had to move on and he carefully brushed the burning ash away to save half his cigarette because this farm of his was not a rich farm, he was a poor man who loved his wife and was sent far away by his government, and I was sent by my own government to sit in a tree and watch him move beneath me, frightened, and I brought him to that moment of falling and blurring.

And I turn the pack of cigarettes over again and I take it into my hand and I gently pull open the cellophane and draw the picture out and she smiles at me now, waiting for some word. I turn the photo over and the back is blank. There is no name here, no words at all. I have nothing but a pack of cigarettes and this nameless face, and I think that they will be of no use anyway, I think that I am a fool of a very mysterious sort either way—to consider saving these things or to consider giving them up—and then I stop thinking altogether and I let my hands move on their own, even as they did on that morning in the clearing, and I shake out the half cigarette into my hand and I put it to my lips and I strike a match and I lift it to the end that he has prepared and I light the cigarette and I draw the smoke inside me. It chills me. I do not believe in ghosts. But I know at once that his wife will go to a place and she will look through many pictures and she will at last see her own face and then she will know what she must know. But I will keep the cigarettes. I will smoke another someday, when I know it is time.

VII.
POSTCONFERENCE
SUPPLEMENTS

18. The War
and the Academy

W. D. EHRHART

The first time I encountered Vietnam as grist for the academic mill, I spent three days walking around Manchester, England, with my mouth hanging open, my chin somewhere down around my knees. The occasion was a 1986 conference at Manchester Polytechnic Institute entitled "Cultural Effects of Vietnam," and I had been invited to give a poetry reading, an offer I had gladly accepted because nobody I know turns down a free trip to England.

I had never been to an academic conference before, however, and I was not prepared for what awaited me. Over the course of those three days, panel after panel—each consisting of two to five presenters—covered topics like "Rockin' Hegemony: West Coast Rock and the Vietnam War" and "Puritanism in Film and Fiction: From *The Scarlet Letter* to *Apocalypse Now.*"

I didn't even know what "hegemony" meant. I kept pinching myself and asking the air, "Are they talking about the war that happened on *this* planet? The war *I* was in? The one with all the dead people and stuff I have nightmares about?" It all seemed so bloodless, so empty of passion, so—well, so academic. It was as if they'd stolen some very personal thing and made it into a coffee table curiosity.

Much of my response, I eventually came to understand, was actually a kind of territorial imperative: the war was mine, it had happened to me, and therefore it belonged to me and my comrades, not to a bunch of intellectuals who hadn't come within 8,000 miles of a shot fired in anger. What authority could possibly equal "I was there"?

I was also, I think, having difficulty coming to terms with the fact that what still seemed so fresh and vivid to me had already become history. The conference was a rude reminder that time was racing by at alarming speed, that I was no longer a young man. I used to think "first you get old and then you die" was a clever expression, but by the time I left Manchester, it had lost much of its charm.

Fortunately, for there is no telling how badly I might have behaved had it not been otherwise, my shock was largely dulled by a severe case of jet lag; for most of those three days, all I could do was gape and scratch my head.

241

And once I got back home and had time to ponder what I'd just survived, I began to consider the conference and what it represented somewhat differently than I had while it was right there in front of my dangling lower jaw.

Firstly, while many of the presenters at Manchester were indeed pure intellectuals whose interest in the war seemed almost by definition academic, others were either Vietnam veterans like retired air force pilot turned English professor John Clark Pratt, or committed activists like Don Luce, who had spent fourteen years in Viet Nam until he was expelled by Nguyen Van Thieu for helping to expose the infamous tiger cages of Con Son Island. Larry Heinemann read from his not yet published *Paco's Story*, and John Balaban read his own poems along with Vietnamese folk poems which he read in both Vietnamese and English.

Secondly, while there were presenters that ought not to have been allowed out except after dark and then only on thick short chains with choke collars, there were others that were quite stunning in their clarity and intelligence and perceptiveness. College librarian, novelist and veteran David A. Willson gave a hilarious and brilliant paper on the cover art of Vietnam War paperback books. Austrian scholar Adi Wimmer demonstrated how *Rambo: First Blood, Part Two* transforms Sylvester Stallone into the Viet Cong and the Vietnamese into the U.S. Army, thereby turning historical reality inside out. And Pilar Marin of the University of Seville gave so lucid a paper on Lloyd Little's *Parthian Shot* that I have stayed in touch with her ever since.

Wimmer and Marin, obviously, are not veterans and have no direct knowledge of the war in Viet Nam, yet both of them taught me a great deal about something I had up until then considered exclusively mine, which brings me to a third observation: If personal witness is the only legitimate lens through which to see the war, what happens when all the witnesses are dead? That question had not occurred to me prior to Manchester, but like it or not, "I was there" only goes so far. Ask any veteran of the Spanish-American War. Oops, they're all dead. Likewise, sooner or later, the only people writing and talking about Vietnam will inevitably be those who have no direct knowledge of it. Shall we veterans encourage and assist them in their efforts while we still can, or shall we be hostile and exclusionary and petulant?

I have come to understand, in fact, that we need the academy very much. In a world where actors make multimillions fighting in Hollywood, the war I fought in the rice fields for $121 a month, where POW/MIA flags fly over every rest stop on the New Jersey turnpike and *Miss Saigon* is all the rage on Broadway, one of the only places young people have any chance of learning anything of value about what actually happened in Viet Nam and why is in colleges and universities where reside those very professors and scholars I first encountered in Manchester.

Indeed, I have come to look forward to the opportunities I occasionally get to participate in such conferences. True, there are always moments of sheer lunacy, like the time in Toronto in 1990 when some professor gave a paper on the social class differences between officers and enlisted personnel using Bob Mason's *Chickenhawk* as her model for officers. When I pointed out to her that Mason was a warrant officer/pilot, a teenaged flying bus driver with neither social standing nor command responsibility, she smiled brightly and replied, "Oh! I didn't know that."

But there are also moments of sheer delight, like the time at the same conference in Toronto, when Professor Paul Lyons of Stockton State College revolutionized my understanding of the so-called Vietnam generation in the space of 20 minutes, convincingly demonstrating that most male members of our generation neither fought nor protested the war, but legally and effortlessly sidestepped it *à la* Dan Quayle and went on about their lives with hardly a pause.

Thus, when Robert Slabey of Notre Dame invited me to participate in the conference he was organizing, "The United States and Viet Nam: From War to Peace," I eagerly accepted the invitation. And a fine conference it turned out to be. The moments of sheer lunacy were mercifully few, and the moments of sheer delight were plentiful. On Saturday afternoon, for example, I joined Robert Olen Butler, Balaban, and Heinemann on Marc Leepson's panel, "The Arts of War and Peace." Meanwhile, among the audience were Lynda Van Devanter (*Visions of War, Dreams of Peace*), Gerald McCarthy (*War Story*), Larry Rottmann (*Voices from the Ho Chi Minh Trail*), John C. Shafer and Dale Ritterbusch (contributors to *Carrying the Darkness*), and Willson (*REMF Diary*), along with H. Bruce Franklin (*M.I.A., or Mythmaking in America*), Arnold R. Isaacs (*Without Honor*), and Elliott Gruner (*Prisoners of Culture*), any of whom could easily have taken my place on the panel.

Indeed, though the academics were mostly a serious and thoughtful lot, some of the very best in the field, many of them veterans, others bright young scholars like Vince Gotera, whose study of American veterans' war poetry, *Radical Visions*, is destined to become the definitive text, Slabey went to considerable lengths to make sure this would not be merely a gathering of academics. Rottmann, for instance, brought his seven-member road crew from the Southeast Asia–Ozark Center at Southwest Missouri State to perform a somber version of his *Voices* book.

Much of the real value of conferences, of course, lies outside the formal program: the chance to renew old friendships and make new ones, the chance to recharge one's emotional batteries, the chance (okay, I admit it) to stay up late drinking beer in the hotel bar while listening to David Willson skewer some unsuspecting novice with his rapier wit (a cliché, but no less true for it).

Each night, in fact, I stayed up later than the night before, which made each morning's 7 a.m. jog around the Notre Dame campus that much harder than the previous morning's run. Once you got going, however, it turned out to be a special time. In South Bend, on the western fringe of the eastern time zone, it's still pitch dark at 7 a.m., and on two mornings it was raining to boot, making it even darker. The ducks on the lake were just beginning to stir at that hour, a mist still lay on the water, and the easy conversation between jogging partner Paul Lyons and me ranged from the rigors of boot camps to the failures of the antiwar Left. Two of the four mornings (when it wasn't raining), Leepson even joined us.

Here are some other things that were special: Former Marine and Oklahoma State English professor Peter Rollins was amazed when I pointed to his miniature ribbon bar and correctly identified his Expeditionary Medal. Not many people know that the first Marines sent to Viet Nam received not the Republic of Viet Nam Service Medal, but the Expeditionary Medal instead. Rollins and I disagree on just about everything to do with the war, but the conversation we struck up that afternoon did much to humanize the distance between us.

It was my turn to be amazed when Professor Catherine Calloway of Arkansas State showed up at the conference with a dozen copies of *Unaccustomed Mercy*. She had brought them because her students wanted me to sign them, and when I did, she acted as if *I* was doing *her* a favor, when in truth she and her students were paying me a compliment I'll remember all my life.

For me, in fact, the whole conference seemed filled with compliments most writers get only rarely in a lifetime, if at all. Certainly nothing quite like it has ever happened to me before. It's a strange feeling—wonderful, but strange—to sit in an audience listening to some scholar say flattering things about your work, and this happened not once but twice in a single morning. Sitting next to Balaban, who was in the same awkward position I was in, I stared at my feet a lot, feeling pleased and embarrassed, thinking, "Geez, I'm not even dead yet." That afternoon I gave a reading to the audience of which the majority not only knew who I was, but had actually read me. *That's* never happened to me before, either.

On our last morning trot around the lake, the conference having officially closed the night before, I found myself thinking back to that earlier conference in Manchester. What a bizarre experience it had been—not strange, like listening to Lorrie Smith's paper about Balaban, Bruce Weigl and me, but truly bizarre—as if I had stumbled into someone else's dream. It had left me ill at ease and befuddled, not knowing quite what to make of it until well after the fact. This time, seven years later, I felt positively exhilarated. What was different? What had changed?

Me, I suppose. I've mostly come to terms with my own advancing years. I'm unavoidably middle-aged now, my hair is graying, my joints are stiff, and I can't arrest or change any of that. I've had to come to terms with myself in ways that occasionally even take on a passing resemblance to wisdom. I know that all of us who lived through the Vietnam years really *are* history to kids who would likely have a difficult time explaining the difference between the last U.S. helicopter out of Saigon and Custer's last stand. Neither Hollywood nor Madison Avenue nor Music Television is ever likely to teach them the difference, and we veterans aren't going to live forever, so if they're ever going to learn anything worth knowing about the war, it will be people like the ones I met at Notre Dame who will teach them. I guess that's why I came away feeling so exhilarated. It was a pretty good crowd. Nice bunch to spend a few days with. I wouldn't mind *my* kid taking a course or two with folks like that.

19. The United States, Viet Nam, and the "Interconnectedness of All Life"

KIM WORTHY

It was in a protean attitude, personally and politically aware and poised for change, that I took the train from New York to Notre Dame for the "From War to Peace" conference. The three days were full of interacting cultural references and emotional extremes. The first epiphanous moment of the conference for me Friday was when John Balaban—a poet and conscientious objector who worked during the war with the Committee of Responsibility for burned and war-injured children in Viet Name—had read from *Remembering Heaven's Face* about a remarkable man called "the Coconut Monk." This monk kept a vow of silence in a "Coney Island of human existence," a peace sanctuary on Phoenix Island near Saigon. In the excerpt John read to us, John interrupts the Coconut Monk looking out over the Mekong River one day, and as he apologizes the monk turns, and John sees he's in tears; the Coconut Monk smiles, points to the tears, then to the sky. John's voice broke, in the auditorium, remembering.

But after I bought and began reading John's compassionate and superbly written book I was a bit disappointed; his talk and readings, both prose and poetry, I had thought indicated a transcendence of "the masculine" (the mythos based on the exclusion of women and "the feminine"). Yet unfortunately I sensed no irony in one story of his, about a woman he calls Kate—a weeping drunk antiwar activist "girl" with a bleeding mouth, fucking the "pig of pigs" (a "war-mongering Major" from a Green Beret camp near Cao Lanh). Kate's bleeding mouth haunts me; I relate it to menstruation as the feminine sexual symbol, and to this woman's voice, removed—through sorrow, oblivion, and a masculine point of view. There was no place in John's story for American women as equals. No wonder Kate was crying. In John's Viet Nam narrative female U.S. volunteers bake pies or are "piled on" by "uninsultable" officers while the men are mobile in boats and jeeps, investigating, adventuring in marketplaces, reinventing themselves, discussing ethics and politics with the players. John bluntly states that he himself would have contended for "the pretty ones" among the volunteers.

Similarly, Pulitzer winner Robert Olen Butler's assumed Viet point of view in his new story, "Salem," from which he read at the conference, signaled to me the kind of transcendence of race that I admire most and that I foresee as the signature of the next century. But regarding gender his reading from *They Whisper* was the same old story, typical of men and women in major American fiction: male pedophilia, men urging each other on to greater (and more predictable) apoplexies of their own maleness.

I was tired of my own recycling of male narratives about women by deconstructing them, "taking them apart" as I jokingly (but it came across as hostile) said I would. For the last seven years I've researched, read, and written about the war as told by men to men or about men. Consequently, I was to be all the more thankful for the women's Viet Nam narratives at this conference. America and Viet Nam, Viet-American women, American women veterans and their true fellow-travelers: these are the people I hear now when I consider the Viet Nam war and its bearing on past and future relations between the two countries. Early Saturday morning I was moved beyond my most remote expectation by war veteran Lynda Van Devanter, the bespectacled mom reading from her memoir *Home Before Morning* and from a volume she edited of voices of other female nurses in Viet Nam. Van Devanter ("Van") that morning earned the right to answer with stunning directness a professor politely asking about the role of God in her experiences in Viet Nam. She had come to Viet Nam, she said, "a good Catholic girl from a big Catholic family" and a proud American—wearing a rhinestone U.S. flag on her fatigue shirt. "Today, Viet Nam," she had felt, "tomorrow the moon." But, she went on, "By about the fourth month I told God to go fuck himself."

Van Devanter had opened her talk saying that the conference was "magical" but also "horrifying" because there were separate panels for gender and race, and "no one came" to the "women" panels.* She later spoke critically but understandingly of the crumbling of her own idealistic compassion under the stresses of treating the wounded. She quoted Sharon Grant who writes grimly in a poem, "By the time I bedded a man / who didn't smell like mud and burned flesh— / He made love and I made jokes." Van quoted another poet who attributed her disintegration directly to a nice young woman's experience of repeatedly losing to pointless death nice human beings like ourselves—specifically, young men with whom she could not help falling in love, even though she was to know them for perhaps only their last few moments

---

*Editor's note: At the Notre Dame conference 20 of 100 participants were women, four with entire sessions. "Gender" was a natural topic-division, though "Women's Poetry" was in a "Poetry" session.

of life. Her respect for these soldiers was palpable. "These honored hands licensed to touch one filthy GI...;" "Goodbye, David—my name is Dusty ... the last person who will love you."

The months changed her into a racist, "a fucking gook-hater," this lady-like speaker said with perfect vocal rhythms. As I listened to her read from a chapter titled "Baby Come," about her unwillingly delivering the baby of a desperate Viet woman—"I was so happy I thought my chest wasn't big enough for it"—for a moment the high windows of the Notre Dame auditorium's audio-visual control rooms seemed to reflect the tops of trees instead of dark, void abstractions. "I loved that woman and her baby because they had broken me out of my protective shell," she went on. "I hated them for the same reason." She threw away the rhinestone flag and "found myself feeling nothing." She was never again to be the same person her parents had loved.

Of nurses she met and talked to after returning from the war Van Devanter said, "Our experience was completely discounted." She herself was not allowed to join Viet Nam Veterans Against the War "because I didn't look like a veteran." Even since the Veterans Administration's counseling programs were initiated, she has felt "a lack of conviction that the experience or vision we shared was important or valid."

"I forgave God," Van Devanter concluded, after her initial blunt response to the professor's question. "Religion didn't help me in any way, shape or form. Today I believe there is a loss of spiritual direction for this country. Healing from this war will come for America when a spiritual direction returns, not just a physical, mental, emotional direction. I believe that if there is a higher power," she said finally, "it only works through people." Van said that "like Dith Pran, I'm not a hero, I'm a witness. I can forget if I choose to—I've come to a point of great peace in my life—but I *will not* forget."

In a report on Viet Nam today, the scholar Douglas Pike said the Viets had "put the war behind them." He was genuinely perplexed as to why "we" couldn't do the same. This stirred a controversy that was, in a way, to define the conference: was it merely childish (or pathological) not to forget it? Or was it true, as Neil Sheehan said later in his address, that "Defeat can be as precious as victory if we can draw wisdom from it. The truth is bitter, disillusioning—but necessary."

From the perspective of many nonwhites and white women (as well as others) perhaps one of the bitter truths about our country is its brutal racism and sexism. Perhaps the country is going to have to go all the way back from Viet Nam through its history and acknowledge its contradictions regarding equality—its exclusions—and perhaps make real its ideals. Maybe citizens of the United States will have to fully recognize, through the Viets and all kinds of vets including nurses, the official concealment of hard facts: massacred Indians, lynched blacks, battered women, bashed gays—"the others" excluded, often brutally, from the dominant straight white world "we" adore in the distorting mirrors of screens and advertising—before Americans can put these humbling and tragic years behind them.

From Hollywood to Hanoi, Thi Thanh Nga (Tiana's) 1992 documentary or "nonfiction feature film" raises these and other interesting questions. It unfolds them in a method familiar by now in documentaries through home movie, television, and Hollywood movie clips, newsreel footage and interviews—all carefully selected and edited for ironic effect—as well as avant-garde techniques, voice-over narration and popular songs. The daughter of the press director for the South Vietnamese government, Tiana and her family fled Saigon in 1966 because her father was certain the North would win. In the United States Tiana tried to assimilate with a vengeance. Her family owned a house with a swimming pool, her brothers played baseball, she called the North Vietnamese "gooks," the GI's "our boys." Elected Homecoming Queen in a San Jose high school, she was forced to abdicate to a classmate with Anglo-Saxon features. She grew defensive, restless, militant; earned a karate black belt; and moved to Hollywood, where she became an actress. When her career began to unravel (she played Rod Steiger's war bride in one film; mostly she was cast in sexy heroine roles in B-movies), she decided to visit Viet Nam.

In Saigon her camera crew explores the "jumping" streets and markets, the homes of Tiana's few remaining relatives, and in an example of the film's uncanny blend of painful human experience and historical metaphor, in the Agent Orange ward of the Saigon Pediatric Hospital they meet Siamese twin boys named Viet and Duc (meaning north and south), about to undergo surgery to separate them. They came from the densely forested highlands where the chemicals were dropped the heaviest. Viet is in poor health and if he dies, "Duc will follow minutes after." Tiana exploits the operation to add suspense, but tastefully. She and her crew return to the hospital after the operation in the context of repeat visits to various other Saigon friends, not merely to learn the symbolic fate of Viet Nam.

Tiana also meets Pham Van Dong, the former premier, at his residence; she asks about her uncle, former minister of defense of South Vietnam, and discovers he's just been released from a reeducation camp. ("What a feisty guy!" Tiana says in her usual joking commentary.) She meets Amerasian children, South Vietnamese movie idols, and a solemnly eloquent, stately woman who as a child survived the U.S. massacre at My Lai and who, as a sacred duty, despite the emotional pain, recounts the events of that nightmare. Tiana teaches the people of Hue how to throw a Frisbee, records a message of peace to U.S. mothers from Dang Bich Ha, the historian and wife of General Giap, and walks on the beach poignantly recalling her childhood, "the most beautiful time of my life."

As seen from interviews with Amerasian children both in the United States and in Viet Nam, a major theme of the film is confused identities. Tiana recognizes the propaganda of both sides in the war: she is hopelessly hooked on U.S. culture, but finds herself degraded by it; her family loathes and fears the new Viet Nam but she is drawn to its center, to its people. Her response to the dilemma is simple. Viet and Duc must acquire separate identities; so must the united Viet Nam consisting today of the surreptitiously busy capitalist South and the aging communist North. And so must the United States and Viet Nam, united for so long in such pain. Tiana's apparent (and convincing) spontaneous love for everyone from the humble to the elite and her participation in all their lives shows by example the path to follow to the central reality of these two unique countries.

From her press kit it's clear Tiana's trip did not occur as represented within the film; she made the film over a much longer time period (five years) than it seems. This opens the filmmaker to charges of misleading the viewers, as did Michael Moore's chronology-shuffling in *Roger and Me*. Also Tiana's beauty and glamour and her roles in American films are always part of the subtext of her documentary, like Michael Moore's prole chic in *Roger and Me*, and Jan Oxenberg's placidness in *Thank You and Good Night!*. Finally, *From Hollywood* also borrows actual footage from Peter Davis's *Hearts and Minds* and Emile de Antonio's *In the Year of the Pig*. How do the ethics and esthetics of Tiana's narrative and its mise-en-scène intersect with the lessons of the war, for both the Americans and the Vietnamese? Answers too often seem left to chance.

In the end, the message of *From Hollywood to Hanoi* was clear. It was reinforced by two presentations at the "Films of Reconciliation" panel: Mark Bigg's raw footage of his film *The Bicycle Doctors* and Mitchell Hart's paper on U.S. films about the war. Biggs's documentary is a day in the life, following, just as the title says, doctors who ride bicycles around as they visit their patients. "I was prepared for poverty, a difficult experience," Biggs told the audience, "not a land of plenty, a place that I would die for." The people need tools, medical supplies and equipment, but as far as basic needs, "Well," Biggs said, "See for yourself." He pressed the play button and unveiled the central market in Hue—beautiful, bounteous. ("I fell deeply in love with that city," Biggs said.) Biggs urges everyone to go to Viet Nam. "Be prepared to become too enchanted and fascinated by what you see. Take twice the film you need, take tape recorders, pens, pencils—take something, anything to bring back what you see and hear. You will meet wonderful and amazing people, you'll come back with lots of incredible stories. And you will be forever changed. Reconciliation," Biggs concluded, "happens one to one."

Like Biggs's film, the clip Mitchell Hart brought in of Barry Levinson's *Good Morning, Viet Nam* brought before Americans beautiful marketplaces; also gorgeous sunrises, "What a Wonderful World" plays on the soundtrack. As Hart pointed out, viewers have generally missed the value of this sequence in the film; most of us in the panel audience were clearly startled by it (judging from the "Oh my Gods," etc.). Intercut with the wonders of the countryside (actually Thai, but in essence Vietnamese) were shots of a bombed village, a bloody sandal, an ARVN execution, and Vietnamese demonstrators viciously attacked by the (U.S.–backed) South Vietnam police. While the misery of American GIs is also prominent, the compassion of the lyrics playing calmly over natural beauty and political turmoil alike is devastating, and the effect is somehow overwhelming sympathy for the Vietnamese people.

"Such a positive portrayal of those who fought against the Americans was not seen since [Peter Davis's 1973 documentary] *Hearts and Minds*," Hart said. Also, *Good Morning, Viet Nam* is "the one film which seriously seeks to foster a reconciliation between Americans and Vietnamese." It is "the only film that shows personal relationships between Americans and Vietnamese." Without some such means of challenging the continuing, perhaps comforting perception of the Vietnamese as the enemy, "there will be little pressure for change."

Phan Nguyen Barker made a similar challenge in her presentation humbly entitled "Seedlings of Peace (Hot Giong Hoa Binh)." In the suddenly powerful conclusion to what was until then an interesting but rather ordinary slide show about her work (flowers pleasingly painted on silk), without warning Phan displayed images—roughly constructed wood and bamboo quilts, of all things—so strong they were like a series of physical blows. Nothing could have prepared me for the toughness and assurance of these quilts made of tree branches from Phan's homeland after she returned there, where she had lost her mother at the age of seven; nor, in contrast to her previous loquacity about herself and her meditations upon her country, the power of her wordlessness. As I watched the slides under an outpouring of my own grief like a torrent tapped into life, I slipped almost literally from my seat to the floor.

Phan's tape deck began to play "The Rose" then, and as she passed around sheets printed with the words to the song a woman beside me began singing. When it was over she turned to me and looking down to where I lay helplessly slumped in my seat, she suddenly waved a telegram at me saying with tears covering her face, "I sang for my dear grandmother; I've only just learned of her death." Phan's object was clearly to invoke this kind of emotional devastation in her audience, but the idea behind it was also plain. An individual must "return" and must really risk everything—ego, identity, even stability—in order to recreate a self that will be conscious of its pain, and henceforward live authentically. By analogy, people whose nations have been in conflict must do the same.

Sunday in Springfield's Amtrak station, waiting for the next New York train, I met the amazing Dr. Nina Lynne who runs a school in Vermont called Children of the Earth and regularly visits New York for meetings of an international group raising awareness of the need for global greening. I asked Nina what message she would broadcast to the world if she could; her answer: "I would like to remind everyone of the interconnectedness of all life." Considering what I'd just experienced, sitting now in perfect intellectual unison with this lovely stranger, I was "whelmed" (as Marc would say). Later Nina and I strode through Penn Station together. As when I'd embarked from there four days earlier, the entire waiting area—all the seats—seemed to be occupied by the urine-soaked and injured. "What a statement on humanity," Nina said quietly.

As John Balaban had signed my copy of *Remembering Heaven's Face* at the conference, he had asked where my brother served in Viet Nam, and I was stunned to realize that twenty years after his suicide I still couldn't answer that. I had always thought he'd been in a secure desk job in Saigon, a company typist or something. It wasn't that I'd forgotten—I'd never really known. Perhaps I had succumbed to the desire of most Americans of our generation to see the tragedies of our lives as something separate from politics. When I returned to my desk in Brooklyn I pulled out a folder with the few letters and records I have of my brother's, and was amazed to find there the precise information that had eluded me for so long. He'd worked as an airplane dispatcher for the U.S. Army 192d Assault Helicopters in Phan Thiet from December 1968 to December 1969. That night I dreamed I met my brother again and he was gorgeous, as if he had been somewhere where he'd received all the love and care he'd needed but was denied by our adored, alcoholic mother (now dead) and our idealized, morally crumbling country, when he shot himself at the age of twenty-one—acne-scarred and bottomed-out on alcohol and drugs—with his Army-issue revolver.

John Balaban writes that in Viet Nam he was given a heart-shaped pin inside of which was a circle containing two more overlapping circles—the top marked "Heaven" ("Mr. Sky") the bottom "the Earth"; and in "the ellipsoid where they overlapped" was "Humankind." "Vietnamese humanity dwelt in proximity to Heaven and Earth, and, indeed, derived from their contingency." I have the sense that to the Vietnamese "Mr. Sky," "the face of heaven" in John's title, means the eternal view, a view not unknown to the West, of course; Troilus found it in the end of Chaucer's "Troilus and Cressida." But Troilus only discovered it after he'd died. The Viets look up and see it many times each day. It is simply acceptance—specifically, human acceptance of our own ever-present mortality. Acknowledgment of one's mortality is also to acknowledge fallibility; it is like surviving a fatal illness, which Chief Wilma Mankiller says has made her more mature, level, calm, and able to lead. So it should be with the U.S.–Viet Nam war. "It was a shared experience," Sheehan says. "It made us part of humanity."

Appendix A
Conference Participants

Craig Adcock, Notre Dame; Robert Baird, Illinois-Urbana; John S. Baky, LaSalle; John Balaban, Miami; Phan Nguyen Barker, Kailua-Kona, HI; Harry Basehart, Salisbury State; Mark Biggs, Southwest Missouri State; Kent Blazer, Wayne State College; Maria Bonn, Albion College; Thomas Bowie Jr., U.S. Air Force Academy; James Brazee Jr., Vietnam Veterans of America; Robert Olen Butler, McNeese State; Catherine Calloway, Arkansas State; James Campbell, Notre Dame; David Carter, Oklahoma Agent Orange Foundation; N. Bradley Christie, Erskine College; Kenton Clymer, Texas-El Paso; Jack Colldeweih, Fairleigh Dickinson; David Cortright, Notre Dame; Arthur Combs, London School of Economics; Joseph Cox, U.S. Military Academy; Paul Daum, New England College; Doan Ngoc Diep, Ho Chi Minh City Polytechnic; Elaine V. DesRosiers, O.P., Notre Dame; Dan Duffy, Yale; Cynthia Edelberg, Cleveland State; Anthony Edmonds, Ball State; W.D. Ehrhart, Philadelphia, PA; Peter Erhard, Andrews; Craig Etcheson, The Cambodia Campaign; James Ferreira, Western Michigan; H. Bruce Franklin, Rutgers-Newark; Stephen Fredman, Notre Dame; Laura S. Fuderer, Notre Dame; Cynthia Fuchs, George Mason; Sonia Gernes, Notre Dame; Marc Jason Gilbert, North Georgia College; Jonathan Goldstein, West Georgia College; Vince Gotera, Northern Iowa; Herman Graham, Pennsylvania; Joseph Gray, Mountain Pictures; John Robert Greene, Cazenovia College; Elliott Gruner, U.S. Military Academy; Jane Hamilton-Merritt, Southport, CT; Mitchell Hart, Penn State; Sandra Hayes, Notre Dame; Larry Heinemann, Chicago, IL; John Hellmann, Ohio State-Lima; Tobey C. Herzog, Wabash College; Theodore M. Hesburgh, C.S.C., Notre Dame; Stephen Hidalgo, Notre Dame; Amanda Howell, Rochester; Charles Howlett, Adelphi; David Hunt, Massachusetts-Boston; Philip K. Jason, U.S. Naval Academy; Larry Johannessen, St. Xavier; Ellen C.K. Johnson, College of DuPage; Eugenia Kaledin, Lexington, MA; Ben Kiernan, Yale; Barry Kroll, Indiana-Bloomington; Jerome Landman, The Indiana Academy; Jessica Lapp, Notre Dame; Marc Leepson, VVA Veteran; Chau T.M. Le, Notre Dame; H. John LeVan, Chicago Medical School; Charles Lindquist Veterans Center, Lexington, KY; Paul Lyons, Richard Stockton College; George Mariscal, California-LaJolla; Suzanne Marilley, Notre Dame; Earl Martin, Mennonite Central Committee; John McAuliff, US-Indochina Reconciliation Project; Gerald McCarthy, St. Thomas Aquinas College; Victoria McLure, South Plains College; Paul Messbarger, Loyola-Chicago; Wilson Miscamble, C.S.C., Notre Dame; Peter Moody, Notre Dame; Felix Moos, Kansas; John Mulvihill, Drake; Martin F. Murphy, Notre Dame; William O'Rourke, Notre Dame; Kristin Pelzer, Hawaii-Manoa; Douglas Pike, California-Berkeley; Mary Sue Ply, Southeastern Louisiana; David E.W. Reed, South Carolina; Edward Rielly, St.

Joseph's College; Dale Ritterbusch, Wisconsin-Whitewater; Peter Rollins, Oklahoma State; John Root, Illinois Institute of Technology; David Rosenberg, Middlebury College; Larry Rottmann, Southeast Asia-Ozark Project; Valerie Sayers, Notre Dame; John Schafer, Humboldt State; Wilbur Scott, Oklahoma; William Searle, Eastern Illinois; Lars-Winfried Seiler, South Carolina; Jonathan Shay, M.D., Tufts Medical School; Neil Sheehan, Washington, D.C.; Robert M. Slabey, Notre Dame; Lorrie Smith, St. Michael's College; Carolyn D. Spatta, California State-Hayward; Phoebe S. Spinrad, Ohio State; Susan Stann-Burke, DeAnza College; Stephen Sullivan, Northeastern; Kali Tal, Viet Nam Generation; C.David Thomas, Indochina Arts Project; Tiana, Du Art Films; Earl Tilford Jr., U.S. Army War College; Lynda Van Devanter, Herndon, VA; Daly Walker, M.D., Columbus, IN; Donald R. Walker, Texas Tech; Tony Williams, Southern Illinois; David Willson, Green River Community College; Brantley Womack, Virginia; Kim Worthy, Wagner College; Jianjiong Zhu, Manitoba

Appendix B
Viet Nam and
the United States:
A Brief Chronology

Year	Viet Nam: Events	U.S.: Events	U.S.: Culture
208 B.C.	Trieu Da proclaims himself emperor of "Nam Viet."		
A.D. 200	Kingdom of Champa.		
967	Independence, after 1100 years of fighting Chinese domination.		
1000		Viking settlement in Newfoundland.	
1070	Temple of Literature (University in Hanoi).		
1211	Mongol invasion of China.		
1492	Dominion extended southward.	Columbus' first voyage.	
1600		Spanish explore Southwest. English settle in Virginia.	
1776	French missionary activity spreads.	Declaration of Independence.	
1803	Nguyen Anh (Gia Long) unifies the country.	Louisiana Purchase.	
1838		Cherokee "Trail of Tears."	
1861	French capture Saigon.	Civil War begins.	
1887	French create Indochinese Union.		
1890	Ho Chi Minh born.	Closing of the Frontier.	

255

Year	Viet Nam: Events	U.S.: Events	U.S.: Culture
1914		The "Great War" begins in Europe.	
1917		The Russian Revolution	
1919	At Versailles Ho tries to petition for Vietnamese self-determination.	U.S. fails to approve Versailles Treaty. U.S. Communist Party formed.	
1930	Indochinese Communist Party formed.	Great Depression.	
1940	Japanese occupy Indochina, but leave French colonial administration intact.		
1941	Ho forms Vietminh to fight both Japanese and French.	Japan bombs Pearl Harbor. U.S. declares war.	
1945	Ho receives American aid to fight Japanese. First Americans killed in Viet Nam. Ho declares independence and proclaims Democratic Republic of Viet Nam.	U.S. drops atom bombs. Japan surrenders.	
1946	Franco-Vietnamese war begins.	"Cold War" begins.	
1949	Communist victory in China.	NATO formed.	
1950	Ho declares the Democratic Republic as the only legal government. U.S. recognizes Bao Dai's State of Viet Nam, sends aid to French.	McCarthy hearings. U.S. sends troops to Korea.	
1953		Korean armistice.	
1954	French defeated at Dienbienphu. Geneva Agreements divide Viet Nam. U.S. supports Diem regime, sends aid.	SEATO formed. School segregation ruled unconstitutional. Civil Rights movement begins.	Elvis Presley's first record.
1955	Diem rejects Geneva Accords, becomes first president of Republic of Viet Nam.		

Year	*Viet Nam: Events*	*U.S.: Events*	*U.S.: Culture*
1956	Diem begins crack-down on dissidents	Montgomery bus .boycott.	Greene's *The Quiet American*.
1957	Insurgent activity begins in the South.	U.S.S.R. launches Sputnik.	
1959	U.S. sends advisers to South. Two are killed by guerrillas.	Castro victory in Cuba.	Lederer and Burdick's *The Ugly American*.
1960	National Liberation Front ("Viet Cong") formed in South with Hanoi's support.	Kennedy elected president.	
1961	More U.S. advisers, Special Forces per-sonnel, and equip-ment sent to Viet Nam and also to Laos.	Bay of Pigs. Berlin Wall. First American in space.	
1962	Chemical warfare. Strategic Hamlet Program. 12,000 American advisers in Viet Nam.	Cuban missile crisis.	
1963	Buddhists protest Diem regime. First monk immo-lates himself. In army coup Diem is killed.	Civil Rights March to Washington. Kennedy assassinated. Johnson President.	
1964	Gulf of Tonkin inci-dent. Khanh coup.	Tonkin Gulf Resolution. Black riots. Civil Rights Act. Johnson declares "war on poverty."	Dylan's "The Times, They Are a-Changin'." Beatles on U.S. TV.
1965	First American com-bat troops land. Troop strength reaches 200,000. U.S. bombs North. Ky coup.	Selma March. Watts and Harlem riots. Berkeley Viet Nam Teach-in.	Moore's *The Green Berets*. Tran Van Dinh's *No Passenger on the River*.
1966	400,000 American troops.		"Ballad of the Green Berets." Phil Ochs' "I Ain't Marchin' Anymore."
1967	500,000 American troops. Thieu regime.	Antiwar protests. March on the Pentagon. Ghetto uprisings.	*A Poetry Reading Against the War*. County Joe's "I Feel Like I'm Fix-ing to Die Rag." Terry's *Viet Rock*. Garson's *MacBird*.

Year	Viet Nam: Events	U.S.: Events	U.S.: Culture
1968	Tet offensive. Siege of Khe Sanh. 540,000 American troops. My Lai massacre. Paris "Peace" talks begin. Johnson halts bombing of North.	Johnson does not run. Martin Luther King, Jr., assassinated. Ghetto riots. Robert Kennedy assassinated. Riots during Democratic convention in Chicago. Nixon elected president.	Halberstam's *One Very Hot Day.* Wayne's *The Green Berets.* Mailer's *The Armies of the Night. In the Year of the Pig* (film). *Hair.* Walter Cronkite and the *Wall Street Journal* oppose the war.
1969	Battle of "Hamburger Hill." Ho dies. "Vietnamization" and withdrawal of U.S. troops.	Antiwar demonstrations across the country. Chicago conspiracy trial of antiwar leaders. Viet Nam Moratorium Day. First draft lottery. Americans walk on the surface of the moon.	Woodstock. Kopit's *Indians. Medium Cool* (film).
1970	U.S. and ARVN attack communist sanctuaries in Cambodia. Coup in Cambodia.	Protests. Students are killed at Kent State (4) and Jackson State (2). Senate repeals Tonkin Gulf Resolution. Vote to 18-year-olds.	Reich's *The Greening of America.* John Lennon's "Give Peace a Chance."
1971	U.S. troop strength down to 140,000.	*Pentagon Papers* published. Lt. Calley convicted of murdering civilians at My Lai.	Rabe's plays: *The Basic Training of Pavlo Hummel* and *Sticks and Bones.*
1972	U.S. bombing of Hanoi and Haiphong.	Watergate break-in. VVAW march on Washington. Harrisburg 7 acquitted. Nixon visits Peking and Moscow, is re-elected.	*Winning Hearts and Minds* (poetry). Casey's *Obscenities.* FitzGerald's *Fire in the Lake.*
1973	Cease-fire agreements signed. Last American troops leave. POWs released.	Nixon announces "Peace with honor." Agnew resigns. End of military draft.	Lifton's *Home from the War.* O'Brien's *If I Die in a Combat Zone. Free Fire Zone: Short Stories by Viet Nam Veterans.*
1974		House Judiciary Committee votes to impeach Nixon.	Stone's *Dog Soldiers.*

Year	Viet Nam: Events	U.S.: Events	U.S.: Culture
1975	Phnompenh falls to Khmer Rouge. Communist forces capture Saigon. Remaining Americans are evacuated. Trade embargo imposed. Communist coup in Laos.	Nixon resigns. President Ford pardons Nixon. Ford pronounces war "finished." Watergate trials.	*Hearts and Minds* (film).
1976	Khmer Rouge kill 2 million Cambodians during genocidal reign of terror.	Bicentennial. Carter elected.	Kovic's *Born on the Fourth of July*.
1977		President Carter pardons most draft evaders.	Herr's *Dispatches*. Caputo's *A Rumor of War*.
1978	Viet Nam invades Cambodia, establishes People's Republic of Kampuchea. "Boat People" flee Viet Nam.	U.S. resumes full diplomatic relations with China, postpones normalization of relations with Viet Nam.	Webb's *Fields of Fire*. O'Brien's *Going After Cacciato* (National Book Award). Films: *The Deer Hunter*, *Coming Home*.
1979	China invades Viet Nam.	Iranian revolutionaries seize hostages at U.S. Embassy.	Hasford's *The Short Timers*. *Apocalypse Now*.
1980		Reagan elected. American Psychiatric Association incorporates PTSD into its manual.	*Tracers* (play). *Viet Nam: The 10,000 Day War* (Canadian TV series).
1981		Viet Nam Veterans protest "Welcome Home" parades for Iranian hostages.	Baker's *Nam*.
1982	First U.S. veterans visit Viet Nam.	Viet Nam Veterans Memorial dedicated.	Delvecchio's *The 13th Valley*. CBS exposé "The Uncounted Enemy: A Viet Nam Deception."
1983		U.S. trains Contras. Assault on Grenada. U.S. Marines killed in Beirut.	*Viet Nam: A Television History* (PBS). Van Devanter's *Home Before Morning*. Ehrhart's *Vietnam-Perkasie*.

Year	Viet Nam: Events	U.S.: Events	U.S.: Culture
1984			Terry's *Bloods*. Springsteen's "Born in the U.S.A."
1985		Court Case: General Westmoreland v. CBS. Welcome Home parade in New York.	*Carrying the Darkness* (Ehrhart's poetry anthology). Stallone's *Rambo II*. Viet Nam War with Walter Cronkite (video series).
1986	Party Congress launches economic "renovation," encourages private enterprise.	U.S. bombs Libya.	*Platoon* (Academy Award). Heinemann's *Paco's Story* (National Book Award).
1987		Movement begun in Congress to normalize relations with Viet Nam.	*Tour of Duty* and *Viet Nam War Stories* (TV series). Kubrick's *Full Metal Jacket*.
1988	Joint U.S. and Vietnamese search teams cooperate in locating remains of MIAs.	Bush elected.	*China Beach* (TV series). Sheehan's *Bright Shining Lie* (Pulitzer Prize).
1989	Viet Nam withdraws from Cambodia. Unrest in China. Tiananmen Massacre in Beijing.	U.S. invades Panama. Berlin Wall demolished. Collapse of Eastern Bloc.	Stone's *Born on the Fourth of July*. *Miss Saigon* (London musical). Hayslip's *When Heaven and Earth Changed Places*.
1990	U.S. and Viet Nam begin discussions to reach a settlement in Cambodia. Vietnamese government publishes new economic plan.	"Operation Desert Shield." U.S. bombs Iraq. German reunification. Unrest in Soviet republics. U.S. Marines in Liberia.	O'Brien's *The Things They Carried*. Opening of exhibition of war art by U.S. and Vietnamese artists. (Exhibit opened in Hanoi in 1994.)
1991	U.N. peacekeeping mission in Cambodia. U.S. opens MIA office in Hanoi.	U.S. and allies defeat Iraq. Bush announces the "Vietnam syndrome" kicked "once and for all." Breakup of Soviet Union. Warsaw (Military) Pact disbanded. Civil war in Yugoslavia.	Puller's *Fortunate Son* (Pulitzer Prize).

Year	Viet Nam: Events	U.S.: Events	U.S.: Culture
1992		U.S. and U.N. forces in Somalia. War in Bosnia. Clinton elected.	Butler's *A Good Scent from a Strange Mountain* (Pulitzer Prize).
1993	Coalition government elected in Cambodia.	Vietnam Women's Memorial dedicated.	Stone's *Heaven and Earth*. Tiana's *From Hollywood to Hanoi*. Komunyakaa's *Neon Vernacular* (Pulitzer Prize).
1994	U.S. companies invest in Viet Nam.	With Senate approval, Clinton lifts the embargo. U.S. troops sent to Haiti.	O'Brien's *In the Lake of the Woods*.
1995	U.S. and Viet Nam establish liaison offices in Hanoi and Washington.	Clinton establishes diplomatic relations with Viet Nam.	McNamara's *In Retrospect: The Tragedy and Legacy of Vietnam*.

Index of Names